T0374166

UPSTAGE, DOWNSTAGE, CROSS

An Actor Emerges in Early English 20th Century Theatre

Bill Thomas

AuthorHouse™
1663 Liberty Drive
Bloomington, IN 47403
www.authorhouse.com
Phone: 1-800-839-8640

Published by AuthorHouse 5/29/2012

ISBN: 978-1-4685-0193-3 (sc)
ISBN: 978-1-4685-0192-6 (e)

This book is printed on acid-free paper.

Table of Contents

Chapter	Title	Page
1	A First Appearance	1
2	Growing Up in Bristol	11
3	The Governess	21
4	The Actor Débuts	33
5	The Runaway	45
6	The Townsends	58
7	The Stowaway	69
8	The Voyage	86
9	Theatre on the Bounding Main	101
10	The Water Wanderer Returns	116
11	The End of Formal Education	129
12	The Acting School	140
13	The Actor Prepares	150
14	The London Theatre Invasion	167
15	The Rehearsal Becomes a Play	186
16	The Birmingham Repertory Company	201
17	The Theatre Apprentices	221
18	The Liverpool Repertory Company	239
19	More Liverpool	256
20	The Unforeseen	273
21	The A.L.S. Travelling Theatre	288
22	Stratford-upon-Avon	301
23	The British National Theatre Conference	313
24	Among the Unemployed	331
25	The Travelling Theatre Again	340
26	The Brighton Repertory Company	359
27	All's Well That Ends Well	376

Chapter 1
A First Appearance

Bristol, 1905

"Mrs. Thronson, Mrs. Thronson," the shrill voice shouted from the dusty cobblestone street in front of the two-story flat at 15 Longfield Road. "Miss-iss Thur-on-son!" it loudly insisted.

Opening the thick, red front door, Elsie Love Wyatt Thronson greeted her neighbor from across the road, Sarah Siddons, a heavyset seamstress. "Sarah, what's the trouble?"

"It's Rupie," was the breathless reply. "He's marching down the middle of Queen's Street with nothing on but a derby."

"Oh, my heavens" was all that slipped out. "How did he get out of the rear garden?" Mrs. Thronson asked as she bundled into her thick afghan overcoat.

"Alphie Goodpasture must'a 'elped 'im ov'r the fence," was Sarah's reply. "'Urry, we've got to fetch him 'fur the bobbies get there."

The two women dashed past the parked horse-driven liveries and wooden two-wheeled carriages lining both sides of the narrow stone street, careened around the worn brick-sided corner chemist's shop, and walked hurriedly towards the noisy crowd gathered in the center of Queen's Street. Horse carriages coming from two directions were prevented from moving forward by the crowd of onlookers, their occupants yelling not-so-nice suggestions to the growing mob.

Moving directly to the center of the fray, with Sarah Siddons panting at arm's length, Elsie Thronson halted in total and complete shock. "Rupert! Rupert Ashley Thronson!" she finally managed to utter in a high-pitched voice. "What in the king's name are you doing?"

Clothesless, except for a large black derby hat which had settled over his head and crept down over his eyebrows, comfortably seated on his favorite rocking horse Penguin, her four-year-old son, face covered by glistening white cream, nose hidden by a round red rubber ball, innocently replied, "I'm playing clown."

As one, several in the crowd roared with instant laughter. A beefy man with a butcher's apron tied around his front laughingly asked of the stunned mother, "Sure 'e's not related to Lady Godiva?" There was collective roar of laughter from the crowd.

"Where's Alphie?" Sarah questioned little Rupert.

"He's picking up shillings," was the satisfied response. Sure enough, to the left of the assemblage, Alphie, at six years, lanky, though fully clothed in his school uniform, was on his hands and knees reaching amongst the cobblestones collecting the monetary gains in a fragile white teacup. He continued muttering softly, "A pittance for a clown. A pittance for a clown." The coins clacked into the coffer.

Throwing her enormous overcoat around the small

boy and whisking him up in her arms, Mrs. Thronson commanded her friend, "Sarah, bring Alphie to my house as fast as you can gather him up. His father and Rupert's are going to hear about this. They're the ones who took the boys to the Clifton Greens' Carnival," she said accusingly.

Off the foursome marched to 15 Longfield, boys in firm armholds.

This was not the first time Rupert Ashley Thronson had made a spectacle of himself (nor would it be the last). Even before he could toddle along on his own, when his doting mother proudly pushed him in a pram through the streets of his birthplace, Weston-Super-Mare, he would coo and sing and laugh, bringing attention to himself in whatever manner succeeded.

"He's a born ham," his father, Rupert Senior, would surprisingly affirm. Though somewhat straight laced, "a lad of the Old English Tradition," Thronson mellowed in the helpless love of his attractive brown-eyed, tousled-haired wife, recently turned twenty-five. Two years older, the already slightly balding assistant grocer had been raised in a deeply religious family headed by a Church of England rector who, like most Victorians, believed that theatres and music halls were literal dens of iniquity. "The people who frequent them are 'seekers of sin,'" he uttered. To Rupert Senior, his equally beloved son was "a beautiful gift from the heavens" for whom a wrong was inconceivable. Suggestions that the boy had theatrical leanings were like Lucifer inviting twelve angels to a celebratory dinner.

The young father had apprenticed as a grocer's helper in Bude, a small village on the Southwest Cornwall coast, which he pronounced "bood." Rupert married the only girl he'd ever cared about as a youth. He met Elsie Wyatt when she was visiting her Welsh cousins in Bude. The relatives were members of one of Rupert's father's tiny congregations, which required Sunday visits to four churches in neighboring towns in the Thronsons' horse-driven landau.

Elsie, having increased her "cousinly" visits, easily won Rupert's heart, and, a few weeks after his first visit to Newton, Wales, to ask her father's permission, they wed there in a simple civil ceremony.

Young, immersed in the precious wonderment of romance, they began their marriage as guests in Rupert's parents' home in Bude. Both, having had to work in various family enterprises during their early years, had not completed primary school but read regularly from the Bible. They also shared a deep affection for music. Rupert taught himself to play the violin; Elsie had learned the piano by ear. Her father was a coal miner near Newtown, eking out a simple life for his family of nine. Her mother was bedridden, having developed internal complications with her last infant.

After marrying, Elsie visited her family by train at every opportunity, occasionally accompanied by her hardworking husband. Five years after their wedding, shortly after Elsie announced she was "with child," the young Thronsons moved to a more northern seacoast Cornish village, Weston-Super-Mare, south of the growing metropolis of Bristol. Rupert had obtained an assistant grocer's position with Charles Kitt Grocers, who ran a busy store at 2 Baker Street just around the corner from the Thronsons' newly acquired flat. When Rupert Ashley Thronson was born on 5 July 1901, at the nearby Memorial Hospital, his father's life was complete in every way, except economically. "I must make my mark, Elsie, for our growing son should have more than we did," he would often remind his adoring wife.

Proudly, the hardworking father wheeled his son's pram on family errands to the boot and shoe maker, the butcher, the greengrocer, the coal and wood merchant, and, of course, to Kitt's grocery store, where the handsome, precocious infant welcomed his most enthusiastic audience of clerks and customers, one of whom imitated famous personages for him. "He always seems to be putting on a type of act now," Rupert Senior boasted to his wife. "He uses a ferocious frown to portray Cromwell when he hears his name. He places his hand alongside his cheek and points his finger to his eye to look like William Shakespeare, and he giggles like Miles Gloriosis in a mediaeval performance. He charms the ladies and entertains the gentlemen. Perhaps we have an Irving on our hands."

British theatre, especially in the provinces, was very sparse. London was the primary cultural center of the country with theatres like the Theatre Royal, Drury Lane, and the Empire featuring playwrights Shakespeare, Shaw, Pinero, William Archer, and Henry Arthur Jones and such actors as George Alexander, Henry Irving, Lewis Waller, Johnston Forbes Robertson, and Mrs. Patrick Campbell. Other growing cities including Manchester, Liverpool, Nottingham, Southampton, and Bristol attracted touring companies such as O'Doyles, Gilbert and Sullivan, the Bensonites, and William Poel's theatrical group, and second and third companies of successful London runs, musical reviews, and an occasional opera or musical concert.

Rupert Senior's only experience in a theatre had been at the Bristol Old Vic when the renowned Shakespearean actor Henry Irving and his equally famous leading lady, Helen Terry, appeared for two nights with a company of twelve, boasting lavish costumes, modest scenery, and a few items of furniture. One of the friends Rupert had met at his bowling club was a distant relative, Edward Gordon Craig, who provided the tickets. Craig, rumored to be Terry's illegitimate son, was then a rising young innovative stage designer. The play was *Richard III,* and Irving's powerful practiced voice, strong physical appearance, and dynamic personality had an overwhelming effect on Rupert. "He was, indeed, Richard III," he later reported to a fascinated Elsie. "And Ellen Terry, she was his infatuating queen."

Rupert continued to describe the style of acting Irving emoted. ""When he polished a table, he would say, 'One, two, three, wipe.' Every sound, every movement, was intentional. It was clear cut and measured. Nothing was real; it was all massively artificial. Yet, he created an overall illusion of truth. In all of his deliveries, he wasted neither words nor gestures. It was as if he presented patter."

"Uh-huh," the small voice bounced back, "One, two, free, wipe," with a gesture.

On Sundays, when Rupert Senior was observing the Holy Day, he, Elsie, and little Rupert would picnic at Clarence Park, let Rupert watch the water playing its squirting tune at the city fountain, or walk the two miles on the sands to the small, very pleasant village of Uphill, with its thirteenth-century church on the summit. Once, when Rupert had just turned three, the trio explored the caves of Barnwell, where father and son pretended they were opposing bands of cowboys and Indians in a Wild West shootout. Elsie laughed and applauded when one of them would grab himself on the chest as if a bullet or arrow had just entered and make a spectacular slow-motioned, backward fall to the ground.

"He looks more realistic than I do," the father observed.

"Where did he learn to do that?" questioned Elsie.

"I showed him," was the reply. "Last month, I read one those large colorful, children's books to him that are published in America. It described all the little details of a real gunfight; there were even drawings on every other page. Rupie loved the stories."

In the late afternoons and evenings, Rupert with his son, sometimes with Elsie, looked forward to visiting the Weston train station less than a mile away. It was here that the commerce of the resort town was determined. Goods for all the homes, shops, stores, pubs, and manufacturers were brought in by railroad car; everything - from boxes of toy soldiers to brooms for the chimney sweep - came to the station, was picked up by horse carriages with open backs and taken to shop proprietors, building contractors, and provision dealers. The small boy adored the haggling, the hustle and bustle, the smells, and the constant din of activity he found at the train yard and, as he learned to speak, shared childlike observations from the train station with his mother and father: "That big man with the cook's apron lifted up a 'ole cow with no hair on." "There was one tall gent in the coal bin I couldn't tell from the ground." "The train that comed in today sounded like a 'chug-chug' song."

One afternoon, young Rupert was all eyes when three large men began unloading a dusty boxcar with the words "The Bensonians" painted across the sides. The first item they removed and roughly threw into a large open carriage was an enormous chair. Next, they brought out a rounded package. Undoing the paper wrapping, one threw a white object to his mate next to the carriage.

"What's that," Rupert inquired of his father.

"It's a skull, Rupie. It used to be a human's head." When the boy grimaced, the father added. "It's all right, it's only going to be used in a play."

"What's a play?" the three-year-old inquired. This was when Rupert Junior first learned about the Black Prince, Hamlet, and how a storyteller named William Shakespeare wrote down words for people to speak in front of other people and that the speakers were called actors. The youngster also heard for the first time about Henry Irving and Helen Terry and how his father had attended their play in Bristol.

"Rupert will soon be of school age," his father reported to his mother one day. "I don't think we can afford elementary here in Weston. Not with the thrupence I make."

"You do work so hard, my darling," mused Elsie fondly. "Have you asked Mr. Kitt for an increase in wages?"

"No, I haven't," was the frustrated response. "Besides his regular clients, he only has the tourists from Bath, Bristol, and Cheltenham in the summers. And it's only April."

"You also have them from Taunton and Oxford, don't you?" asked Elsie.

"Yes, but we're not close to a large city or the Grand Atlantic or Imperial Hotels, so we don't get a lot of the tourist trade really," pondered Rupert. "I'm going to have to look elsewhere."

For the next several weeks, Rupert Senior inspected the "Postings Announced" sections of the *Weston-Super-Mare Gazette*, the *Clevedon Journal*, and *Somersetshire Advertiser* available for guests in the hotel lobbies. "I can't find anything in the newspapers," he reported to Elsie over dinner one evening. "I talked to Charles Kitt today and explained our problem. He was most sympathetic and commended me on my work. But he said the store's income was at somewhat of a standstill. He was thinking of letting someone go, not me, but someone less dutiful. He spoke of a possible opportunity in Bristol. He told me of a grocery distributor's son he knew who supplied him with some canned wares, whose father owned several groceries throughout Bristol. Charles said he'd give me a letter of introduction, and next Tuesday I'm off to take the train to Bristol to visit him."

The following Tuesday, at dawn's earliest hint, with Elsie's encouragement, a finely pressed wool suit, a jaunty bowler, and a slurpy kiss from his son, Rupert set off for Bristol. Elsie was so nervous all day that she kept bumping into closed doors she thought she'd opened, forgetting where she'd laid down her sewing, her scissors, her spectacles, or little Rupie's rag doll. She even forgot to read her son a western story after his afternoon nap from the American children's book. "Where's father?" she asked of no one in particular for the nth time in the early evening. "It's getting dark, and he's not here yet."

"He's gone to London to see the queen," offered young Rupert trying to help, remembering one line from a favorite rhyme.

Finally, an hour after the sun had set, the rapping on the closed front door pronounced Rupert's arrival. "I may have a posting. I may have a hiring," opening the door, he excitedly voiced to his anxious wife. Hugging her tightly and lifting her from the floor, he added, "Edgar Shirley liked me. He's recommending me to his father. They're adding to their employees in Clifton."

"Clifton," Elsie repeated. "Clifton's the nicest section of Bristol. It's where all the swells live!"

"That's right," her husband responded, tickling his smiling son under the chin. "And I'm going to be there next Tuesday to meet Mr. Samuel Shirley, Mr. Edgar Shirley's father."

Next Tuesday came and went. The young father had made a favorable impression on the senior Shirley, who hired him as an assistant grocer for his expanding store on Whiteladies Road at the bottom of Camdon. The year was 1905, and Rupert Senior would remain an employee of Shirley's for the next twenty-five years.

Renting a room for himself near the store for a short

time, Rupert eventually found a suitable new dwelling at 15 Longfield in St. Andrews Park. It was a two-story flat with four large front windows, three bedrooms, a kitchen, dining room, and living area. There was a small stone-fenced yard for little Rupie in the rear. Nearby was a large, tree-laden park in front of St. Andrews church, with rambling, rolling grass-covered hills especially useful for young boys who loved to run after imaginary friends, tumble like the monkeys in the Bristol Zoo, and climb amongst the branches of a friendly elm.

Chapter 2
Growing Up in Bristol

Britain, 1906-10

After Elsie and Rupie were settled in their new home, the Thronsons visited several primary schools, including the famous Bristol Cathedral School behind the Abbey Gateway, founded in 1140. Finding it and others too expensive for their means, they enrolled their six-year-old son in Christ Church Elementary School in Clifton. It was conveniently close to Shirley's Grocers and had a good reputation for providing a sound education.

Young Rupert's schooling fell into the normal pattern of riding to school with his father in a public horse-driven carriage over Cobden Hill, down Whiteladies, and up to the school off of Queens Road in the mornings; and walking home from school in the early afternoon with his mother who faithfully trod the three miles from Longfield to Christ Church School, then back again with her son. In the late afternoons, when the weather allowed, the young boy would play in the park or, during the rainy season, draw or play games in his home or at Alphie Goodpasture's flat. Their favorite game was pretending that they were Knights of the Round Table. They would trade off playing the evil Black Knight, the brave White Knight, and, sometimes, one would even be King Arthur. They had so much fun with these play games that their mothers had made little costumes and their fathers cut impressive-looking swords from the soft wood of crates Rupert Senior brought home from Shirley's. When other children joined them, each would chose a knight's, page boy's, or squire's role, or even the Maid Marian, or a hand servant part that was always reserved for girls.

After the Queen's Street episode, little Rupert had gained the local reputation among his peers of being quite fearless and not at all ashamed of nudity, which he would willingly display at any of his friends' requests at the drop of a pence. After entering at the unveiling part of one of these performances, his mother insisted that her husband have a long serious talk with his impetuous son about the sinfulness of the naked body and the shamefulness of the public houses where people exhibited themselves for money. Rupert Senior did his best to speak in terms his son would understand, and, though listening intently, the boy couldn't think of any other ways to be rewarded but to remove his attire at the plunk of a coin. In any case, he now knew what "stripper" meant.

During the late afternoon and on Sundays, after church services and depending on the weather, the small family either walked home, hailed a horse-drawn cab with a coachman, or took the trolley which ran on either side of the metal, electrically powered poles, which curved along the middle of Whiteladies Road to the center of Bristol. Sometimes, they boarded the double-decker buses that had replaced the horse-drawn buses running up and down Queens Road from in front of the Victoria Rooms to the downtown area. On the top of some of the buildings or over the doors of shops, colorful advertisement signs announced the available goods and services. Rupie's favorite was a large Fry's Chocolates poster featuring a ten-year-old boy, who was pictured identically five times in the same pose in his striped child's sailor suit and scarf, but with five very different facial expressions. His father read the poster's announcements to him: "Desperation - he wants to taste the chocolate; pacification - he has to earn the privilege; expectation - it's almost time; acclamation - he's getting ready; and realization - he's chewing on it - It's Fry's." Other signs promoted Masons, the jeweler, Miss Madin, two sisters who sold dairy products, restaurants like the Italian Trattoria, La Couch's Bar, Bon Appetite with French cuisine, and Rossi's, which specialized in Greek food.

Leaving Rupie with Mrs. Siddons, Rupert and Elsie attended a lecture or concert at the massive Victoria Rooms. They also saw an occasional play, which Elsie would dutifully describe to Rupie. At Shirley's, customer visits were regularized. Mrs. Cecil Watson came on Mondays; Mrs. Peter Stockworth collected her purchases on Tuesday; Mrs. Petersen on Wednesdays; and so forth. Sometimes, a housemaid or cook would come in place of her employer. Many years later, the daughter of Sir George Oatley, Bristol's most prominent architect, who had designed the University of Bristol Tower and fifteen other major buildings of the industrial city, was to write: "A trip to Shirley's was always a special occasion."

On Saturdays, when little Rupert was out of school, he sometimes accompanied his father to Shirley's and helped pour rice or meal into barrels, stacked canned vegetables on shelves, or packed boxes with debris for the dustbin man to pick up. He often watched his father greet one of his female patrons at the bottom rung of her expensive carriage's steps and with a welcoming outstretched hand lead her into the front of the well-stocked grocery store. where checkered-cloth-covered tables were arranged to provide tea to the grocery's mostly lady customers.

Rupie would watch his father enjoying measuring the different blends of exotic Indian tea, Shirley's specialty, into decorative metal strainers and pouring the always boiling water into delicate Westmoreland tea cups. Invariably, the matronly woman would remove a paper sheet from her ever-present handbag, unfold it, and read it aloud while his father, pen and paper in hand, would write out the order. Rupert Senior, in turn, though still an assistant grocer, would call one of his aides, ordering him to prepare the requested goods in wickered reed baskets while he added up the price of each item. Conversation covered the weather, the latest pronouncements of the Lord Mayor, and what theatrical companies were visiting the Hippodrome or Bristol Old Vic theatres. Often, the young grocer would select a container from a special shelf of goods and introduce his buyer to a new product In those days, long before the introduction of "supermarkets," one bought meat and poultry in a local butcher shop; bread and rolls in a bakery; vegetables and fruit from a greengrocer; wines from an ale and beverage trader; sugar, spices, rice, meals, tea, coffee, chocolate, and canned and packaged goods from a grocer; and cigars from a tobacconist.

When the two Ruperts, young and old, returned home on these special Saturdays after little Rupie helped his father at the shop, he often imitated the mannerisms, gestures, and speech patterns of his father's customers to entertain his parents. Both, somewhat apprehensive that they might be encouraging negative behavior, found their son's miming so engaging they succumbed as a willing audience and actually looked forward to Rupie's interpretations of Shirley's fashionable patronage.

When the boy was seven, his teacher, Miss Fanny Usherholme, sent an invitation to Mr. and Mrs. Thronson to visit her on a Thursday afternoon after school. The following Thursday, with no idea what Miss Usherholme had in store for them, they placed Rupie in the competent custody of Sara Siddons and apprehensively walked to Christ Church School. Once there, the anxious couple entered Miss Usherholme's classroom on a very cold, gusty, and rain-filled, darkened day. The news they received was equally dreary.

"Your son has many talents," began the portly educator with a tied-back gray-hair bun. "He has a definite gift for drawing pictures and coloring. However, he's a born 'cut-up.' Not only does he make fun of his fellow students by repeating almost everything they recite in class in a loud whisper, but every time I turn my back on him, he's imitating me. Not only that, but look at this!"

The teacher opened a large brown folder full of child-scrawled sketches. From amongst them, she pulled out a large linen sheet and held it in front of the subdued adults. What looked like a drawing of a bilious Humpty Dumpty with dark hair drawn at the back into a bun, a distorted face twisted into a vicious smile, and wearing a dress similar to a ballet dancer's tutu, was, without doubt, the very lady in front of them. "I'll not tolerate this type of behavior in my class. I've spoken to the headmaster about it. Mr. Beavons is waiting in his office to discuss this matter with you." And, with that, she turned, and exited the room.

"I'm afraid Rupie has gone too far," Rupert sadly remarked to his wife. "We'll have to find him another school." Agreeing, his wife led her dismayed husband down the long dim corridor to the headmaster's office.

In the carriage on the way home, the parents were somewhat relieved. Mr. Beavons, though sternly in support of his teacher, had provided a solution to the problem. There was another class of the same grade as young Rupert's, which had just gained an opening due to a departing pupil whose family was moving to South Africa. A male teacher, Mr. Hadley, who was very popular with the boys, was the teacher. "Perhaps," offered Mr. Beavons, "young Rupert will fare better in a new situation."

So it was that the youth moved into a new phase of his life, which was to influence his future. "Mr. Hadley's a corker," he reported to his eager parents at dinner after his first day in the new class. "He told his class that a talented artist had been invited to join his twenty brilliant students and asked that, during the next few weeks, I draw a picture of each one of them to post on the front wall of the classroom. He told the boys to treat me like a mate, to tell me about themselves as I drew each of their sketches in the cloak room behind the class. That's all I did - the whole first day. It was keen."

The Thronsons soon realized Hadley was a "gift from God," Elsie's term. He took a genuine interest in each of "his boys," learning as much as he could about their individual skills and interests. "A weakness may be an overdone strength," he often said. "But we must build on our strengths."

Instead of standing in front of his class all day like most teachers, he was right in the middle of a chaos of noise and activity much of the time. Every boy was engaged in some kind of personal project: carving a wooden statue with shavings whittled into a large storage box, putting together a four-string instrument, or painting a "Happy Birthday" sign for a parent. Oh yes, they'd recite their lessons, repeat Biblical verses aloud, and do their "times tables." But outside, rain or shine, they'd play such games as hopscotch, catch-one-catch-all, and a modified version of cricket, a sport Mr. Hadley had played at Oxford. Rupert flourished.

Hadley, a dark-haired, handsome, raw-boned young man, encouraged him to draw. He also read pieces from Shakespeare and had the boys choose their favorite parts to read. When Mr. Hadley suggested his students try acting out some of the roles in King Arthur's Court, the classmates all made their own costumes, and Mr. Hadley wrote a short play in which everyone had a character to perform. Days went by too fast, weeks turned into months, and, in August 1908, promoted upwards to the next level, Rupert had to say his farewells to his very favorite teacher.

During the next two years at Christ Church Elementary School, Rupert made so many friends he was always visiting someone else's house. His deportment in school was exemplary; his marks in literature, mathematics, English, Latin, and history were good; and all of his teachers encouraged his drawing.

As a reward, Elsie had, after much persuasion, condescended to taking little Rupert, now growing at a Jack-and-the-Beanstalk pace, to a Saturday matinee at Bristol's Hippodrome theatre. Dan Leno, the great early twentieth-century comedian, was featured in a musical revue called *Hip, Hip, Hurray!* It included a dog act, jugglers, a female opera singer, a classical pianist, a balancing act, and a dancer in a giraffe costume.

Following the previous opening night performance, the *Bristol Globe* review reported: "Last night a star company of 50 talented artists in all sorts of acts and ten real bloodhounds graced our local stage. The dogs were excellent, but they had very little support." This wasn't boy Rupert's impression. To his parent's consternation, but to the delight of his neighborhood playmates, he replayed every moment of the review he could remember, making up the parts he'd forgotten, pretending he was catching the imaginary bowling pins of the juggler, somersaulting if a flip off the ground was warranted, and wearing his father's coattails to imitate Leno jokes he didn't even comprehend.

"The boy's going to be an actor," his mother pronounced on one of the few balmy Bristol nights when the stars could be viewed from the tiny Thronson backyard.

Sherry glass in hand, Rupert said firmly, "Over my proverbial diseased and debauched dead corpse."

"Rupert, how awful," his surprised wife responded.

"No, Elsie," Rupert continued. "Our son is going to be a barrister, a chartered accountant, or a government servant."

"Not a grocer's assistant?" his wife queried.

"Well, that's not such a bad situation, is it? The occupation's treated us quite well," Rupert responded somewhat defensively. "Besides, Rupie's been helping out quite famously on Saturdays. I've decided to put him on wages."

"Have you told him, ducks?" his wife said fondly.

"No, not yet. I'll surprise him next Saturday."

The following Saturday, Rupert Senior opened the grocery store promptly at eight, gathered his seven assistants and clerks for a brief meeting to plan the day's business activities, and announced, to the boy's great surprise and delight, that his son would be, henceforth, a clerk's helper. As Rupie followed his taller and stronger fellow employees around that day, he learned to imitate their actions, even though they took him longer and he worked harder to accomplish them.

At one point, in a storage room, when he was underneath a large wooden carton attempting to lift it upward from one shelf to another, a rough low-pitched voice said gently, "May I assist you, my lad?" As the boy looked up, a kind hand ran softly across his head, and the large well-dressed man picked the carton from his hands and placed it gently on the upper shelf. Clasping his hands together, the gentleman suggested, "You must be Rupert Thronson's son. Where is he? I've got a nice surprise for him."

At that very moment, the father entered the back room, "Oh, Mr. Shirley, I didn't know you were here. I see you've met Rupie."

"Yes, I see he tries to lift boxes bigger than he is. He'll make a fine grocer, don't you think?"

"Of course, Mr. Shirley. If you say so."

"I don't actually, Rupert. He's going to make us all proud," Shirley offered with a wide grin. "You see, his father is going to be able to send him to a splendid school that grocers' sons can't often afford."

"I don't know what you mean, sir," said a cautious Rupert.

Clasping his assistant grocer by the upper arms with his strong hands, the large store proprietor said, "Bring in our Shirley workers. I have an announcement to make!"

Once the assembly had hastily gathered in the box-filled room, Shirley addressed them. "My accountant has just reported the profits from our seven Bristol grocery stores for the year. This store, our Clifton branch, has outperformed the others by a wide margin. Accordingly, each of you will receive a generous Christmas bonus, and I'm making Rupert Thronson a full manager, moving Mr. Shelgrave to a new position in my central office." The din of collective pleasure was infectious. "Let's all have a cup of tea," Shirley suggested, "so we can toast our newest manager."

Before Shirley left the store, he sat privately in the Shelgrave office discussing well-laid-out plans with Rupert.

"And I don't want my key store managers living in shabby digs. We're moving you to Clifton. As a matter of fact, my solicitor, Henry Anderson, has a flat for let on Melrose Place, just down the street, that you and the missus might be interested in."

Reporting the happy news to his astonished wife that evening, Rupert Senior poured out his long-cherished dreams to his attentive listener. "I can't wait for you to see the flat at 11 Melrose Place. I never imagined we could afford anything like it. It's huge, has three bedrooms, there's a sitting room for you, an immense drawing room, and a spacious rear garden for Rupie and our new dog."

"Our new dog," Elsie repeated.

"Yes, and it's time we had a governess for Rupie. You've become very busy sewing for the hospital committee and helping out at the Bowling Green. Besides, I'm going to need your help with the store accounts as the new manager. I don't trust anyone else to review the receipts."

CHAPTER 3
The Governess

Bristol, 1910

In good time, the Thronsons were settled in their new quarters, just two blocks from Shirley's. They had acquired a new dog, a lively cocker spaniel, which Rupie named Daisy, and they were conducting interviews for a governess.

"I liked the last person I met today," Elsie reported the minute Rupert Senior had placed his derby on the hat stand by the carved-oak front door with the oval, stained window at the top. "She has excellent letters, even though she's only seventeen. She also comes from a family of butlers, maids, cooks, governesses, and hand servants. They've taught her everything they know."

"Hire whomever you want, dear. You know what's best for Rupie," her husband acquiesced. "What's her name?" he inquired.

"Angela."

Now nine years old, the young Thronson was soon to worship his new governess. Her primary duties were to entertain Rupie after school, feed him when his parents were unavailable, play his favorite games, toss the ball with him in the park, and see that he recited his school lessons.

The worst job was training Daisy to take care of her bodily needs in the proper places. Every time the puppy made what looked like a pained expression, the closest one would rush the poor dog out the back door and place him on the lush green lawn. Father did not tolerate puppy "accidents." It didn't take Angela too long to teach the pet how to scratch lightly on the door when the need arose, but this was after Rupie began taking Daisy on regular walks with a lead.

On Saturdays, Rupie still went to Shirley's to help his father, and Angela had the day off. Saturdays, too, were the only times Elsie had to herself to wash the Thronson clothes, iron, clean and pick up the house, and conduct the essential weekly shopping. Sundays were for church and family outings, and often Angela was invited to walk on the quay, picnic at the Downs, stroll through Castle Park, or watch the ships sailing up the Avon from the Clifton Suspension Bridge, although she always refused.

With Angela's insistence, Rupie reviewed his lessons regularly, even though hers was a limited education and she could neither read nor write. Rupert was fulfilling his promise in school. Angela had a bright and active mind, a remarkable memory, and flair very much like young Rupert for imitating people. Through drilling Rupie on his lessons, she began to learn the rudiments of addition and subtraction, the alphabet, and simple word formation. Reminded of Mr. Hadley, he made this a mutual project for the two of them. Her new position, Angela firmly believed, would take her out of the foulness in which she lived. Illiterate, she knew that if she could read and write, she could flee from her present conditions. She was determined to succeed as a governess.

What Elsie didn't know about Angela, as well, was that her letters of recommendation were false. A product of the waterfront, the ninth child of eleven, eight girls and three boys, she had grown up in squalor, which her forged documents for employment did not indicate. Her mother was a cleaning woman for a pub, one of the most popular on the quay, the Plough and the Bow, loudly frequented by scores of dock workers and seamen from the maritime fleet of the world: Spain, Portugal, Brazil, Canada, America, Japan, and China. Angela's father, whom she had never known to be sober, made his paltry family contribution by running messages or providing supplies, primarily whiskey and rum, to the sailors minding their ships in the harbor. His sons, aged five through ten, were, more than often, his go-betweens, collecting currency for the tobacco, drink, weapons, or clothing desired by his sea-worn customers. Angela's father, on occasion, provided prostitutes, among them, beginning as young as nine, his supple daughters. His family's ramshackle flat served as the brothel. Their mother had trained the daughters, who also provided income to the family through sewing, cooking, and cleaning the homes of the upper class, in the wiles of lovemaking. But, strangely, Angela's parents honored their own faithfulness to one another. To them, part of survival was bringing children into the world to help provide for the family in any way they could contribute.

As Angela and little Rupert grew more accustomed to one another, one of their favorite pastimes was to make up stories about people they knew and then act them out. They pretended they were beggars in the park, outside vendors in the Old Market, horses pulling a rich lady's posh carriage, customers at Shirley's - any situation they could find to make fun of. They were both good at mimicking their characters, though it was difficult for one not to laugh when the other pulled an outrageous stunt, such as Rupie getting honey stuck in his hair when he was imitating Winnie the Pooh or Angela's sour demeanor as Queen Elizabeth. Daisy would always portray the horse, the lion, or the monkey in the jungle.

Although the boy had many friends at school, he now lived in a more exclusive area where the inhabitants tended to be older, and there were not many children his age. Without a brother or sister, young Rupert learned from Angela what it was to share the same chocolate, sit on another's lap so you only had to buy one seat on the now-motorized public autobus, and negotiate who wanted to do what, when, and for how long. Occasionally, Angela would walk the four miles to the waterfront with little Rupert. He would pick out words on signs such as "the," "old," "king," "prince," and have Angela recognize the letters and pronounce them.

Rupie would hear the whispered comments from among the many vendors selling their wares spread on blankets at shipside along Baltic Wharf: "Angie, 'ow 'bout a toss, lass," "Are ye better than yur sis?" "I've got a lovely shillin' that's ready for yur palm." There were even loud calls from the railings of the many vessels loading or unloading huge bundles of goods by large winches fixed to the heavy masts. "When'll we meet tonight, Angie?" "Do I see you or your pa for the fix?" and even with thick accents, "Senorita, iss it a fiesta or no?"

On one of these outings, Angela met a young, hairy-faced British bosun's mate, Marsh, at the front door of her home near Canons. She told Rupie to wait outside while they talked inside. With a stick in the dirt, Rupie painstakingly drew the silhouette of a three-master he could see just by the old two-story building the couple had entered, pondering what Angela could be discussing with the young man.

Within only a few minutes, the bearded man opened the solid-oak front door and came out of the house. Tossing a trupence to Rupie, he muttered, "Wasn't as good as las' time," then loped off with a grin.

Several weeks later, on another visit to the quay, Rupie was in the disorderly common area of the house when Angela greeted a man at the front door, this time a solidly built, uniformed carriage driver who had left his horse and buggy on the street. Addressing Rupie, Angela excused herself. The door to the bedroom into which the mustached man had lifted her was ajar. When the giggles and sighs attracted him to the opening, Rupie could easily see a trouserless man bouncing atop the naked governess. He watched as long as he was undetected. Through the door opening, he saw the coach driver place several coins in Angela's hand before he left. Although he felt it was wrong, and he didn't know what to call what they were doing, Rupie was jealous. He wanted Angela to himself.

Weeks passed, but the weather precluded returning to the quay, and much of the time was spent indoors in the Thronson household, which Daisy thoroughly enjoyed. Rupie didn't tell Angela what he'd observed.

One especially stormy day, Rupie decided he'd like to play one of his old knight roles from King Arthur and asked Angela to play the queen. They were in Rupie's upstairs bedroom formally decorated with pictures of foxhunts. Outside, Daisy was in the back garden. "I'm going to return from the Crusades. I've been wounded and you feel sorry for me," said Rupie, donning a blouse from his wardrobe and placing it over his Christ Church school uniform as he went into the hall. Angela reclined, as regally as she could, on Rupie's small quilt-covered bed. Closing then quickly opening the bedroom door, Rupie entered with a stately swagger holding his father's nightstick as if it were a sword. "Oh my queen, my queen, I've returned from the wars. But I've been wounded."

"Alas, where have you been injured, my brave knight?" Angela said majestically raising both her arms.

"In the flanks, damsel. In the flanks." Dropping his trousers and undershorts abruptly, with no embarrassment whatsoever, Rupie pointed to a freckle on his upper right thigh, exposing himself

"Rupie, put your knickers back on," Angela demanded. And Rupie obeyed, quickly pulling his trousers up from the shoes upon which they had fallen. "Now don't do that again," the governess said, testing her authority. Rupie was slightly amazed at her anger. She had seen him naked, having bathed him sporadically when he had encountered mud or dirt during their play times.

Over the next few weeks, Rupie refrained from exposing himself again, but, one afternoon, after she had drawn the bath, and he lay in the warmly soaped water, he shut his eyes and tried to remember how his friend Angela had looked without her clothes on. If she went to the loo, he'd try to look through the cracks in the door. This didn't work, but he always tried it when he could. If she put on or took off a sweater, he always stopped what he was doing to eye her maturing breasts.

Angela was not unaware of Rupie's curious stares and ignored the noises she had heard at the loo's door. She, too, had stirring feelings when she hugged Rupie, or they tangled themselves up wrestling on the floor.

One day, young Rupert questioned his governess, "Wouldn't you like to be a stripper?"

"A what?" was the response.

"A stripper, someone who takes her clothes off for money," Rupie answered.

"Now, why would I do anything like that?" Angela inquired.

"Like I said - for money," Rupie said coyly. "I've got

three shillings I earned at Shirley's. Would you take off your clothes for me?"

They were in the living room of the Thronson flat. Rupie's parents weren't scheduled to return for another hour. "Come on upstairs to your room," said the teenager as she led her smaller ward up the staircase.

Once in the closed room, Angela confronted Rupert, and with a serious tone said, "Rupie, no one must know about this. But I will do it for you, for the money, because I need every pence I can gather to escape from my father, but only, only if you teach me to read."

Rupie nodded happily. Angela slowly removed her garments.

After the first time, each week Rupie would take three shillings out his eight-shilling weekly earnings to give to Angela. In return, and only when they were assured to be alone, Angela would take Rupie to one of the rooms in the Thronson home, bolt the door, slowly remove first her sweater, then her blouse, next her skirt, and, standing in a slip, a brief upper garment, and soft white underpants - take them off in turn. "Now read, Rupie, and let me see the words as you pronounce them?" They began with Dickens and then read *Treasure Island*, agreeing, without question, that the pub across from the Old Vic, the Stars and Angels, was where Robert Louis Stevenson had his villains plot their kidnapping. The "reading" sessions went on for three months, during which time Angela, naked, began reading the simplest words aloud herself. Several weeks into their sessions, Little Rupert, too, removed his clothing. Infrequently, they would touch and lightly fondle one another. Once they even wrestled on the floor. Rupert was uninhibited; to Angela, nakedness was neither embarrassing nor necessarily a prelude to a sexual encounter. From her earliest years, when the weather was warm, her family members ran about their home unclad without a thought about it.

During the fourth month, when they were alone one afternoon, Angela said, "Let's pretend that you're an oil painter, Rupie, and I'm your model. You can draw a picture like we saw at the City Art Gallery by the university." And with that, Angela removed her shoes and stockings and gracefully danced slowly across the room with Rupie's eyes taking in every move. Within a few minutes, Angela announced, "Posing session's over. Let's read!"

For the next month, they both enjoyed reading together without their clothing, followed by their drawing session. For their drawing encounter, Angela posed on a bed, a chair, or on the carpeted floor, each time, totally naked, striking a different position which would best accent her breasts, her face, or the bushy triangle joining her upper legs. The ten-year-old, now pushing eleven, always brought his special notebook with the large Chinese patterned paper sheets, his sketching quill, and a tiny bottle of India ink. Certainly not an accomplished artist, Rupie, nevertheless, showed a knack for capturing the natural proportions of Angela's attractive body. After their regularized sessions, he would faithfully hide his sketchbook under his bed, and, for the rest of the week, no reference would be made to the sessions until Angela's next invitation to an empty room.

One Saturday morning in November, Mrs. Thronson was dusting her son's room while "her men" were at the grocery store. Losing the grip on her duster as she brushed it against the gas lamp on the table next to Rupie's bed, she bent to pick it up, noticing the edge of the tell-all sketchbook peeking out from the comforter.

In twenty minutes, she was in her husband's office, abruptly pulling him away from his order-taking from an elderly widow. Rupert had only the hasty opportunity to call out to one of his supernumeraries: "Take Mrs. Radcliff's grocery order, will you?"

Once the office door was closed, the obviously agitated woman opened the sketchbook she'd been tightly clenching to a page with an easily recognizable full frontal view of an unattired Angela, held it up to her astonished husband, and declaring firmly, "She's sacked!"

The parting did not entail the "sweet sorrow" Shakespeare referred to. Angela was crushed by news of her dismissal, and Rupie was not only devastated and embarrassed, but also heartbroken that their pleasant rendezvous had been abruptly terminated. The Thronsons never saw Angela again. She had saved enough to escape her circumstances.

Rupert Thronson had confronted his son with the sketchbook, throwing it into the fireplace, and angrily pronounced, "The devil in you drew these filthy pictures." After Angela's departure, Rupie went on a hunger strike for a short time, and, for one solid week, a silence strike.

Concerned about her son's remorse, Elsie decided to present him with a surprise for his forthcoming 5 July birthday and phoned for tickets for Empire Theatre on Old Market Street. Wilkie Bard, a famous comedian, and a family of acrobats called the Sisters' Act were the headliners. After reviewing the variety show's line up in the *Bristol Times*, Rupert Senior hadn't objected. Sitting close to the front of the stage, Rupie was enthralled. He thought Bard was the funniest man he'd ever seen since he could make the simplest activities quite silly, such as miming a search for money in his pockets while purchasing a block of ice and then trying to carry it home. He whispered to his mother that he thought the acrobats, in his judgment, were "impossibly brave to risk their lives throwing themselves about." There was also a skillful bird imitator "whose owl sounds were the best," an opera singer who could vocalize "the highest notes I've ever heard," a "real, live lion," and "a comic who changed into women's' clothes right before our eyes." There was even a silly sketch from Oliver Twist where the boy Oliver dressed up like a villain and an evil-looking actor played the part of the boy.

Silence broken, Rupie talked of nothing else than his theatre experience and kept asking when they could attend again. The whole thrill of sitting among two thousand people in a fabulously ornate hall, surrounded by Greek statues, the huge curtain rising, the smell of the gaslights illuminating the performers, being amongst the laughter and applause, happily watching the skills and talents of remarkable people and even animals, provided him with memories that stretched through the following weeks as he shared his experiences with schoolmates and verbally relived the moments with his patient parents. "When can we go again?" "Can I use the shillings I've saved?" "What's coming to town?" were among his constant questions.

Finally, his parents consented. The Karro Troupe would soon be arriving in Bristol performing in *The Football Match.* Elsie assured her husband that the content found in a sporting event could not have a questionable influence on their young son. Because it was about rugby, which Elsie didn't understand, Rupert Senior was assigned to accompany Rupie to the People's Palace Theatre on Baldwin Street.

Rupie could hardly wait until the Saturday matinee arrived. He insisted that he and his father arrive one hour early in case there was a mistake about their seats. The moment the front doors to the impressive theatre opened, Rupie and his father were the only ones to present their tickets to the attendants. Shortly after they were seated in an empty theatre, one hour before the performance was to begin, Rupie asked if they could explore the building. Together, he and his father examined the colorful murals on the sides of the theatre. They depicted Chinese dragons with long necks and outstretched arms walking over the tops of trees in a forest. Next, they studied the murals of the Palace's past performers. Fortunately, for Rupert Senior, their names were embossed in brass plates at the bottom of each picture.

"They're only actors," his father reported, "not important people. Performing in a theatre is not thought to be an honorable type of employment." Even so, Rupie read the names to himself as he thoughtfully perused their images, posed in the costume of a character for which each was noted: Mrs. Patrick Campbell, Gladys Cooper, Seymour Hicks, John Martin-Harvey, George Robey, Ellen Terry, Sybil Thorndike, Herbert Beerbohm Tree, David Garrick, Henry Irving, and William Shakespeare were all in handsome frames.

Little did the boy know that within their lifetimes, save one, all of the male actors framed will have been knighted and each of the women titled as "Dame." Mrs. Campbell was a stage queen who became famous for her leading role in Pinero's *The Second Mrs. Tanqueray* and was George Bernard Shaw's first Eliza in *Pygmalion*. Dame Gladys Cooper had graduated from being a chorus girl and pin-up to becoming one of Britain's greatest actresses of her time. Sir Seymour Hicks, an actor-director-writer-comedian, wrote the first musical revue ever performed in London. Sir John Martin-Harvey, an actor-manager who was a pupil of Henry Irving, later touched theatrical greatness as Oedipus Rex. Sir George Robey became known as the English musical hall "Prime Minister of Mirth." Dame Ellen Terry was easily the leading Victorian actress of her time. Shaw's greatest St. Joan was the accomplished actress and tragedienne Dame Sybil Thorndike who helped first spread the prominence of London's Old Vic as a performing house. Actor-manager Sir Herbert Beerbohm Tree, because of his elaborate Shakespearian productions during the latter part of the nineteenth-century, was to be the founder of His Majesty's Theatre in London and the first Higgins in *Pygmalion* opposite Mrs. Campbell. David Garrick was the great eighteenth-century Shakespearean actor who managed London's Drury Lane theatre for the majority of his career. Sir Henry Irving would become known as the finest of all Victorian actors. In William Shakespeare's and David Garrick's times, knighthood for men of the theatrical cloth was unheard of.

When they returned to the auditorium, there was still only a smattering of people in the audience and only a few more wandered in before the house lights dimmed and the new electrical lighting instruments brightened the stage. The aris had been drawn. The performance was more than Rupie could have hoped for. *The Football Match* was a comedy about a team preparing for an important game with its major rival. It had all the drama and elements of a real squad preparing for and engaging in a rugger contest. But, for him, he recognized his first stage hero, an impossible little man who emerged as the prize athlete of the game that had been performed on the Palace stage, a comic who captivated the audience with his gestures, his facial expressions, his acrobatic falls, and his struts across the stage as he won the game for the home team. That actor, whose father had played all the Bristol halls before his son, was easily the funniest person Rupie had ever seen. His name was Charlie Chaplin.

Chapter 4
The Actor Débuts

Bristol, 1913

Every year, in August, the Sawyer Brothers' Circus came to Clifton Downs. On the first Saturday afternoon of its arrival in 1913, after all the horse-driven vehicles had completed their journeys from a week at Bath and were assembled at the top of grassy parklands next to the famous Clifton Bridge and across the Avon Gorge from Leigh Woods, it was a wondrous treat for children to watch the "set up." They were permitted to view all of the intricate pieces that together composed the entire circus - the canvas bags, rolled up cloth, lumber, and wooden stools - pulled out and unfolded from the backs of the carts and the beds of wagons that the parade of workers, men as well as women and children, readied, rapidly and efficiently, wasting no motion. Within a minimum of time, right before the spectators' eyes, appeared a gaily colored hodgepodge of booths, tents, cages, and fenced areas for the animals - all surrounded by the horse-driven house carts for the tents, scenery, and performers.

When the massive doors of the largest wagon were opened, and Jumbo the elephant emerged, "oohs" and "ahs" dissolved into spontaneous applause. The enormous pachyderm appeared to recognize this adoration with a polite nod and upward swing of his massive trunk. Small tents were reserved for the side shows - "Ronald Ripley, The Terribly Shrunken Man," "Nadua, The Fire Eater," and "Let Cockney Jack Guess Your Weight."

The huge main tent, as high as a schooner's masthead, was where the two-ring circus headlined a one-hour performance of gymnasts balancing on white horses, clowns pantomiming skits in their colorful suits and ridiculous make up, acrobats swinging over the audience on ropes and hanging bars, Jumbo performing like a trained dog, and the lion tamer playing with the occupants of his cage of huge jungle cats.

Rupie and his father were among the spectators observing the assortment of Sawyers' Circus being assembled. Rupie was in total awe of the many scenes unfolding before him. Excitedly running from place to place, he didn't want to miss anything, causing his father to often lose the boy in the increasing crowds that grew around each activity occurring simultaneously. Rupie rushed from cage to cage to view the different animals all nervously and variously adapting to their new surroundings for the two-week run - the monkeys, the horses, the lions, the black bear, and the penguins. He witnessed the erection of the three-sided tents, each fronted by a small stage for the sideshow performers. After the sizeable canvas walls had been raised over the wooden framework that held up the main tent, Rupie peeked through one of the flapping curtains as several workman hammered the forms which were to be the circus rings, others unhinged risers that would hold ticketed spectators, while still others were up in the rigging securing the many ropes which hung from the high central canvas steeple.

For two hours, Rupert Senior followed, lost, then found, followed, lost, and eventually again found his awestruck son. With patience at an end, he pointed Rupie towards College Road and said, "It's time to go home, Rupie. Supper's waiting." Reluctantly, the twelve-year-old scanned the busy scene for a final look, and then followed his father across the spacious, well-manicured green lawn.

Once the supper plates, filled with roast beef and potatoes, were served, Rupie, knowing full well that he needed two adult votes for confirmation, asked eagerly, "When are we going to the circus?"

His father answered first, "In this household, son, we work for our amusements. We just don't receive them for doing nothing."

"Yes, Rupie, with Angela gone and you still on school holiday, you're occasionally going to have to stay at my sewing lady's, Mrs. Dickson's home. You can help her with her mending business," his mother added. "She needs someone to pick up the clothing and drapery she sews, take it back to her customers when she's finished, and collect the payments."

"It'll be good employment for you," proclaimed his father. "You'll learn how to handle money. If you get right to it tomorrow, you'll have enough shillings to buy a ticket for the circus in a fortnight."

"Couldn't you lend me enough to go tomorrow," little Rupert implored.

"Tomorrow's the Holy Day. We can't allow you to attend a circus on Sunday," his mother responded.

Begrudgingly, Rupie compromised. "How about Monday after school? I'll ask Phillip if he can get permission to go, too. Please take us, Mother. Please take us," he pleaded."

"Rupert," she turned to her husband, "I have to attend the prayer service planning meeting with Rector Evans on Monday. Could you take him?"

"So, that means you'll allow him to go on Monday," her husband said curtly.

"I really don't see why not," Elsie responded softly as if to sooth her husband's slight hint of ire. "You can write Rupie's first business contract, a credit for the price of a circus ticket."

Thoughtful for a moment, the father finally responded: "That is a splendid idea, Elsie. It's about time Rupert learned something about the business world. Being a debtor before he's a profiteer makes substantial sense. Rupie, is it a bargain, then?"

The boy nodded his head in affirmation, as his father went in search of paper and pen.

Sunday went by rapidly. First, church services; then, lunch and Bible-reading; hymn music at home with Elsie at the baby Steinway and both Ruperts playing violins; a short walk with Daisy; a brief visit by Rector Evans on his way to a sick parishioner; a walk to the Victoria Rooms for a lecture on "Modern India"; supper; a game of whist, which Elsie won; then, bed. Rupie had trouble sleeping. All the different visions of the circus being mounted filled the recesses of his mind, blending together in a mass of confusion before he fell into unconsciousness.

After his mother had accompanied him to Ann Dickson's flat across from the Thronsons' previous residence, Rupie listened intently as the jolly, plump, middle-aged woman showed him how to fold men's shirts and women's dresses, how to wrap newsprint around them into packages, tying string across the edges to make them secure. She took out a large map of the streets around St. Andrews Park and showed the boy where the houses were as she checked five names on a list she withdrew from her small cedar desk.

"Now, first, I want you to take these curtains to Mrs. Cecil Raymound on Lofhlin Road, and then around the corner is Mrs. Feeney's house. She only receives this blouse I sewed," Mrs. Dickson instructed. "Then, come back here; I'll have three more places for you to visit with mending to return. On each of these sheets of paper, I've written the amount of money you're to collect. If anyone gives you a little extra, you can keep it, but let me know who it is. All right, dear?" she added.

Under the weight of the large package of curtains and the smaller one for Mrs. Feeney, Rupie edged his way down the five sets of stairs, and with his back supported by the brass banister in front of the connected two-story dwellings that ran down the entire block, headed for his first assignment. His thoughts, naturally, were on the circus.

Promptly, at three o'clock, Rupert Thronson's loud knock was heard on Mrs. Dickson's front door, and Rupie, accustomed to the widow's home, anxiously opened it for both his father and his old friend, Phillip Maggs. "Let's go. Let's go," he urged.

Thanking Mrs. Dickson, Rupert Senior followed the excited boys into the waiting horse-driven landau and called to the driver seated in front of the covered cab, "The circus, please. The circus at Clifton Downs."

Forty minutes later, the trio was inside the six-foot temporary canvas fence that now encircled the circus grounds. "First, we'll see the show in the main tent. Then, we'll visit the sideshows. All right, boys?"

After a short wait, Rupert and the two boys found front stools on the platformed seating next to one of the two thick wooden rings that designated the sawdust stages over the ground that depicted the performance areas. In a two-ring circus, performers first gave their acts in one ring for one audience and then repeated them in a second ring to the other group of ticket holders. A small man with an unexpectedly booming voice announced each act through a large red megaphone. "Lay-dies and gen-tle-men, boy-ys and gi-rls," he broadcasted loudly. "May I have the attention of the audience in ring one? Entering the ring is our first act of the afternoon, Helena and Her Hearty Horsemen!"

A beautiful young woman, resembling a Greek goddess, outfitted in a shiny pink sequined military uniform, rode into the ring atop a handsome white steed, ornamented with red and blue ribbons tied to his sides from mane to swinging tail. Helena's long dark hair flying behind her, the woman galloped skillfully around one turn of the ring. She beckoned to the entrance that she had just left, and first one red-uniformed cowboy, then another in blue, followed by one dressed all in green, and still others in richly colored costumes depicting the wild west of America, galloped into the large tent.

Smiling widely as they waved to the cheering crowd, the cowboys, each in order, directed their horses around the ring in front of the audience, climbing down one side of the horse and up the other while the steed was in full stride. Performing further feats of skill while mounting and dismounting with the horse running, standing with only one foot on the saddle, and then drawing silver pistols and firing into the air drove the thrilled audience to unceasing applause.

Next were the clowns whose crazy antics included pretending to throw water on the crowd from buckets which turned out to be empty, shooting one another with rifles that shot banners with the word "bang," and conducting a mock safari into a forest of fake trees held by local Bristol boys to face and run from the emerging large hairy gorilla, another clown in costume. As the clowns jumped over the short barrier separating them from the laughing crowd to enter the audience area, Rupie thought he recognized one of the boys holding the profile of a cedar tree. *Yes,* he thought to himself, *that's Richard Bates. He was in the upper class at Christ Church when I started. I'm certain that's he.*

Bates, like the other boys, wore dark clothing and a black seaman's knit cap. After the clown act, Rupie noted that Richard Bates and the others set and removed the implements that the performers used, even the stool and the whip that the lion tamer, in his kingly outfit, carried into the feline cage, after Jumbo had danced his mammoth's jig and carried his master atop his enormous back. Choosing from amongst the side shows, they learned that Ronald Ripley was an ancient midget; Nadua an extremely dark Indian with a distinct British accent, who took only a very small lighted stick into his mouth; and Cockney Jack, according to his father, probably had a hidden scale under the carpet when he guessed a person's weight.

"Did you notice that before he made his prediction in stones," his father whispered. "He was looking at someone standing by the opposite wall? Maybe they were signaling."

Neither Rupie nor Phillip had noticed anything so dishonest, but they soon learned about illusion when they filed into a black-and-white-striped tent as spectators of "Martin the Magician, Master of the Mystic." After three large gas lamps were extinguished and the tent was dark, a bright circle of light suddenly appeared on the dark blue curtain hanging at the rear of the stage. Into the circle stepped Martin, a tall, mustached, handsome dark-haired man dressed in a black suit partially covered by a flowing black velvet cape. Martin performed one astonishing trick after another. He invited volunteers from the audience to choose playing cards from a deck that he would shuffle and, time after time, select the exact card that the volunteer had initially chosen. He took off his hat, turned it onto its top and drew out a small rabbit. He tied colored scarves together, tugged at them to insure the knots were secure, and then, miraculously, pulling them through a tube, brought them out singly - red, blue, green, purple, and magenta.

A pretty young woman, with a wide smile, wearing a long white gown with a hood almost covering her blond curls came onto the small stage from behind the curtain and announced, "For his next act, Martin, the greatest magician in the entire world," she paused as if to encourage the clapping spectators to unanimously agree with her, "will now perform the most dangerous and difficult act in his fabulous repertoire."

Martin bowed graciously and the applause grew louder.

Waving an arm for silence, the woman, scanning the audience with a dazzling smile, requested, "We're going to give out five shillings for this one. I need a volunteer, a boy." Small hands rose impulsively from the crowd of sixty. Among them was Rupie's.

"Take me!"

"Me, I volunteer!"

"Hello, over here!"

The woman's eyes settled on the Thronson boy. "Come up here, little man." she invited.

"Is it all right, father?" the boy asked.

With a nod of affirmation, Rupert followed his son along the raised platform and helped him up the three steep steps at the left side of the stage.

Alighting the stage floor, surprised by the brightness of the one light illuminating it, Rupie felt his hand gently taken in the warm grasp of the pretty woman who, after asking his name, turned, and said: "Martin, this is Rupert Thronson."

After shaking the larger hand that the wondrous magic man extended, Rupie was led off the stage to a small room behind the curtain where an older boy was adjusting a long wooden box over a curtained table with wheels. While Martin performed several scarf tricks for the audience, the woman informed Rupert he was about to be sawed in half.

Repulsed, Rupie started to run for safety. "No, no, you're not really going to be hurt. It'll just look like it. We have a trick box and table. That's why we have to have small boys to do it." She explained how Rupie would be tucked face down into the box with his head hanging out a hole at one end and two shoes sticking out the other end. He was to make his body into a ball bringing his legs to his stomach. Then, at her signal from the side of the stage, when a large cloud of smoke had concealed Martin and the box filled with Rupie, just after two saw strokes by the magician, Rupie was to bring his legs down and push open a concealed trap door that was covered by the curtained table. He would then slip under the curtain and stand next to Martin.

"But you must be an actor, Rupert. It's the main part of the act. The audience must believe that you're really being sawed in half."

"Even my father?" queried an uncertain Rupie.

"No, both your father and your friend know that it's just make believe. We told your father we'd selected you when he bought the three tickets for the show. I'm sure he's told your mate," she added. "Richard, will you show Rupert how to move in the box?"

"I know you," Rupie said as the tall boy helped him into the box. "You went to Christ Church Elementary, didn't you?"

"That's right, lad. I went there before I became an actor. Now just slide in here and crimple yourself up. Good. Now put your head into this one in the front, and I'll wrap a cloth around it so it won't hurt your neck."

"You're an actor?" Rupie asked just to make certain he'd heard right.

"Oh yes, mate. I'm just helping out at the circus. Martin's my uncle. And he is really a good magician. Actually, he helped me get started doin' just what you're doin' now." Continuing, "Now push down on this little door right by your belt. That's it. Do you feel the square opening? Now, crunch yourself up and get ready to put your feet through the hole." And as Rupie followed his instructions correctly, he said, "That's good. Are you ready to drop down?"

Rupie nodded.

The woman returned from peeking around the main curtain and bent down to address Rupie, whose head was extended from the front end of the brightly painted rectangular wooden box. "Do you know what to do with your body in the box?"

Rupie said: "Yes, miss."

"Now, I want to tell you how you're really going to earn your five shillings. Hopefully, you're going to become as good an actor as Richard is."

"How?" was the cautious answer.

"After you hear two long strokes of Martin's saw, you must scream and yell just as if you are actually being sawed in two. You must convince the audience that the steel teeth of the saw are really tearing your flesh. Is that understood?"

Rupie nodded.

"We can't make any noise back here so you'll have to save your screaming for the audience. Let me see you contort your face?" the girl asked.

Rupie scowled.

"No, that's not at all believable. Richard, bend down and show him what a tortured face is all about," she ordered.

Squatting in front of Rupie, the older boy squinted his features into a pained grimace, mouth open, upper lip curled at one end, eyes widened.

Rupie laughed nervously.

"Now you do it?" requested the woman.

Rupie complied, and both said as one, "Capital."

Just then, a female's terrified shriek was heard from the audience.

"What's that?" asked Rupie.

Richard replied, "Nothing, lad, it's uncle's knife throwing act. He pretends to throw at a volunteer who's tied to a wooden panel. The lady who screamed didn't realize that the knives spring up around the victim from behind the board, and Martin tucks the blades from his hand under his cuff as his arm comes forward in the throwing motion."

"The spectators watch where the blade will stick, fearing it will puncture the volunteer," the woman added. "They don't even look at Martin's hand as he throws."

Richard closed the two side hatches tightening the cover over Rupie's box. Loud applause indicated that the knife-throwing scene was concluded. As Richard wheeled Rupie out onto the stage in his box, head sticking out at one end, shoes at the other, he whispered, "Good fortune, lad. I'll talk to you when you're done."

Once the box was placed in the middle of the stage under a very bright light, Martin the Magician rounded it like a wolf sizing up his prey. Speaking to his audience about the numbers of unfortunate accidents that happen to great magicians who take such risks, he explained that, although he would definitely separate the top half of young Thronson's body from the bottom half, the trick itself was repairing the damage without a trace. Naturally, he did not reveal that not only had Rupie tucked his legs into a concealed trap opening, but the large saw he initially showed the audience would be hidden in the back of the box to be replaced by a trick saw which had a handle end and a saw blade end but no middle to sever Rupie, only an unseen rod inside the box holding the pieces together.

Introductory remarks at an end, the veteran trickster changed tools in a blink and began sawing. At the start of his third thrust of the blade forward, an inhuman wail rose from the throat of the head at the front opening of the box, a scream so frightening and unbelievable that the magician was not sure he'd made the proper exchange of saws.

The audience was in frenzy, some laughing, some crying out nervously to stop, others unconvinced that this was not an illusion, talking in loud warning voices. There was loud screaming. Soon after Rupie had forced his face into a hideous expression, smoke filled the stage and, quickly, he squeezed his legs down through the un-trapped door opening and onto the stage floor.

"Over here," Richard called as he helped Rupie out of the box. "Walk right through the center of the curtain and join Uncle Martin," he commanded. "Good show, Rupert," he called as the boy opened the curtain to meet the din of appreciation voiced by the overwhelmed audience.

Martin the Magician, beaming as he bent to shake Rupie's extended right hand, held out a five shilling silver piece in the other. "You've certainly earned this, my boy," he commended. "If ever you're looking for an acting job, come see me," he volunteered.

Receiving praise from both his father and a somewhat envious Phillip Maggs, throughout the rest of the afternoon and early evening, strangers approached Rupie to tell him how convincing he'd been. Rupie was in heaven.

Chapter 5
The Runaway

Bristol, 1913

Rupie entered the lower division of the Middle School of the Bristol Grammar School, well known locally as BGS, in September 1913. He was twelve, one of twenty-one boys in his class. His teacher, a Mr. Andrew J. White, was 40ish, a stout, fair-minded, granite-faced, strict Christian man who had served the British Army in India and still had a pronounced military bearing. Rupie's subjects included the following:

The Old Testament: Psalms and The Ten Commandments

Geography of the British Isles

World History from 1485 to 1832

Readings from Dickens

French Literature and Composition

Arithmetic

Geometry

Manual Training, an elective

Arithmetic covered decimals and proportions, algebraic equations, identities, graphs, multiplication and division; geometry introduced triangles and parallelograms. Manual Training involved the use of various workman's tools, water coloring, and pencil drawing.

An average student in the solids, Rupie immediately showed promise in his elective. He preferred learning from doing rather than listening. With almost five-hundred boys in the school, and lacking the higher prestige (and expense) of Clifton College, also a boarding school, BGS was, none-the-less, gaining greater repute and establishing conscientious standards. Its facilities included the Great Hall, a huge, impressive assembly room, where several classes could be held without disturbing one another; nineteen classrooms, four science laboratories, an art room, a carpenter's shop, lavatories, cloakrooms, a sizeable library, and a gymnasium. There were also two pavilions, the Fives courts, the rifle range, and playing fields. Blue uniforms and ties were required at all times except during sporting activities when the athletes were in playing attire and the spectators wore jerseys and long trousers.

Bristol Grammar School was originally founded at Bartholomew's, near Bristol, in 1561. After 230 years, it was re-opened at its present site adjacent to the University of Bristol. When Rupie entered BGS, Dr. Cyril Norwood, eventually Sir Cyril Norwood, led it. After leaving BGS to become headmaster at Harrow, one of England's most prestigious university preparatory academies, he eventually became the President of St. John's College, Oxford. Upon

Norwood's arrival in 1906, the school was in such poor straits that he was said to have saved it from extinction. During his tenure, lasting until 1916, Rupie's final year as well, the energetic headmaster had reformed the curriculum, removed unnecessary rote and redundancy, revitalized the School Board with distinguished men from commerce and academia, and encouraged involvement of faculty and staff with educational bodies of all kinds. In fundraising, he had made strong appeals to the generosity of the friends of the school, physically resulting in doubling its size. He developed a merit system to replace a punitive one and formed the largest troop of Boy Scouts in Bristol.

The school agreed with Rupie. There was reciprocation. He enjoyed his classmates, especially his friend, Phillip Maggs, son of Bristol's now leading furniture dealer, and Peter Gibbs, whose father was a loading master on the wharfs. The Maggs boy, who was to become Rupie's friend for life, was strikingly handsome, blue-eyed, well built, athletically gifted, sandy-haired, and uncommonly bright. Peter, in contrast, resembled a young Falstaff, large in every proportion, though he was keen of mind, saw humor in any action, and was loyal to the core, both in friendship and purpose. Rupie was now of average height, robust, fairly good-looking, talkative, and witty.

Beyond total immersion in school, each of Rupie's weekdays was additionally filled by one hour of violin practice, two hours of homework, and three hours of custodial chores at Shirley's.

Somehow he still found occasional bits of time to visit with Richard Bates, now a regularly paid employee at Bristol's Old Vic Theatre. Richard would meet Rupie for a brief chat through the fence at BGS, or they would have a rendezvous late at night in the theatre when Rupie could steal away from his parents' flat. Richard had embarked on his own personalized theatrical training program. He'd moved from backstage work to selling candies to the patrons in the front lobby of the theatre, providing him the time and funds to begin serious acting study with a private teacher.

"Mine's a good position, Rupie," he assured his younger friend late one evening as they sat against one of the brick walls in the alley behind the Old Vic. "It gives me a chance to watch different actors perform and see all the plays that come to Bristol. I know the stage doorkeepers at the other theatres, so I can see the daily rehearsals of understudies and supernumeraries practicing the current play. If a company's in repertory, I watch the whole new play before its evening performance. Every evening and on matinee afternoons, I'm viewing the real live performances," he reported cheerfully.

"That's ripping, Richard. That's really ripping," Rupie commented with genuine admiration.

"Also, I'm attending a new acting school," Richard said. "Saw an advertisement in the *Bristol Times and Mirror*. 'Miss Joyce Russell holds classes for acting, dancing, and calisthenics.'" Richard stood up, swung his body around and pranced like a graceful circus horse. "I signed up. Five quid a week for two classes. But, Rupie, I'm bursting apart with this one."

Returning to his sitting position against the wall, Richard asked, "Guess what? Last week, I saw Johnston Forbes-Robertson as Caesar in G. B. Shaw's *Caesar and Cleopatra*."

"Johnston Forbes-Robertson," Rupie gasped.

Richard described how Shaw had written the part especially for Forbes-Robertson, how he'd already played the role for three months in London, had been in Bath, and had brought the touring company to Bristol.

"His wife's in the cast. She's beautiful and an unbelievable actress." Richard had Rupie's full attention. "Gertrude

Elliott's her name. They met on a tour of *Romeo and Juliet.* They were married on the stage, just as if the characters they played never died. You sure can call that 'a storybook wedding.' I heard when they performed several of Shaw's new plays in America, their reviews were beyond belief."

"What's a review?" Rupie inquired.

"Haven't you ever read a review?" Richard responded with amazement. "If you get bad ones, the show closes. A review is what a newspaper's drama critic writes about a performance. It's his impression about a play and the performers. If it's good, people come. If it's not, they don't."

"Wasn't Shaw a drama critic?" Rupie asked.

"Yes, and a good one. He started as a book critic. Then he moved into music and drama reviews. He started writing plays when he believed he could do a better job than the dramatists he was reporting on. His first success was *Arms and the Man.*"

"But didn't he get in trouble with the Lord Chamberlain?" Rupie thought aloud.

"Good for you, Rupie. He did. The censor didn't like some of his subjects and some of his characters. He writes about social issues and promiscuity - things like that. That's why most of his plays were performed in America before they got though the censor here. Ever heard of a closet drama, Rupie?

Rupie shook his head.

"That's what Shaw writes. When he doesn't expect the Lord Chamberlain to give him a license for a play to be performed, he makes it into a book and sells a reading version," Richard said with certainty. "For a long time, he was a dramatist whose plays most people read instead of seeing."

"What's promiscuity?" asked Rupie.

"Promiscuity. It's just that." Richard slowly pronounced the syllables, "Prom-is-que-ity. We don't have to get into that. I want to tell you about Oscar Asche."

"Who's that?" Rupie inquired.

"Well, for one thing, he's Miss Russell's favorite actor-manager of them all. She's very fond of him. Says he reminds her of me, even though I'm still a lad."

"Why is that?"

"He was a rugged sort. He was born in Australia." Richard went on to tell Rupie about Asche's having lived alone in the bush country as a youth, killing and cooking his own food, and reading Shakespeare to his greyhound dog. When he decided on acting as a career, his Norwegian father, a rough and tumble man who'd been everything from a policeman to a gold seeker, sent Asche to Norway to learn acting. When he came to England, he joined Frank Benson's Bensonians, primarily because of his brawn and his ability as a first-rate wicket keeper. According to Richard, Asche's first role was in *As You Like It,* because he was the only actor in the company who could wrestle with Benson and make it look believable.

"That's the kind of actor I want to be, an Oscar Asche. Rupie, you'll never believe it. Asche started just like me. He took odd jobs no one else wanted. He worked his way up from being a super to second leads. After touring with the Bensonians for several years, he joined Tree at His Majesty's Theatre in London. There, he played more important roles, finally becoming hugely successful in *The Taming of the Shrew.* It was a breathless, knockabout, rampageous performance. They played it as a farce; the audience couldn't stop laughing. He's also the best Othello I've ever seen. His immense voice and physique are just right for the role. He certainly beat the devil out of Iago."

Rupie's interest piqued when Richard told him of Asche's

keen interest in authentic scenery. Rupie shared his own new success in drawing at BGS. He asked Richard to describe Asche's design of the Forest of Arden in *As You Like It.*

"He had artificial forest glades that you couldn't tell from the real thing. There were masses of ferns two feet high he changed every week after the actors had trod over them. The ground was covered by thick autumn leaves, fallen logs lay half hidden by real moss, and there were clumps of bushes that looked like they were growing among the larger green trees. Rows of pines disappeared into the distance. And Asche," Richard, rising again, pretending he was on stage, continued, "He delivered the 'seven ages' speech chewing on an apple." Richard munched on an imaginary apple. "You see, he's very keen on natural settings."

Rupie, as always, listened, wide-eyed, taking in every syllable. Richard who was well read in the subject, had described the individual styles and performance techniques of the nine most prominent actor-managers in the kingdom on stage with Rupie. When Rupie began asking insightful questions about their facial expressions and gestures, Richard said, "Who could say you're not going to be an actor?"

Rupie studied hard at Bristol Grammar School. His talents were apparent in drawing and sketching any of the subjects the art teacher set before the class: bowls of fruit, statues of Greek gods, a dueling pistol, a bouquet of flowers, as well as working with tools, metal and wood. His parents always looked forward to his bringing home a new example of his craftsmanship. By no means a graceful athlete, Rupie still held his own in most sporting contests and had a particular fondness for cricket. He, Phillip, and Peter usually managed to be on the same side. By June, he'd completed a surprise present for his mother in manual training class, a drawing of a theatre. But his parents also had a surprise for him.

"My lad," his father addressed him alone one night, as the rain raged outside their front windows. "Your mother and I are sending you on your school holiday to Coventry to visit your Uncle Charles and Aunt Gladys and your two cousins. You're to spend the early part of your vacation fortnight with them. Mother and I will join you later."

Rupie was elated. He had hoped his father might want to visit his only brother as he often did in the summer. This might provide him with the chance he was waiting for. Although he and his cousin James, who was close to his own age, were friends, better yet, he'd learned from Richard the previous day that Martin the Magician was performing in a theatre in Birmingham, which was very close to Coventry.

"Phillip, Peter, come over here," Rupie called to his mates during a Thursday afternoon cricket match the last week before vacation, "I want to tell you something."

"What is it?" inquired Phillip as he and Peter sat on the grass on either side of Rupie.

"I'm running away. I'm going to become an actor," Rupie announced confidently. "And you two are not to tell my secret," he added sternly.

"How are you going to do it, Rupie?" Peter whispered huskily, as if the crowd of boys gathered near them on the cricket field might overhear them.

"Yes, how?" added Phillip.

Rupie told them about his planned seasonal visit to his uncle's cottage in Coventry, but he had a scheme to find Martin the Magician instead. "I'm going to send my uncle a message that we're going to Weston to holiday with old friends. Look, isn't this convincing?"

Rupie produced an engraved Shirley and Sons envelope with the typewritten address of his uncle Charles. Opening the unsealed envelope carefully, he slipped out a single sheet of paper and read to his attentive friends:

> "Dear Charles, I am sorry, dear brother, but we have changed our plans for our holiday. My former employer, Charles Kitt, is gravely ill, and I must be at hand in Weston-Super-Mare in case of the worst. I look forward to seeing you at Christmastime. We will sorely miss you and Gladys and the boys."

The letter was signed with a flourishing "R."

"Ripping! Simply ripping," Peter remarked with genuine admiration. "Rupie, this looks like the real item." Phillip nodded his approval.

"Father will take me to Clifton Downs Station to board the train on Saturday. When I arrive in Coventry, I can deliver this message to my uncle's post and get back on a train headed for Birmingham. I've saved some shillings, but, Phillip, do you have any money you can lend me?" he implored.

"I've got five pounds to buy Christmas presents. I'll bring it to school."

"That'll do it. Thanks, Phillip."

On Friday, Phillip handed his friend the money, and, with Peter, wished him success in his acting adventure.

On Saturday morning, Rupie's thoughtful strategy unfolded without a hitch. His mother bade him goodbye after an especially delicious breakfast of soft-boiled eggs. His father took him by horse-driven cab to the train station. His train arriving in Coventry at four, Rupie walked to his uncle's cottage and left the false document without detection. He returned to the station to catch the next train for Birmingham.

By eight-thirty that night, travelling handbag in tow, Rupie sat in the balcony of a darkened theatre in Birmingham waiting for the purple velvet front curtain to be drawn upward to the sides. A poster in the window of the Prince of Wales Theatre announced *The Fabulous Follies,* and among the featured performers, in large black letters, was the name "Martin the Marvelous: Wonderful Wizardry."

The majority of the over 18,000 performers in British theatre at the time were employed in melodramas and musical and variety reviews rather than dramatic theatre. Instead of the ground level pits in the rear of the theatre for the standing attendees, orchestras were now seated in lowered pits directly in front of the stage. As the house lights dimmed, the orchestra played a thunderous introduction Rupie recognized as Beethoven.

The first act of *The Fabulous Follies* included a French pantomimist who was trying to find his way into a flower shop through an imaginary door in a glass window, who was prickled by an imaginary porcupine. Madame Emma Albani sang a burlesqued aria from *La Traviotta*. Next was a comedy sketch by the popular Archie Pitt, called "Mr. Tower of London." He was dressed in a large costume exactly like the structure, and two dogs relieved themselves on his red brick-colored trousers. A woman named Gracie Fields sang two amusing songs about her long lost lovers. A handsome couple performed scenes from three different Shakespearian plays, the best when the woman, playing the role of a highly emotional man-hater, melted before his eyes professing her newfound love, and the actor responded with a booming, "Why there's a wench! - Come on and kiss me, Kate."

After the interval, a large black-bearded man, dressed like a western cowboy, had an hilarious boxing match with a huge brown bear wearing a Little Miss Muffet outfit. Next, at long last, as far as Rupie was concerned, the moment he'd been waiting for arrived. The sign placed on the forestage easel by the front curtain read "Martin the Marvelous." And he was...

Martin, arms raised in a u-shape, entered the curtained stage from the wings wearing an impressive green, regal robe and a gold crown. He sported a smart-looking Van Dyke beard. The crowd rose, cheering as one. "Marvelous Martin. Marvelous Martin," they shouted.

Upstairs, high in the balcony, the young boy couldn't see the playing cards that Martin first displayed with a series of magic tricks with selected members of the audience, but he did recognize the numerous colored scarves that he pulled from a supposedly hollow tube, and the spectators filling the auditorium applauded for more.

A pretty young blond lady in a sailor's outfit, topped with a round white cap, took center stage and asked for boy volunteers for a special act that Martin was preparing to perform, sawing a boy in two, and the chance to earn five shillings.

"I'm Doreen Swift, Martin the Marvelous' assistant," she announced. With a bright incandescent spotlight following her, she walked up one of the two main aisles beneath the single balcony, scanning the audience for a prospect. "Eenny, meeney, miny, mo," she said loudly. "No, I'm going upstairs to find a boy. Someone up there can use the money more, I believe."

As the orchestra crescendoed, and Martin the Marvelous preened, Doreen walked down the balcony stairs towards Rupie, who, in an aisle seat, was waving his hands wildly as he called, "Miss Swift. Miss Swift. Look over here. Please."

She recognized him immediately, giving him a wink. But not wanting the other eager hand-wavers to know of her identification, she walked several rows past Rupie, before moving back up the stairs. Then, casting her eyes on him, she said, loudly enough for everyone in the theatre to hear,

"Aha! I've found him! Here is Martin the Marvelous' new associate. What's your name, young man?"

Thinking quickly, Rupie responded, "My name's Edward, Edward Johnston," aware that someone in the theatre might know his father.

After hustling Rupie backstage to a small dressing room, as the onstage Martin continued drawing oohs and ahs from his doting audience for his sleight-of-hand tricks, pulling item after item from a supposedly empty top hat, Doreen hugged him tightly and said sincerely, "Oh, Rupie, how good to see you. You're our best actor. Are you ready to be sawed in half again?"

Rupie nodded happily.

A boy, in his late teens quietly entered the room. Doreen introduced them. "Edward Johnston, if that's who you want to be, this is Thomas Jackson. His father's forming a repertory theatre here in Birmingham, and he's been helping us with costumes." The boys shook hands amicably.

Martin immediately recognized his nephew Richard Bates' friend, and Rupie repeated his initial role as the victim to be sawed in half the second time. He outdid his first performance, and at least one lady fainted when the smoke began to fill the stage, Rupie's hideous screams ringing to the rear of the theatre walls.

At the end of the act, when Rupie appeared smiling and unscathed, the applause was thunderous. Marvelous Martin shook his right hand vigorously, "Rupie, you're sensational. The stage will have to be your profession!"

Offstage, Thomas Jackson congratulated him. Doreen hugged and kissed him.

"The stage my profession? I wish my father believed that," repeated Rupie, gratefully.

"That's right. Where's your father?" Doreen inquired.

"Did you see him, Doreen?" Rupie asked with a

frightened expression, as Martin the Marvelous joined them after taking his bows.

"No, I didn't, Rupie. That is, young Mr. Johnston," she corrected herself. "You were alone in the balcony. Isn't that so, Rupie?"

"I've run away," the boy confessed. "I'm leaving school. I want to become an actor, but my father won't let me."

"Rupie, we're going to have to return you to your father. You know that, don't you?" the magician declared sympathetically.

"No! Why can't you be my pretend father?" Rupie protested. "I can be your human sacrifice for every performance. You won't have to ask for volunteers to saw in half. I can live on five shillings a day."

"I'm sorry, young man. This country has regulations about young performers. Your parents must provide written permission to the local magistrate for you to be a child actor. I can't take the risk. We must return you to your home. What's your real last name, Rupert?"

"I won't tell you," Rupie pouted, moving towards a backstage corner just as the costar comedian Wilkie Bard took center stage to a rousing round of applause. Doreen told Martin she couldn't remember Rupie's last name either. He remained tight-lipped sulking against the backstage wall. Discussing the matter further, she and Martin decided to send a message to Richard Bates that Rupie was with them and to contact his father.

"In the meantime, why can't he continue to be sawed in half?" said Martin. "He's the best sacrifice we've ever had to date, don't you think?" And Doreen couldn't agree more.

Chapter 6
The Townsends

Birmingham, Bristol, 1913

After Rupie finally confessed his last name was Thronson, Martin introduced him to a couple in the touring review who had a spare bed in their portable living quarters. They agreed to have Rupie, who they recognized as a sprouting teenager, stay a few days with them until his father fetched him. The couple, named Townsend, had a song and dance act, a clever take-off on Shaw's Pygmalion. Mrs. Townsend played the part of Professor Higgins, and her husband was the flower vendor. Audiences loved the role reversal, and steady employment with a touring review gave them the opportunity to perform in melodramas and dramatic presentations for the rest of the year. They were both dedicated Shakespearean actors. They described their challenging lives as stage players to their ardent young listener between performances of the review. The first evening, before taking him to his temporary living facility, the trio sat in a booth in a pub around the corner from the theatre.

"We were very fortunate," Fannie Townsend, a slight brown-haired woman in her late twenties wearing a pigtail, recalled. "Teddy, my husband, took a small role with Herbert Beerbohm Tree at London's Haymarket Theatre. Tree founded the Academy of Dramatic Arts, don't you know?"

She bubbled with her memories of the highly regarded Tree, gaining Rupie's rapt attention. She related how she and her husband considered Tree the second coming of Irving, his expensive stage settings, using splendor and realism at the same time, even real rabbits, grass carpets, fresh roses from the forests, and completely built ships rocking at sea with waves splashing on deck.

"I've never seen the likes o' that," Rupie exclaimed.

"Once he drove a golden chariot drawn by two gorgeous white steeds right onto the stage," she mused. "His best role was as Fagin in *Oliver Twist*. He also made a terrifying Svengali. He always wears the most realistic make up; his acting is always clever and imaginative. Sometimes, it's difficult to act on the same stage with him because he's so inventive. Every performance, he tries different physical techniques and speech deliveries," she remembered. "You never know what he'll do next."

"I thought Tree only acted in Shakespearean plays, so he could play the leading roles," Rupie interjected.

Mrs. Townsend responded, "You're right. You're a smart laddie. Mostly he does. His Shakespeare productions are most lavish. Also, he employs the best actors around him, including Lewis Waller and Oscar Asche."

"I know about them," Rupie contributed eagerly. "They brought their own companies to the Bristol Old Vic."

"Fancy that," remarked Mrs. Townsend. "Theodore, did you know that? This young man knows Lewis Waller and Oscar Asche!"

"Well, I don't really know them, but my friend, Richard Bates does," Rupie offered. "He's studying to be an actor."

"Good show," said Mr. Townsend, a bit older than his wife, a tall, dark, blue-eyed man with noble features. "Finally, I'm able to get in a word. If you know about Shakespearean actors, do you know anything of Henry Irving's sons, Rupert?"

Shaking his head that he didn't, Rupie turned on the bench slightly to face Theodore Townsend. "They were the last of the great actor-managers," Townsend explained. "They followed Johnston Forbes-Robertson, Herbert Tree, George Alexander, Frank Benson, Lewis Waller, John Martin-Harvey, Oscar Asche, and Harley Granville-Barker."

Counting the names he recognized on his fingers, Rupie boasted, "I think I've already heard about their acting feats."

"For someone your age, that's quite an achievement, son. These are the greatest theatre men of England. They've taken their companies all over Britain, Scotland, Wales, and Ireland. Three have also toured America. Mrs. Townsend and I were with Martin-Harvey's Shakespearian triumph in the colonies."

"We were there three years ago," Mrs. Townsend announced proudly.

"You've been to America?" Rupie asked in awe. "Oh, how I've dreamed to go there. Cowboys and Indians, gold mines, no king or queen to worship, much more freedom than in Britain."

When they arrived at the Townsend's living carriage, Rupie realized it had at one time been a horse-driven lorry, with a covered driver's cab in front seating two. Townsend had removed the partition between the cab and the lorry bed and built a wooden, two-foot vertical wall around the bed, added four posts and a wooden framework and covered the whole structure with large canvas sheets. It was cozy and rainproof with just enough room for two people to pass one another without saying "Excuse me."

Inside, dainty pillows marked the double bed dominating the limited living space. Townsend, a skilled carpenter, which made him additionally more useful to theatre managers, had cleverly installed shelves of various heights, which enclosed the travelling room, except for a canvas flap opening in the rear that served as a door.

Their clothing was neatly folded within the shelves, and books, artifacts, and shoes filled the rest. A tall, paneled armoire held the hanging garments, several of which were costumes for the Townsends' dramatic sketches. A small round table was in the center of the wagon room with three wooden straight chairs around it. Two undersized, upholstered wing chairs, decorated in a colorful multi-flowered cloth design, were at the sides of the portable dwelling, and, behind the former driver's seat was a metal container with a pump on top for water. A large, much worn wooden table, upon which were carefully stacked dishes, silverware, and cooking utensils, completed the couple's quarters. Rupie slept on the floor under the worn table, warmed by two blankets and a feather comforter.

The several days Rupie had with the Townsends provided him valuable insights into the lives of travelling actors.

Fannie Whiteside Brough and Theodore "Teddy" Townsend had met in one of Frank Benson's companies bringing Shakespeare to small villages in England. After a year of alternating plays and portraying townspeople, couriers, messengers, servants, and other minor roles, both had graduated into supporting parts, while understudying principal performers.

Fanny could recite any of Shakespeare's published plays

word for word, while Teddy, once reminded of a passage, would fill in all the action. Fanny had the envious ability to memorize her parts with almost only one reading, while Teddy forgot his lines almost as soon as they were uttered. She had an ingratiating laugh, a pleasant soprano voice, and engaging beauty. Teddy was over six feet in height, regal-looking, always smiling, and he delivered his character's words like a military officer urging his troops to engage the enemy. Eight-hour-a-day rehearsals by the demanding Benson and their own free time learning lines together began a warm professional relationship, shortly turning to love. They were married by a city official between a Saturday matinee and an evening performance in Hull. Leaving Benson after a two-year stint, they toured for another two years with Ben Greet and George Alexander companies. They also acted for two seasons with Herbert Beerbohm Tree in London at the Lyceum and did a stint in America. Dedicated to the stage, Fanny and Teddy were both experienced experts in the language of Shakespeare, with a little Shaw and Galsworthy thrown in.

The Townsends made Rupie aware of the realistic economics of the theatrical world. On a tour, an actor was always hunting for new "digs" at a reasonable cost in every village and hamlet. To satisfy physical needs, one often had to search outside or in a darkened hallway for the loo or use whatever was available for a chamber pot. If you dined in a tawdry kitchen in your lodgings, you had to eat whatever was served. In pubs or small cafes, the fare wasn't always tasty. Actors had to purchase and care for their own costumes. More than often, they dressed before stage entrances in drafty, filthy dressing rooms. Worst yet, what they told Rupie about performing for unappreciative audiences tarnished some of the allure the profession held for the young boy.

"One reason we married was because we could live more cheaply together on the road," said Fanny as she sat on the bed threading a needle to mend a tear in her husband's lavish courtier's costume.

Theodore Townsend walked to the round table in the center of the lorry, placing a large, leather-covered packet in front of Rupie, who was seated in one of the straight-backed chairs. Townsend said,"Rupie, this is a collection of reviews and handbills about our theatrical travels. Fannie and I left the London stage and Tree after we became aware of how many performers there were in Britain and how few could actually make a living, much less become successful. Do you realize, Rupie, that in 1901, probably about the time you were born, there were over 12,000 actors throughout the kingdom?"

"Yes, Mr. Townsend, you're right. I was born that year," Rupie answered.

"Half were men and half were female performers," Townsend reported.

"Are you trying to frighten me away from acting? How many are there now?" asked Rupie.

"Twice that number. At this very minute, all over England, there're between 200 and 250 theatrical companies covering every town in this country. When Fannie and I were in America, Benson had six different Shakespeare companies touring in both countries at the same time."

"We were just two young Thespians among many. We didn't think melodrama or a song-and-dance act were our fortes," added his wife.

"That's why we decided to go off on our own. We were so familiar with the bard's work, having spent several years struggling to master his plays, it soon made sense that our best lot was to stay with Shakespeare. We'd just move over into the more lucrative variety circuit with popular representations," Townsend intoned. "So we hired a London agent, William Locklear. He made the rounds on our behalf while we were on tour."

"Made the rounds?" Rupie repeated curiously.

"That's where good agents excel," Townsend responded. "If they can convince a producer to attend the performance of one of their clients, the producer can see an actor in action. That's how they earn their ten percent commission. That's why the best agents do so well."

"That's far better than having to audition for every role you seek," his wife added.

"It's also cheaper than advertising in *The Performer*," suggested Townsend.

The Townsends presented only Shakespearean theatrical sketches in the touring variety show, varying acts on their presumptions of audience tastes. They alternated between Romeo and Juliet, the parts of Julia and Proteus in *The Two Gentlemen from Verona*, Anthony and Cleopatra, and Petruchio and Katherina in *The Taming of the Shrew.* They were Ariel and Prospero in *The Tempest,* the dark prince and his mother, Queen of Denmark, in *Hamlet*; and the King and Cordelia in *King Lear.*

"We converted this lorry into travelling quarters because we're putting all our shillings and pounds away to buy a small farm in the Lake District," Fannie Townsend contributed happily. "We're going to raise little Shakespearian actors and livestock."

"You're going to leave the theatre?" Rupie asked, disbelief written on his face.

"Yes, Rupie, the theatre's no place to raise children," nodded Townsend to his wife. "We don't want to continue our lives as social outcasts. Actors have neither class status nor public respect."

"Sometimes, I'm even treated like a, like a prostitute!" Fannie Townsend uttered sadly.

"Now, Fannie, not in front of the boy. Don't use that word," her husband corrected.

"Forgive me," she responded, not looking as though she meant it.

"Let me show you these photographs and posters we collected in America, Rupie," offered Teddy Townsend, opening the folder in front of Rupie. "We first opened to a rousing crowd at the Belasco Theatre in New York." One by one, Townsend exhibited programs and playbills of their tour and pictures of the couple standing in front of theatres in Baltimore, Philadelphia, Boston, and Chicago, names to Rupie that had never been places. He was enthralled.

"Theatre has an immense future in America," suggested Townsend. "If we were younger, that's where we'd be. It's bigger than England. It has wider spaces, growing cities, and far more opportunities for actors and managers than here. Right now, more than two hundred theatrical companies are touring somewhere between the east coast and California."

"And there are ample trains to carry you," added Fannie, as she finished sewing the mend on her husband's costume. "And they like British actors."

"I'll file away that added knowledge," Rupie proclaimed, smacking his hand loudly on the table, before beginning the preparation of his temporary bed.

The following morning, an early morning knock at Martin's luxurious hotel room door awakened him. Star billing guaranteed comparable quarters. "Sir," a voice called out. "I have a message for you."

Martin, donning a sleeping robe as he strode to the door, opened it and reached for the brown envelope extended to him. From his pocket, he removed a ten-pence piece and dropped it into the outstretched hand. Glancing briefly at the note he had unfolded from the envelope, he closed the door to his room quietly and walked down the dim, candle lit hall to Doreen's more modest room. He rapped on the door. A yawning voice said, "Just a moment," before opening the door to let him in.

Wiping her eyes with a finger, Doreen insisted, "Martin, it's quite early. You had a late performance. What are you doing up at this hour? It's Christmas Eve." Doreen turned, returning to her place under the inviting, warm bedcovers.

Martin, sitting at the side of the bed, waved the note. "This is a message from Richard. He sent it to our hotel. Rupie's father and mother are arriving at the train station at ten o'clock. It's nine now. We'll have to hurry."

"Oh, goodness me. We must find the Townsends as soon as we can," Doreen said as she rose from the bed and moved towards the closet.

"Their lorry's parked behind the Prince of Wales. I'll get dressed and get the boy. I'll meet you at the station."

"Wait for me! I want to go with you," Doreen said, as she slipped a dress over her head.

It was a difficult task to wrest Edward Johnson, the convincing victim of a saw blade, known to his cohorts as Rupie Thronson, away from the Townsends. Rupie had convinced them of his ambitious scheme to continue as Martin's accomplice and be trained as a Shakespearean actor by the willing Townsends.

Martin and Doreen, hailing a horse-driven taxi, escorted the reluctant boy to the Birmingham Train Station to await his anticipated parent's train. "Rupert, my boy, you mustn't be so disappointed," the bearded mystic cautioned. "You can still be an actor. You'll just have to wait a little longer. Besides, you've got to learn how to play a role other than a screaming hyena who's being skewered."

"True," contributed Doreen. "There aren't too many roles for hyenas!"

Both had made numerous suggestions as to how Rupie could pursue his dream. He could engage in school dramatics. He could enroll with Richard's teacher for acting, singing, and dance classes. He should see as many theatrical performances as he could to study how actors act.

"My father won't allow it," Rupie kept insisting.

"Let's see if I can convince him to the contrary," offered Martin. "Now, let me demonstrate a card trick with which you can entertain your classmates." Martin laid out a brand new deck of playing cards on the metal bench on which they were seated. Rupie chose three different cards, placed them back into the deck, and Martin, with his eyes closed, repeatedly informed Rupie of the cards he had selected.

"How did you do that?" Rupie asked.

"Doreen was right behind you and gave me hand signs," was the answer.

Just then a loud voice interrupted them.

"Rupert Ashley Thronson! Come here at once!" His father insisted as he rushed towards him, his wife several feet behind him.

"It's a pleasure, Mr. and Mrs. Thronson," Martin said in friendly fashion as he moved towards the intense pair.

"Rupie! Rupie! How could you? How could you run away like this?" His mother cried as she hugged him tightly. "My darling boy, you've been so naughty."

Ignoring the magician and his assistant, Rupert Senior directed his obvious ire at his son. "Rupert, you'll be punished severely for this. It's shameful how you've frightened your mother. And you, sir," finally turning to Martin, "are guilty of kidnapping. I'll have you in irons for this!" he proclaimed.

"Hold a moment, m' lord. We meant no harm, my dear

man. We didn't even know the boy's name," the wizard replied. "We sent for you immediately we learned Rupie had run away. Wasn't it my nephew Richard who contacted you?"

"That young actor? He's the one who's been the bad influence on Rupert. It's all his fault," the anxious father intoned.

"Please, sit down. Let's relax. We can all have a nice cup of tea, can't we?" Doreen wisely suggested. "And, Rupie, wouldn't you like some nice hot cocoa?"

Still upset, Rupert Senior said angrily, "We're leaving. But you haven't heard the last of this. I don't approve of my son mingling with people of your ilk."

With that, he grabbed the arms of the sniffling Rupie and forcibly pulled him towards an arriving train. His wife followed him dutifully, not knowing what to say.

Rupie managed a weak good-bye to the magician and his assistant as he was dragged up the stairs to the train. Elsie Thronson muttered a tearful thanks.

The red-faced Bristol grocer angrily stomped up the stairs with Rupie in hand. The three were leaving for a wordless trip to Coventry. It was not a happy family reunion.

Chapter 7
The Stowaway

Bristol, 1913-14

When Rupie returned to Bristol Grammar School to begin the winter term after his Birmingham escapades, his schoolmates unanimously agreed he took the cake for having the most adventuresome holiday. He was the hit of the recess periods with his masterful card tricks, insuring that, as his mentor had told him, a good magician never reveals the secret of a sleight-of-hand. In the school library, he had a favorite table and chair, where he became a vociferous reader of Shakespeare, taking particular attention to the scenes he had seen the Townsends so artfully perform.

At home and at his cleanup work at Shirley's, he was very quiet around his father, speaking only when entirely necessary, for he was still in a snit about not being allowed to see Richard Bates or mention anything to do with acting or the theatre. Faithfully, he took Daisy on daily walks. Rupert Senior never threatened Rupie with any type of punishment, but the boy felt as if he were in some sort of detention and his father was the institutional guard. His mother bridged the lack of communication between father and son, attempting to be, at all times, as cheerful as possible. Rupie knew she had to side with his father. He also knew she, too, believed the theatre to be a place of sin, and hoped that Rupie would outgrow his fixation.

Rupie's art classes enabled him to apply touches of his dormant creativity. Most of all, he enjoyed conjuring up ideas for stage settings of Shakespeare's Hamlet. His sketches of parapets at the top of the Ellsinore Castle and of the throne room garnered plaudits from his teacher, Mr. White. "Mr. Thronson, you have an admirable proficiency in drawing in perspective. I once knew a fellow officer in Calcutta who had a similar flair; he'd studied architecture at Cambridge. If you did as well in your '6's and 8's' and the sciences, that might be a challenging discipline for you to pursue." While the rest of his classmates were each engaged in his own drawing activity, Mr. White asked, "Have you ever made a model of one of these sketches?"

"No, sir, I'm not sure what you mean by a model," Rupie responded.

"Well, you obtain a large sheet of heavy paper or cardboard, something like this."

He pulled out a piece of matting from a drawer under the drawing board Rupie was using. "You must first trace out a silhouette of what it is you're modeling. Take this throne you've drawn." After drawing his own rough image of the royal chair, Mr. White, removing a small knife from his vest pocket, demonstrated how the pieces could be brought together to form the miniature stage setting. "Of course, you need mucilage to fasten the sides together but this is the general idea. Why don't you try it yourself?" he said as he walked to the next student's station to observe his progress with a watercolor painting of a dead lizard he'd brought to school that morning.

For the next two hours, Rupie was lost in sketching pillars and statues and exterior castle walls and then cutting them into replicas of his drawings. Mr. White stopped by several times to comment on his progress and provide him with cement, and he showed Rupie how to cut out triangular pieces, which, when placed vertically, supported his miniature cardboard setting.

"In theatrical terms, these are called stage braces. They're what hold up the scenery. But it's best to paint your model when you can lay it out horizontally. Ordinarily, you can't do that with real scenery, you know, what they call flats. You have to paint them upright," Rupie's teacher said with authority.

"How do you know so much about stage settings, Mr. White?"

"Oh, perhaps because I'm a frustrated Thespian myself, Rupie. They say that there's a little ham in every teacher."

"Ham, sir?"

"Yes, Rupie. Ham. The tendency to over-dramatize something. Using an abnormally affected voice, gesturing broadly, exaggerating every move."

"You do do that, sir, if I might say."

"You certainly may, Rupie. I don't mind. It was a way we officers often spoke in the military if we wanted to insure that an important concept be thoroughly understood. If we added a few theatrics, soldiers seemed to remember better."

"I'll take note of that, sir," nodded Rupie, returning his attention to his imaginary throne room.

Directly at three o'clock when the bell, ringing the end of the school day, sounded, Rupie headed for his father's store, which was less than a mile from BGS. Once there, he changed his school uniform for his grocer's uniform, a pair of white coveralls over a long-sleeved pale blue shirt with

"Shirley's" embroidered in black small scrolling letters across one side of his chest. Next, he would report to the grocer's assistant, a friendly eighteen-year-old, Percy Montrose. Percy, a muscular, tall, redhead, would read from a task list Rupie's father prepared for each employee every day. Percy always looked forward to Rupie's daily arrival because he could leave the store-cleaning, produce-stacking, and provision-loading chores to the younger boy and spend his own time filling orders for the ever-arriving customers who never seemed to subside. Rupert Senior was usually in the front of the store, seated in a small tearoom at a round, cloth-covered table chatting with customers while they sipped tea from fragile china cups. The tea was always Horniman's, Shirley's specialty.

Once Rupie told Percy of his father, "He drinks tea and the rest of us sanitize and take grocery orders. I don't see how he can drink so much. Someday he's just going to float down Whitladies and disappear," laughing to himself at the forbidden thought.

After the grocery store closed at six, and his father locked the front doors, the two of them would walk silently two blocks down Whitladies, turn right on Melrose Place, and enter the front door to the Thronson flat where Daisy always greeted them happily. One or the other might try to start a conversation with "The weather's quite pleasant," which wasn't usually the case, or "How was school today?" the answer to which was always "Tolerable." Conversation between the two of them had definitely waned, and Rupie's father knew quite well that it was his intolerance of the acting profession that had caused the boy to build a wall of non-communication between them.

Occasionally, Rupie was invited to have supper at the Maggs' house. To the young boy, the residence was a mansion. The owner of Maggs Furniture and Moving,

Ltd. lived in a fashionable, two-story Victorian house with a bright yellow exterior and intricate white trim framing the doors and windows. "It has eight bedrooms and five bathrooms," Rupie reported to his mother. "The living room looks like it's owned by the Royal Family, and the furniture is all handmade from India. Even the arms of the oak chairs have carvings of serpents wrapped around them."

His mother replied, "Well, our flat would be better furnished, too, if we owned the biggest furniture store in Bristol. It's so pricey there, Rupie, I can't afford to buy at Maggs. It's also in the dearest part of the city," she added.

"Mother, I think the window curtains are all made of velvet. They're thick and shiny. I'll bet the chandeliers are covered with real diamonds."

"It's nice you pay attention to those types of things, dear. Your future wife will appreciate good taste when you're married. Good chartered accountants can afford fancy houses!"

"Chartered accountants? What's that have to do with the Maggs' house?"

"That's what Phillip's father studied in school, Rupie. That's why he's so good at the furniture business."

"He inherited it," Rupie exclaimed. "Why do you have to be good in anything if you're going to have a furniture store given to you anyway? What's this about a chartered accountant, though?"

"Your father and I have discussed it, Rupie. If you aren't successful enough to qualify for Oxbridge, then we think you should become an accountant. You do very well with figures."

"Don't I have anything to say about it?" asked Rupie.

"A son must do what his father wishes," interrupted Rupert Senior who had just entered the living room. "Since you're serving as an apprentice at Shirley's, you can become a grocery manager just like me."

"But I don't want to work in a grocery store. Besides, I couldn't drink all the tea you do."

"Your father has to socialize with his customers, Rupie. They can't think he's unfriendly. Besides, they drink the Horniman's. Your father just sips," she stated emphatically. Addressing her husband, she said, "Rupie's very impressed with the Maggs' home, dear. Says they have velvet curtains."

"That's elegant. Oh, that reminds me. I picked up a letter for you at the Mail Post. It's from your sister Val, in Toronto."

"From America? I didn't know Aunt Valerie was in America, mother."

"She's not been there long," Elsie answered her son. "Her husband, your Uncle Horace, has a position with the Canadian Railway. He's posted in Toronto as a mechanical engineer."

"Read us the letter, Elsie," requested Rupert, handing it to her.

She refused the letter. "You know how poorly I read, dear. You read it aloud to us."

Rupert read the rather general letter about how her younger sister and her husband Horace had sailed from Plymouth to New York, visited Philadelphia, Washington, D.C., and Boston, and had trained to Toronto, which, she related, was very much like London.

Listening intently to Rupert Senior, Elsie sighed. "Poor girl, she was seasick for her entire eleven-day trip across the Atlantic."

The seed of an idea sprang to Rupie's brain.

Over the next several months, with his father's reluctant permission, Rupie would sometimes meet his friend Peter at Bristol's main wharf. They walked from one ship to another watching the loading and unloading of sacks of potatoes and yams, barrels of grain and whiskey, stacks of lumber, and boxes of bottled lotions, perfumes, and liquid. The huge ships bore flags of almost every nation in Europe, many from Canada and other commonwealth countries. Peter and Rupie guessed the names of the countries represented by banners hanging from every stern, with Peter usually having the edge. Peter's father, a former seaman himself, arranged permission for the two boys to board a vessel on occasion, ever under the watchful eyes of soldiers patrolling the wharf. They enjoyed inspecting the cramped crew's living quarters, the captain's office, the bridge, the engine room, and the tremendously large holds in which so much cargo was stored.

"Who watches the cargo when the ship's afloat?" Rupie asked Peter one day as they were taking one of their pleasurable vessel tours.

Peter laughed. "No one, silly. Why would they have to watch the cargo if the ship was afloat? There's no one to steal anything nor anywhere to take whatever you've stolen."

"Do you think it would be hard to stow away on a ship like this?" asked Rupie.

"It's not easy," answered Peter. "It also depends on how long you have to stay stowed."

"What do you mean?" Rupie inquired.

"Well, you have to take care of your own necessaries. Where do you go to the loo? What do you have to eat? Then, there's also the problem of water," Peter mused.

The boys descended a circular ladder further down into the hold. "There's something else, too," Peter added. "You've got to get on the ship in the first place."

"That's true. That is a problem!" Rupie admitted.

Over the next several weeks, Rupie improved his limited knowledge of the commerce of a seaport like Bristol and the great dependency on imports for an island empire. One evening, when he was dining with the Gibbs at their modest flat on Front Street near the docks, Mrs. Gibbs was busy putting dishes on the kitchen table readying them for her husband's favorite meal, filet of halibut. Rupie, Peter, and Peter's older brother Oscar were playing Whist in the living room. Nearby, Mr. Gibbs was perusing a list of products, which he would be responsible for loading the following day. Reading aloud to himself, he said softly, "We've got coal from Wales, wheat from Yorkshire, apples from Nottingham, wheat from Leister, lumber from the Lake District, smoked fish from Brighton, and potatoes from Italy. I've got one ship that's departing for Cape Town, South Africa, and another bound for New York, the *Lusitania.*"

"How long is the voyage from Bristol to New York?" asked Rupie.

"It could take seven to eleven days," answered Peter's father, a brawny, bearded, red-faced native Bristolian. "I've made that trip many times. It's faster the other way with the wind behind ya. I was ten years old when I first shipped out." Sparking his memory, he continued to mesmerize the boys telling them about several of his adventures in the stormiest of seas.

Oscar, a tanned, long-dark-haired eighteen-year-old, grinned at his father. "Dad, you went to sea when you were ten, and you won't let me go when I'm eight'n."

"I was an orphan, m'lad," his father responded. "That's different. I had to go. Was no other choice. The orphanage was a hellhole, worst than Calcutta. There were no other onshore jobs for a boy as I've told you many a time. It was easier to be a cabin boy in those days. We didn't have all those bloomin' rules about child labor we got now. Besides, your ma and I like havin' you around. Even Peter does, don't ya, son?"

"Of course," answered Peter. "Even if he does bully me." Oscar playfully patted the scruff of his younger brother's neck.

"Come into the kitchen, boys," Mrs. Gibbs gently commanded as she placed a huge platter of zesty smelling fish in front of the male contingent.

After dinner, the three boys sat on the stoop in front of the Gibbs' flat throwing their pocket knives into a circle drawn in the dirt. "Oscar," Rupie asked quizzically, "How could someone get aboard a ship without anyone seeing him?"

"It's pretty hard. Almost impossible," answered the older boy. "There's usually only one way to come aboard and that's up the gangway. There's always a bosun there to check people on and off. Seamen patrol the ship and stand watches all day and all night. They're usually in four-hour shifts, and soldiers are on the wharf. It'd be pretty hard," he repeated.

"I think…I think I know a way," pondered Rupie aloud.

"What's that?" Peter asked, Oscar peering with interest over his shoulder.

Rupie told them how he'd been watching the loading and unloading of cargo over the past weeks. He thought he could stow away on the ship bound for New York without being detected.

Excitedly, Oscar exclaimed, "You're right. It's possible. But it's risky."

"Not if every step's planned carefully," responded Rupie.

For the next three months, Rupie and Peter, and, occasionally, Oscar, would sit together to put the pieces of their secret plan together. Asked to accompany Rupie in this new adventure, neither of his friends wanted to go. Oscar worried that, if he were arrested, he'd sacrifice obtaining a seaman's license. Peter wanted no part of it.

On the fourth of August, England declared war on Germany, but, despite the rationing of petrol and selected food items and the enlistment of thousands of males, little changed for Rupie and his family. He still intended to make the voyage.

He told Peter, "I've asked Phillip to go with me. He's always wanted to go to America. But he can't make up his mind."

The next day, while sharing sandwiches, Rupie instructed Phillip about his final plan. Again, he invited him to go. "We'd have a place to stay, Phillip. My aunt lives in Toronto. I've got her address."

"Why do you want to run away again, Rupie?" Phillip asked intently. "England has declared war on Germany."

"I want to go on the stage. You know that. My father will never permit me to be an actor here. I have to go!"

"You still want to be a stupid actor, Rupie? You're insane!"

"Do you want to go with me? You've always said that you wanted to visit America."

"I will, Rupie. My father says that we'll be going next year. He wants to look into exporting furniture to some of the major American cities. He's taking the whole family. There's no reason for me to go with you, is there?"

"I guess not," answered a disappointed Rupie, "but you're not to mention my plan to anyone. Is that clear?"

"Of course," his friend answered.

With Oscar's having talked to members of the ship's crew, Rupie had learned that the *Lusitania* was leaving the Bristol docks on the twelfth of September, down the Avon, en route to New York. At three that morning, Rupie quietly crept out of his flat with a small overnight case containing a few tins of food, a change of clothes, a pen knife, a heavy dark sweater, his toiletries, a rope for emergencies, a candle and matches, a copy of *Midsummer Night's Dream*, a sketchbook and pens, the envelope with his aunt's address on the flap, a painted pillowcase, and a large burlap sack he had taken from the greengrocer.

After awaking Peter and Oscar without their parents' detection, Rupie and the boys hurried to the wharf and stopped in the unforgiving fog in a narrow brick alley two blocks from the *Lusitania*. "The last loading of the ship will start at six," said Oscar. "I need time to set up things, find a wheelbarrow, and learn the lay of the land."

"Good, when my father finds me gone, he'll have no idea where I am. Just as long as the ship still sails at twelve noon."

"It will," responded Oscar. "Everybody here follows a strict timetable. Wait, what's that noise? Hey, you, who are you?" He whispered loudly through the still dark early morning fog.

"It's me, Phillip," a soft, rather frightened voice responded. "I've come to help Rupie." Their sleepy classmate stepped out of the darkness.

"Greetings, Phillip," said Rupie giving him a hearty handshake. "I'm almost off."

"Hello, Phillip," greeted Peter, "Do you know my brother, Oscar?"

The boys acknowledged one another.

"Well, it's time," said Rupie. Help me, gentlemen. I have to snuggle into this burlap sack. Oscar, can you fetch the wheelbarrow?"

"Right-o. It's just where I left it." Oscar took off in a sprint down the dim alleyway.

"Mates," addressing his friends, "promise you won't tell my father where I've gone?"

"I promise," Phillip acknowledged.

"And I as well," Peter confirmed.

"No, it has to be a stronger commitment than that. I want you both to sign a sacred vow in blood." Rupie reached into his case and pulled out his sketchbook, a bottle of India ink, and a quill pen. He quickly jotted a note in ink. He wiped off the pen and plunged the sharp tip into his wrist. A drop of blood immediately appeared. He dipped the pen into the blood several times, writing his signature at the bottom of the page. "I've just written. 'We vow not to tell Mr. Rupert Thronson the whereabouts of his son. Signed in a blood oath.' Now take the quill pen, stick yourselves, and sign at bottom." Rupie urged his friends. They followed his direction in turn.

The sound of wheels in the cobblestone alleyway attracted their attention. Oscar appeared out of the mist pushing a handcart. "Rupie, they've started to arrive for the final loading. We must hurry. I'm going over to engage the only soldier standing guard." Handing the cart to Phillip, he approached the soldier and soon had him moving towards the other end of the wharf.

Rupie said, "Help me get into this sack. Goodbye, my friends. I'll cable you when I get to New York." With that, he wrapped himself and the overnight case into a white sheet and then wiggled into the brown potato bag Oscar held open for him.

From his pocket, Peter pulled out a large sewing needle into which a thin string had been strung through the eye and began seaming the top of the bag. Phillip, holding the edges of the top together, asked Rupie, "Are you all right?"

A muffled voice responded, "Aw wite."

Phillip, bringing the wheelbarrow forward, said, "Peter, you take the bottom of the sack and I'll take the top. Lift up, and I'll move the barrow under Rupie. Careful," he said, as the boys gently placed Rupie into the bed of the cart. "Now,

Peter, you go ahead and signal me when the coast is clear. Oscar has the soldier's back to us. Let's go now."

"Here we go, Rupie," Peter reassured his be-sacked burden.

Arriving in the dock's loading area, boxes, trunks, sacks of all shapes and sizes were haphazardly piled on the shipside of the dock. Thick ropes hung from every sail, threaded through three-to-five-inch winches extending from them with one end dangling down the side of the main mast held securely to the tall support. A boson's knot was tied around the eight pin, and the other end of the rope was divided into equal strands and secured to the pallet sides.

Pushing the wheelbarrow to the side of one of the pallets on which innumerable sacks of potatoes were neatly piled, Phillip said in a loud whisper, "Here, let's load Rupie onto this pallet. He'll fit right into the middle. These are all gunnysacks. The longshoremen shouldn't notice his. Are you still all right, Rupie?" he asked.

"Cheery-o," seemed to be the reply.

The boys carefully picked up him up from the wheelbarrow and eased him between the sacks of potatoes.

"That's good, he's almost hidden now," announced Peter. "Let's move those sacks beside him a little closer." And, as they complied, he said, "Good...good...that's perfect. They'll never see him. Let's stand to the side and wait until the dockworkers arrive. We don't want to attract attention to these potatoes."

"Rupie's really brave. I'd never want to be lifted up that high and swung into a ship," said Phillip.

"Nor I," aped Peter.

In less than ten minutes, several longshoremen arrived and donned their gloves. Seamen appeared on the ship decks overlooking the wharf, some giving familiar orders to prepare for cargo loading, others lifting weighty covers opening the holds to the warming sunlight beginning to fill the cloudy skies.

"Over here," called Oscar to the black-stocking-capped *Lusitania* boson's mate. "Let's pull this one up next." Oscar moved to the pallet on which Rupie was hidden. He attached the smaller ropes holding the pallet to the thick hemp that had been looped through the winch. He gave a hand signal to the two sailors who had begun pulling the dockside rope hanging from the mechanical apparatus. His brother and Phillip stood in shadows nearby, fearing for Rupie's life.

"Heave-ho! Heave-ho!" said Oscar as the pallet began rising from the ground, swinging slightly from side to side. He lifted a long pole to the pallet's side and neutralized the motion, softly whispering, "Goodbye, Rupie. Bon voyage."

The potato-laden pallet rose gradually as the seamen pulled the rope hand over hand. As the pallet rose to deck level, two sailors moved to the side and grabbed the sides, firmly guiding the load towards the large opening in the center of the ship leading to the almost-full hold.

As the pallet disappeared below deck, Phillip whispered, "There he goes!"

"Quiet." whispered Peter almost as loudly. "We'd best leave this place."

They waved farewell to Oscar, who had started the preparation of another pallet for loading.

"Let's come back at noon to watch the ship depart," suggested Phillip.

"I'll see you then," responded Peter.

The two boys left the Bristol wharf bound for their respective and warm homes, tired, excited, and happy for their friend Rupie.

As the pallet settled heavily onto the hundreds of potato bags stacked one on top of another, it landed unevenly; Rupie slid slightly to his left feeling frightened, alone, and somewhat stifled in the warm bag. *I'll open it with my knife to get more air. I think this is the last pallet to be loaded in this part of the hold,* he thought to himself, removing the knife from his pocket and cutting the thin rope threaded along the top of the sack.

Sticking his head through the hole, Rupie gasped to inhale the welcome air. No one was in sight. *So far, so good.* After that, there was a long wait.

Precisely at noon, a soulful horn wailed to acknowledge the time of the ship's departure. As the crew lined up on the dockside of the ship, a number of women and small children waved to them from the wharf, throwing kisses and shouting their farewells. To the three boys watching from behind the wharfside crowd, the "goodbyes," "safe trip," "God be w'thee," were all adieus for Rupie on their behalf.

Pulling the huge ship by three enormous rope lines, the tiny tugboat chugged down the Avon. The huge vessel groaned its slow progress directly behind. Rupie felt the ship's movement. At last, we're seabound, he thought.

Returning to his luxurious Clifton home, Phillip, engaged in his regular piano lesson with Professor Borloff, his elflike, delicate music teacher, had trouble concentrating on the keys.

"Master Maggs," said his mentor, "You're playing Bach like a carpenter with a hammer. Be gentler with the notes!"

"Professor, I don't feel like practicing today," Phillip stated. "I don't feel very well."

"What's the problem, my boy? It's a rare beautiful day today, a day when young men should be very happy, not melancholy like you."

"What time is it, professor?"

"Don't worry about time, Phillip. We have another hour of practice. Remember, the church recital's next week. You're not close to being ready."

Phillip tried to concentrate harder on his lessons, becoming more involved with thinking about Bach than Rupie. The professor nodded his approval as Phillip became more absorbed in the flow of the classical piece. Finally, pulling his round pocket watch from beneath his vest, the professor noted, "Ah, that was much better, Master Maggs. You see, that old saying 'Practice makes perfect' does make sense."

"What time is it, professor?"

"Five o'clock," was the answer. "Do you have an appointment somewhere?"

'Not really, but I have to ask my mother if I can go back to the wharf."

"The wharf, what have you been doing down there? That's not a place for boys."

"My friend, Peter Gibbs, lives near there. I really must see him. I'm worried about someone."

"Phillip, you must spend more time practicing your piano. I can't be with you all the time. If you do poorly at the recital, your father will be quite upset. Promise me that you'll spend more time on your scales, " he said as he picked up his light brown walking stick from the wooden butler beside the Maggs' front door, "Goodbye Phillip. Promise me?"

Phillip answered, "Of course," as the music teacher shut the finely carved oak door behind him.

With his mother's permission, Phillip rode his older brother's two-wheel bicycle to Peter's house, parking it by the front stoop.

Peter's mother called her son. "A friend's here, dear."

The minute he arrived, Peter asked, "What's the matter? Why are you here?"

"Come outside, Peter. I want to talk to you," Phillip demanded seriously, ignoring Mrs. Gibbs who stood nearby.

Once they were alone in the narrow street in front of the Riggs' small house, Phillip confided his anxiety about Rupie's well-being to his schoolmate. "Peter, he only had food for four days, and I don't think he has enough water to last two. He can't make it through the voyage!"

"Didn't you put that bag of food under the potato sack next to Rupie?"

"What bag?" Phillip answered.

"The one Oscar had in the wheelbarrow," Peter responded immediately.

"I didn't even know it was there. Oscar didn't say anything to me."

"Oh, this is pretty bad! You're right! Rupie'll starve to death. We can't let him!"

"We must tell his father, Peter," Phillip said after a moment. "He'll have to cable the captain. They're already in the Atlantic. They can't turn the ship back."

"But we signed a blood oath," Peter protested.

"That's not worth a pile of spoiled strawberries," answered Phillip. "Rupie's life's more important than any oath."

Pondering the consequences, Peter finally had to agree. "Yes, you have to go home anyway. You can tell Mr. Thronson on your way. His flat is near Shirley's."

Chapter 8
The Voyage

At Sea, 1914

Daniel Dow, the wiry, sun worn, mustachioed fifty-eight-year-old captain of the *Lusitania,* read aloud the wireless Sparks had just handed to him. His first mate, Lewis Moody, a medium-sized, eager-to-please, twenty-eight-year-old officer, was the sole listener.

> Captain Daniel Dow (stop) Son Rupert Ashley Thronson (stop) age 13 stowaway forward hold in potato sack (stop) Have deposited round trip 3rd class passage at Barclay Bank for Cunard (stop) Please place boy with temporary guardian (stop) Will reimburse fully on ship return to Liverpool (stop) Tell Rupert Junior parents love him (stop) Signed Rupert Thronson

"Moody, take four men to the hold and fin' the lad! Bring'm ta me forthright!" Dow ordered in his heavy Welsh accent.

"Aye-aye, Captain"

"And Moody. You're now 'is guardian."

"Aye-aye, sir," Moody replied without enthusiasm.

It took an hour to locate Rupie, even though his name reverberated through the cavernous hold with five seamen shouting it and peering into every crevice. Rupie had worked himself into a crude cave formed by the bags full of potatoes. As he heard his name called repeatedly, he thought, *Some blood oath. The lads perjured themselves.*

"Rupert Ashley Thronson. We know you're here. Where are you?" Lt. Moody called loudly. Turning to his men, he said, "Disperse yourselves, gentlemen. Turn over every potato sack if you have to." Again, loudly, "Rupert, please answer me," he bellowed. "We received a cable from your father. We know you're here. Say something!"

A weak, undistinguishable murmur broke the silence. "I'm he-er. Up he-er," it said.

"Mr. Moody, on this side, on top of this potato pile. Blimey, the sack's moving," one of the seaman observed. "Over here, sir." Moody and the others rushed to the sailor who had spotted the wiggling burlap sack.

"Very clever, Mr. Moody," crewmember Ross remarked. "He's under a cloth that's painted like real potatoes." Climbing to the sack in question, Ross pulled out a knife and carefully cut an opening along the top of the hemp material. "Now, come out slowly, laddie. Oh, you've got a bag full of things, have you? Here hand it to me."

Rupie slowly and carefully pulled the burlap and its potato-painted cover off as he unfolded himself from his hiding place. "Don't shoot," he said. "I'm coming out with my hands up." He scrambled down from the high pile of potato sacks and held his arms in the air. All the crewmen chuckled.

Moody said, "We're not a western posse, lad. We just

want to add you to the regular passenger list. Your father arranged for a third-class fare. There's no way we can get you back to England. We're too far out at sea. Besides, you're my responsibility now. Are you hungry?"

"No, sir. I'm fine," Rupie responded.

"All right," Moody said. "Let's pay a visit to Captain Dow. He'll want to know how you smuggled yourself onto the ship in the midst of wartime. Men, you can report to your stations. I can handle the situation from here."

The crewmembers disbursed. Moody led Rupie through a maze of wide passageways and up several ladders until they arrived at Captain Dow's quarters. He knocked on the door.

"Captain, it's First Mate Moody. We found the stowaway."

The cabin door opened, and Moody led Rupie into a sumptuous compartment resembling a large conference room with an adjoining kitchen and sleeping quarters that could be seen behind the opening for a walnut-paneled door. Rupie, though docile, shivered with fright. Nevertheless, not looking directly at the captain, he asked, "How did you know where to find me?"

"We received a cable from yer fatha," responded the captain. He's also arranged for yer third-class passage. Sit down, Mr. Thronson. I must admit it's quite a suprise to see ya, an unauth'rized passenger on my ship. What, pray tell, brought ya t'us? Wait, before ya respond, I'd like to know where Mr. Moody found ya. Mr. Moody, please."

Moody spoke right up, "Well, sir, he was very clever and well prepared for the journey. He had a candle, food and water, and a change of clothing. He had painted potatoes on a white sheet, which looked very real, and hid inside it and a burlap potato sack cover. It was difficult to detect him. One thing bothered me, however..."

"And wa was that, Moody?" the captain asked.

"The loo. I didn't know how he planned to go to the w.c."

"D'ya 'ave an answer to that, son? Holds don't have loos."

"No, sir. It never entered my mind. Besides, I wasn't hidden away long enough to have the urge," Rupie responded.

"Well, be that as it may. D'ya 'ave the urge now?"

"Yes, sir. I do," a nervous Rupie replied. The captain pointed to an adjacent door, which Rupie entered.

The captain and Moody discussed how a repetition of such a stowaway plan could be averted in the future. "We'll just have to double our military security at the docks," the captain summarized. "Imagine, hidin' in a potato sack... very ingen'ous."

Rupie returned and sat, tentatively, between the two officers.

"Mr. Thronson, let's hear yer story," the captain requested.

Rupie, at first, recited his tale slowly but gained confidence as he unveiled his intent to become an actor in America, his careful planning and observations at the Bristol wharf, and his engaging trusted friends who broke a promise of secrecy. This completed his confession.

"Now, that 'as quite a saga, wasn't it, Moody?" The officer nodded. "Mr. Thronson, why don't ya tell us something about yerself, yer family, yer schooling, and why ya want to be an actor?"

Rupie responded, gaining more confidence in realizing that he would not be imprisoned as a stowaway. He briefly told of his family life, his studies, and his few experiences in the theatrical world. "Sir," he concluded. "I'm really sorry. I know I shouldn't have stowed away. But, I didn't know how else I could escape to America."

"Well, young fella, Mr. Moody and I 'ave no choice but to return ya to England and yer parents. Ya've been quite convincing in yer desire to enter the actin' profession. However, this is a ship. We're at war. We're at sea, and ya have no official auth'rization to be on this vessel. Ya see? Ya have passage, but no passport. Ya're going to have to stay aboard the *Lusitania* while we discharge passengers and cargo in New York and sail back with us on the return voyage."

"Is that final, sir? Can't I leave the ship in New York? I have relatives in Toronto," Rupie appealed.

"Yes, that is final. The *Lusitania* will be your home for the next fortnight. Now, do ya think we should place ya in the ship's gaol?" the captain added.

Realizing the folly of further protesting, Rupie, becoming subservient, asked pleadingly, "Sir, I want to make it up to you. I'm terribly sorry I snuck onto your ship. Could I work my way across? Isn't there some job I can perform as a crewmember?"

"I'm going to leave that up to Mr. Moody. But…I do have one suggestion."

"What's that, sir?" Moody inquired.

"We 'ave the Bensonians, that group of Stratford actors, aboard, Mr. Moody. Why waste an opportunity for Mr. Thronson when Thespians abound in our corr'dors rehearsin' Shakespeare in our public places? Now, take Mr. Thronson to his third-class quarters. Perhaps, ya can lodge him in a cabin with actors. Farewell for now, Mr. Thronson. Ya're in good hands with Mr. Moody. Welcome aboard the *Lusitania*." The captain rose and beckoned them to the cabin door. "Farewell for now, Mr. Thronson. Happy sailing."

Moody led Rupie along the corridors, located a steward in the third-class section of the ship, and handed the boy his few belongings. The steward unlocked cabin 516 and moved aside when Moody and Rupie entered. Moody dismissed the steward. There were two double bunk beds in the cabin, two small desks, and four chairs. There was a small round porthole.

Moody addressed Rupie, "Your bunkmates aren't here right now. It's lunchtime, and you must be hungry. Why not eat this apple and drink this cup of water sitting on the table. I'm going to have to locate some more food and a few more items of clothing for you, laddie," he said. "Now, Mr. Thronson, if you are to become a crewmember, it is essential that you follow all the rules and requirements of the ship's master. Is that clear?" he asked.

"Yes, sir," Rupie responded.

"I'll return within the hour," Moody said, leaving Rupie sitting on an upper bunk.

Rupie following the first mate's orders, slowly ate his first luncheon aboard the *Lusitania* and inspected his new, rather basic naval surroundings.

When Moody returned, he placed a clothing bag on Rupie's upper bunk and requested that he follow him to his own officer's quarters.

Once settled in his own large comfortable cabin, resembling a fully-equipped civilian hotel room, Moody addressed Rupie in a friendly manner. "Mr. Thronson, what do your friends call you?" he asked.

"Rupie," the boy replied.

"Fine. Rupie, I think I've found a way to keep you busy during your cruise with us. In fact, I've discovered two responsible opportunities, but you must fulfill them as competently as possible. Do you understand?"

"Yes, sir," Rupie answered, eyebrows raised with interest.

"In all your activities, you are responding to me as your commanding officer. Each morning, you will report to this cabin at six a.m. We will review the day's assignments. Every night, precisely at ten p.m., you will again report to brief me on your day's activities. Your quarters will be in cabin 516. You will have your meals in the crew's mess. Your first position will be as a bellboy on the *Lusitania* crew. In that post, you will be under the supervision of Seaman Gustifson. Your working hours will be from seven a.m. to five p.m. each day. This responsibility will require that you become familiar with every inch of the ship since you will be delivering cablegrams to passenger quarters and to public gathering rooms, as well as directly to Captain Dow. Any questions?"

"Yes, sir," Rupie responded with an enthusiastic smile on his face. "Do I get to wear a uniform?"

"You do. It's in the bag I gave you in your cabin," answered Moody, with an equally enthusiastic grin.

"Now for the second position. Are you ready?" Rupie nodded affirmatively.

"I've made contact with Mr. Randle Ayrton, stage manager of the Bensonians. They're travelling to America for a series of Shakespearean productions. He has agreed to your serving as a stage prompter prior to docking in New York. He's very pleased to have someone besides his actors following the written scripts for his rehearsals. All of his performers are still memorizing their own parts. They have to prepare nine different plays in readiness for their American performances. The first play will be presented two days after our arrival. Each additional play is to be performed in succeeding days."

"Oh, Mr. Moody. That's smashing news!" Rupie announced happily. "Thank you. Thank you so much."

Moody continued, "Once we leave my cabin, I'll take you to the Enquiries Office for instructions. At five p.m., I'll fetch you, and we'll find the Bensonians. Then, you can learn what the responsibilities of a prompter are."

Moody and Rupie made their way to the Enquiries Office where the boy was introduced to Seaman Gustifson. Moody bade farewell.

"Well, lad, I understand you're known as Rupie, so that's what I'll call ye," Gustifson said. "Andrew! Andrew Larson!" he called. Immediately, a boy, a few years older than Rupie appeared. "Andrew, this is Rupie Thronson. He's our new bellboy. Stowed away in the hold he did. But the captain decided to put him to work as a regular crew member. I'd like you to give him a thorough tour of the ship. Take two hours this morning and another two this afternoon. In the meantime, I want you to brief him on what a bellboy is supposed to do."

In a short period, Rupie learned that the *Lusitania* was an immense and beautiful ship. Its four large funnels and two masts spanned the 787-foot length of the vessel. For the newest crewmember, Andrew gave Rupie a full tour of the ship. Rupie drew all the locations of cabins and public rooms in the first-, second- and third-classes in a notebook, as well as the officers' compartments. He would be delivering messages at all times in all locations.

The first-class entrance had a colorful carpeted floor and heaters throughout the lobby. Oak-paneled corridors led to the smoking room and lounge, revolving doors provided entry, and all around were mirrors, fancy lighting fixtures, draperies, and both practical and decorative furniture. Suites were furnished in period décor. The broad outside decks were enclosed from the wind and ocean spray, and there were lifts to be used by both first- and second-class passengers.

The second-class corridors and public rooms were also luxurious and comfortable, with oak paneling in the smoking and dining rooms, sycamore in the library, green and red upholstered furniture and the same colors in the carpeted corridors. Staterooms uniformly had white enameled walls and mahogany furniture, with carpeted or linoleum floors.

For the third class, there were two dining saloons, two bars, a comfortable oak-paneled smoking room with teak tables and chairs, and a general assembly room similarly furnished.

More than 1,200 passengers filled the corridors, decks, and public rooms. Since there were few organized activities, people talked in small groups, played cards, smoked, and a great majority read books. More than a few would always be found staring out into the ocean, studying the moving waves and clouds, some searching the waters for ocean life. The only scheduled events were meals, eight-thirty to ten-thirty a.m. for breakfast, one to two-thirty p.m. for luncheon, and six to eight p.m. for dinner. Each morning, noon, and night, the bugler would summon passengers to their meals in the large dining saloons. In addition to the regular dining rooms for each class, for first-class travellers, there was a fancy restaurant with walnut paneling and French décor.

Also, in the upper class there were Turkish and electric baths open to the ladies and gentlemen at different times during the day. Additionally, the 32-foot by 15-foot swimming pool also had selective hours for men, women, and children. A small gymnasium with lifting apparatus and mats and a squash racket court were located on a first-class deck. Both first- and second-class passengers had access to libraries. Decks for all classes were covered for promenading purposes.

When they returned from the exhaustive tour, Seaman Gustifson provided a review of the ship's message center. He explained that, by 1912, most transatlantic passenger liners had wireless equipment. Here in the Enquiry Office at the starboard side of the ship, passengers would compose handwritten messages. They would pay twelve shillings, six pennies for the first ten words and nine pennies for each additional word. Messages were sent by pneumatic tube to the wireless cabin where Sparks worked. He would note the word count, transmit the message, prepare a bill for the customer, and return it to the Enquiries Office. Incoming messages were handwritten by the receiving operator and typed on a Marconi form by the relief operator before being sent to the Enquiry desk. Upon receipt at the desk, they were delivered by the bellboy to the passenger cabins or one of the public rooms. Messages regarding navigation or communications from the Cunard Line were taken directly to the bridge, a few steps down the corridor on the port side of the officers' quarters.

Andrew accompanied Rupie on his first three deliveries and one message pick-up. Satisfied that Rupie could function on his own and appeared to have a reasonable familiarity with the ship, Andrew and the third bellboy went about their own duties, each trading off with both incoming cables and passenger requests for new wireless messages.

At five o'clock, Lt. Moody entered the Enquiries Office and led Rupie back to his quarters. "I want to tell you more about our ship," he told Rupie, seating himself and pointing to a desk chair for Rupie.

"The RMS *Lusitania* is owned by the Cunard Steamship Line Shipping Company. It was built at the same time as its sister ship, the *Mauretania*. She was launched on seven June 1906. Both the ships are smaller than the White Star's *Titanic*, which, as you must know, was sunk by an iceberg on fourteen April 1912, two years ago. The loss of life totaled 1,517 souls." Moody bowed his head before continuing, "The twin ships were built to enable Cunard to offer weekly service between Liverpool and New York, both making the one-way trip in seven days. The *Aquitania*, built a year or so later, provides their third ship. It's larger and slower than the *Lusitania* and the *Mauretania*, but far more luxurious."

"Really?" Rupie interrupted. "More luxurious than our ship?"

"Most assuredly," answered Moody, continuing with his narration. "Another reason for building the two sister ships was to compete with other countries' liners, particularly Germany's. Germans dominated the Atlantic speed record for ten years. The *Kaiser Wilhelm II* liner was the king of the ocean until the *Lusitania* overcame its winning time across the ocean. In October 1907, the *Lusitania* averaged 23.99 knots westbound, returning in a close rate of 23.61 knots eastbound. Later, she increased her record to 25.85 knots, but the *Maurentania* was even faster, and still is.

"Are we trying to break a record on this voyage, Mr. Moody?" Rupie inquired.

"I'm afraid not, Rupie. We'll travel fast, but we're also always alert to the possibility of German submarines. Remember, we're at war. Also, we have a large number of Americans travelling with us, returning to their homes, away from the war zone. The Germans have also recently provided us a warning to share with our passengers. Here," handing Rupie, a large poster, "read this."

Rupie's eyes widened as he digested the words on the poster.

NOTICE!

TRAVELLERS intending to embark on the Atlantic voyage are reminded that a state of war exists between Germany and her allies and Great Britain and her allies; that the zone of war includes the waters adjacent to the British Isles; that, in accordance with formal notice given by the Imperial German Government, vessels flying the flag of Great Britain or any of her allies, are liable to destruction in those waters and that travelers sailing in the war zone on the ships of Great Britain or her allies do so at their own risk

IMPERIAL GERMAN EMBASSY

"And that includes you, too, Rupie, as a crewmember," Moody cautioned. "We must be very careful on the ocean these days. When out on the deck, always be on the lookout for unwelcome objects on the water's surface, especially large ones. Rupie, be reassured. Despite the fears, our last captain, 'Bowler Bill' Turner, told me, upon reading this German warning, 'Don't worry. The *Lusitania* is safer than trolley cars in New York.' Just be cautious anyway."

Moody continued, "Depending on the weather and the speed of the vessel, our progress is measured at approximately 440 knots a day from Thursday to the following Tuesday, and we cover the final 300 miles to New York on the next day, Wednesday. We'll lay over in America for five days and make the return trip in another seven. So you'll be back in England in a fortnight. That means you'll become a real sailor, many days at sea and in port. At 75 revolutions per minute, our four huge propellers are driving us through the smooth sea at about twenty-one knots, or almost twenty-four land miles per hour. We're still a very fast ship. So, now, Rupie, why don't you go to your seaman's mess and meet me in the third-class public gathering room in one hour?"

Rupie nodded and took his departure.

When the two of them arrived in the third-class lounge, they immediately noticed the large room had been clearly divided into two very different arrangements. On the port side, passengers were scattered around their section in comfortable chairs, seated around tables, or on large sofas talking softly, reading or playing cards or other board games.

On the starboard side, a group of people, mostly young men and women, were seated on two rows of benches, one directly behind the other, facing three men and a woman in front of them. All had sheaves of paper in their hands, each reading aloud as his or her role in the play required. Rupie and Mr. Moody took seats at the side of the two rows and listened intently to what was being read. No one seemed to notice them, since they were studying the written papers before them.

After an hour, one of the gentlemen in the front, announced, "All right, everyone, let's take a bit of an interlude." As one, the group rose, and left the room, heading towards the bar area.

Moody approached a large, goateed man in front who had just risen. "Mr. Ayrton, I'd like to introduce you to Rupert Thronson, our stowaway, budding actor. Come here, Rupie, meet Mr. Ayrton, the stage manager of the Bensonians."

Ayrton hurried over to Rupie, took his hand warmly, and said, "Oh, yes, our young prompter. We've been expecting you. Have you ever prompted before, young man?" Rupie shook his head. "It's really rather simple." Demonstrating with the packet in his hand, he explained, "You see, this is a script. It has all of the stage directions as to when and where actors enter and cross the stage, stand and sit, but, most importantly, it tells who speaks when and what they must say. We call these the actor's lines." Noticing Moody looking somewhat impatient, Ayrton said to him. "Oh please, run along now, Mr. Moody. Mr. Thronson will be fine. We'll take good care of him."

Moody thanked him and turning, said, "Rupie, I'll see you in my quarters at ten. All right?" Rupie, eyes glued to the pages in front of him, merely nodded.

Ayrton introduced Rupie to the assembled actors as

their new prompter. They gave Rupie a friendly round of applause. The rest of the evening, as the actors read or recited their lines, some letter perfect, others gesturing or calling for help or misreading the words, Rupie, seated behind the two rows of benches, soon learned which of them were familiar with the play they were reading, Shakespeare's comedy *Much Ado About Nothing,* and which were still memorizing their roles. Ayrton would introduce each new scene and explain where the action took place, who entered from where, and where and how the actors moved on stage. Rupie learned that this procedure was known in the theatrical world as "blocking."

During another interval, Ayrton reviewed the theatrical company's American repertory tour with him. "You see, Rupert, the cast was together for only one performance of *Hamlet*, when we were in Bristol, before we departed on the *Lusitania*. We were told it would be safer for us to board there because of the possible submarine danger in Liverpool. We'll be performing nine plays, a different play every night, with up to three matinees in some places. Our actors must thoroughly know their roles before landing in New York. We'll be playing six comedies, a tragedy, and an historical play, *King Richard II*. We have only seven days to discuss each play and try to learn our speaking roles. Each day, come to my cabin in the morning. I'll give you the script to read for that evening. Is that clear?"

"Yes, sir," Rupie said enthusiastically.

"And Rupert, we'll be paying you thirty shillings for your valuable assistance. Is that satisfactory?"

"Oh, yes, sir. Very much so, sir," Rupie happily responded.

The play the cast was rehearsing, *Much Ado About Nothing*, was very entertaining to Rupie, who had seen it performed by a touring company at Bristol Grammar School. He'd remembered that the plot concerned two very different sets of lovers, Beatrice and Benedict, and Claudio and Hero. It was a merry war of the sexes, where all kinds of obstacles arose between the couples. Benedict and Beatrice acted like they hated one another, but, in the end, their love was most apparent. However, he was concerned that Aryton read two roles, one of which was the leading role of Benedict.

As the cast was being dismissed, Rupie asked Aryton, "Which character are you actually portraying, sir? Why did you have to read two parts?"

Aryton responded, "Oh, I'm sorry, Rupert. All the leading roles in our repertory will be performed by Pa, the great Frank Benson. He's busy responding to correspondence this evening. Besides, he's performed these Shakespearean plays for years and knows the words for all the parts."

"Oh, that's wonderful, sir. I know all about England's actor managers, and Mr. Benson is well known for having brought Shakespeare to every village and school in Great Britain," Rupie remarked. "I even know two actors who worked with him," he added.

"He also toured the rest of the Commonwealth, South Africa, India, China," Aryton said. "That's why we're all going to America. You'll meet Mr. Benson tomorrow night, Mr. Thronson. Now, run along. You prompted very well this evening."

Promptly at ten, Rupie rapped on Mr. Moody's cabin door. It was opened immediately and Moody said, "No need to report tonight, Rupie. You've had a most lengthy day and need your sleep. Ta-ta." He closed his door tightly, and Rupie returned to his quarters. Entering, he was pleased to see that his cabinmates included the younger members of the Bensonians, and it was only after an hour of further conversation that the candles were extinquished and the four lads fell asleep. Rupie's first day at sea had been rather fulfilling.

Chapter 9
Theatre on the Bounding Main

At Sea, 1914

The following morning, Rupie stood before Seaman Gustifson in his bellboy's attire. The smart, grey uniform fit him perfectly. He had had a welcome bath the night before, and his hair was combed. He stood very straight before his Enquiries supervisor, and saluted him. "Rupert Thronson reporting for duty, sir," he stated proudly.

During the morning, occasionally referring to locations in his notebook, he carried messages throughout the ship. At eleven a.m., he was surprised to see Captain Dow entering the passageway adjacent to the Enquiries center leading several uniformed officers. "Good day, Mr. Thronson," the captain said pleasantly. "Enjoy your first day aboard? Have any sea sickness?"

"Oh, no, sir. I had a marvelous day. Thank you again, sir," Rupie responded.

Mr. Moody had not mentioned to him that Captain

Dow made a thorough inspection of the ship each day, a requirement of the Cunard Lines. It was a reassuring sight to the passengers, especially during wartime, knowing that safety, speed, and satisfaction were uppermost in the minds of the ship's officers. Gustifson informed Rupie that sometime after ten a.m., the *Lusitania*'s chief engineer, purser, assistant purser, surgeon, and chief steward would make their reports to the captain in his quarters. They had already completed their own departmental inspections an hour previously. After listening to the reports, noting needs and deficiencies, the entire entourage would sweep through the corridors and public rooms of all classes: kitchens, pantries, dining saloons, hospitals for passengers and crew, barber's shops, bakery shop, and other compartments. The impressive group of uniformed officers covered the entire ship, examining, observing, and noting cleanliness, condition, and performance. They went from deck to deck, downward to the great storage rooms, cargo spaces, and engine rooms, where the captain was attended only by the chief engineer, and along the open decks where winches, cranes, and ventilators were checked and tested. Upon completion of their tour, the group re-assembled in the captain's quarters to discuss the inspection results and the required navigational tasks for the day.

Seaman Gustifson, standing next to Rupie at the door of the Enquiries Office, informed the captain and his fellow officers that his department had never been so busy. "Many of those cabling are concerned about submarines in the Atlantic, sir. Have any sightings been radioed to us?"

"No, Gustifson, we've heard nothing about submarines from Sparks. Hopefully, passage will be clear all the way to New York."

"Let's hope so, sir. Thank you, sir," Gustifson said, as the assemblage headed down the corridor.

The days flew by for Rupie. From the nightly readings, he learned the plots of the nine plays the Bensonians would be performing, recalling several he had seen in school. He made new friends among the younger cast members besides his three cabin mates. He took special interest in an actress, Rosie St. John, only a few years older than Rupie, who played a boy in *Much Ado About Nothing,* a page and third player in Hamlet, and two small roles in two other plays. She had told Rupie that her father had paid Mr. Benson to teach her how to become an actress, and he had invited her on the tour to gain experience. Rupie also began initial acquaintanceships with the older key actors in the company. He was greatly impressed by their obviously fine acting abilities.

The second night aboard, he was introduced to Frank Benson, the company's prominent leader.

"Oh, I know of you, sir," Rupie said immediately. "I even know the Townsends who toured with you in America." Benson was pleased and spent a brief few minutes questioning Rupie about his former performers. Rupie told Benson about his short stay with the Townsends and their mutual affection for the famous actor-manager. Benson told Rupie that they had been "great troupers."

As the rehearsals began, Benson would occasionally rise from his seat on one of the actors' benches, and tromp up and down the imagined stage area before them, delivering his lines with force and gusto as if he were already on stage. Rupie had heard many stories about both the varied experiences of Benson's touring companies and his desires to turn Stratford-upon-Avon into the center of Shakespearean theatrical literature and performance. He also knew that Benson was the person most responsible for taking Shakespeare to every hamlet on the British Isles and into any school that invited him. He could learn much from this great Thespian.

The second night out, the cast read their parts in *The Merchant of Venice.* The play introduced the vengeful creditor, Shylock, a Jewish moneylender who seeks everything he can possibly gain from his Christian opposite, the generous, faithful Antonio. The play's Christian heroine, Portia, defends Antonio from Shylock's horrid legal suit. In the end, the villain renounces his faith and his fortune. Rupie especially liked the line, "All that glitters is not gold," which Benson inadvertently changed to "All that's golden does not glitter," and he thanked Rupie for his correction.

The third night, the comedic *Taming of the Shrew* was rehearsed. This time a small audience had formed around where the actors were gathered, with passengers moving their chairs from the leisure part of the third-class public room. The *Shrew* is a farce about female submission. According to her father, the strong-willed, independent Katherine must marry before her younger sister, Bianca, can choose from among her many suitors. These same suitors persuade a fortune-seeker, Petruchio, to court Katherine, vowing to pay all costs, and Petruchio would be rewarded from her dowry. Despite their constant fighting over anything and everything, the two marry. Denying Katherine food and sleep, while continuously singing her praises, Petruchio finally browbeats his wife into submission – she is tamed. Bianca marries suitor Lucentio, and suitor Hortensio marries a widow. At a banquet with wagers on who has the most obedient wife, Petrucio wins because of his wife's faithful lecture on the importance of wifely submission. There was laughter and applause on occasion when the small group of spectators reacted to particular actors' deliveries. The cast enjoyed having an audience.

The second offering of the evening introduced the jovial, self-assured, scrupulous, overweight knight Falstaff, who attempted to charm several married women into accepting his insincere love. Deceiving them in the play, *The Merry Wives of Windsor*, the rare folio taking place in England, Falstaff is only interested in their money. The ladies turn the tables on him, and he receives his just reward. Rupie couldn't contain his laughter with the delightful Edward Warburton's skill in making Falstaff such a believable dolt, and neither could the growing audience.

During the days, on his missions with messages, Rupie observed Benson running in his briefs around the decks in the mornings and late afternoons, swimming in the large pool, playing cricket with members of the cast on the top open deck, and practicing sword fighting. Each time they met, Benson would toss out lines from Shakespeare's plays as a form of mutual enjoyment. Cast members told Rupie that Benson was famous for his formidable background and continued interest in sports. He had competed as an athlete at Oxford and, even in his leading roles, he added physicality to every portrayal, hurtling himself into chairs, jumping over a piece of furniture rather than walking around it, and vigorously greeting cast members as they entered the stage arena.

The following night, Rupie was totally immersed in and amused by the farce, *Twelfth Night*. He found the continuous confusion of jealousy, mistaken identity, fights and duels fully enchanting during a play-reading night that involved two rehearsals. Shipwrecked on an isolated island, Viola, disguised as a man, Cesario, tries to make her way in the world of men. She becomes a servant for Duke Orsino. The duke is smitten with a neighboring countess, Olivia, who is in mourning for the death of her brother, Viola's supposedly perished brother. Olivia's uncle Sir Toby Belch, a Falstaff-like character, further confuses the plot in presenting another suitor for her, chiefly to get his hands on the gentleman's money. In the end, Orsino decides his real love is the undisguised Viola. Her long-lost brother, Sebastian, marries Olivia. And even Sir Toby finds romance with Olivia's handmaiden, Maria.

The other reading that evening was *As You Like It*, another comedy. As Rupie described the play to Andrew the next day, "Rosalind, the daughter of a banished duke, is banished herself by her evil uncle, Duke Frederick. She must leave her pursuit of the man she loves, Orlando, the disinherited son of another banished duke. She switches genders and, as Ganymede, travels with her loyal cousin, Celia, to the Forest of Arden, where her father and his friends reside in exile."

Andrew asked, "Isn't this sort of complicated?"

"That's Shakespeare, Andrew," Rupie related. "He had his characters provide their very different views on such subjects as love, aging, the natural world, and death. New friends are made and families are reunited. By the play's end, Ganymede, once again Rosalind, marries her Orlando. Even the mean uncle reforms and marries Rosalind's cousin, Celia. All of the paths open so that Rosalind's father can rule his fiefdom once again."

That day, the fifth at sea, Rupie began leaving each passenger with a special Shakespearean quote when he delivered a message. *From the Merchant of Venice,* he borrowed, "I'm gone within a twinkling of an eye." In the second-class public lounge, waiting for a cable recipient to answer his page, he declared, "I'll not budge a step – until Mr. Patterson answers my call," a paraphrase from *Taming of the Shrew.* He weaved in other Shakespearian lines from plays as different occasions arose. When he delivered one message, he stated, "That's the short and the long of it," from *The Merry Wives of Windsor.* With another cable going to a name he had trouble pronouncing, he said, "I cannot tell what the dickens his name is," from the same play.

In the evening, the cast ran through their parts in *Romeo and Juliet* and *Hamlet,* both quite familiar to Rupie.

The following day, he told Andrew that the actors playing the parts of Romeo and Juliet were "absolutely brilliant." He had been moved to tears by the touching balcony scene and noted to his friend that this was the only play in which Benson was not appearing in a lead role. The impresario had remained in his cabin answering letters for the first rehearsal of the evening. He had returned, however, to act out his magnificent interpretation of Hamlet for the second rehearsal that night. Rupie, the cast, and the increasingly growing audience had been mesmerized by Benson's commanding delivery and powerful stage presence. Benson received a standing ovation from those gathered in the third-class public room, commanding the attention of everyone in the large space. No passengers played cards, read, or conversed. The Bensonians had had all their attention.

On the sixth and last night of rehearsals, the only historical Shakespeare play in the company's repertoire, *King Richard II,* was delivered by the cast. Benson was again superb, and, because of the increased interest of the passengers, the entire reading was moved to the second-class public lounge, which seated far more seagoers.

Rupie was unfamiliar with the play and followed his script intently, speaking up immediately if an actor misread a line or was slow to pick up a cue. He learned that King Richard II, king only by virtue of his family status, was intelligent but weak. He has banished his rival, Henry Bolingbroke, fearing that he was a threat to the crown. Waging a war in Ireland but needing funds, Richard confiscates funds from the wealthy John of Gaunt, who happens to be his former rival's father. Bolingbroke and many nobles rebel against the King, confining him to the Tower of London, and Bolingbroke ascends the throne as Henry IV. Assuming that their newly-crowned king wants Richard dead, his friend, Exton, and his two assistants murder Richard, who dies bravely. Henry, full of guilt, banishes Exton. From this play, Rupie would borrow "Eating the bitter bread of banishment" and "The ripest fruit first falls" and somehow weave these quotations into his message deliveries.

Since Rosie St. John didn't have lines in the play, she sat next to Rupie, turning pages for him in the script. Between intervals and the stops for stage directions for the actors, they jabbered together like two birds in a juniper tree. Rupie told her he'd miss her and couldn't wait for her to return to England and he could visit her in London. At the end of the rehearsal, Mr. Ayrton thanked Rupie for his services, and presented him with his promised wages.

The following day, the last at sea, the *Lusitania* covered the remaining 300 miles at full speed, arriving in New York in the early afternoon. A large orchestra and hundreds of greeters met the ship at the Cunard pier. Rupie stood on the top deck with Andrew and other crewmembers calling and waving farewell to the passengers they recognized. Luggage had been delivered to the passengers' cabins, and they carried their bags down the gangway, many with their stewards assisting them. The entire Bensonian troupe, many of whom Rupie had said goodbye to the previous night, were loaded onto two large buses. Scenery, costumes, and properties for their plays were stacked in two sizeable trucks, which followed the buses towards the towering buildings seen in the distance – the City of New York.

During the five days in port, while other crewmembers were able to take liberty in America's largest city, Rupie, admitting to Mr. Moody that he enjoyed drawing, was assigned to the paint detail. Each day, the detail moved from place to place, covering bulkheads that were corroded or needed touchups with grey, wartime-colored paint. Rupie had taken new quarters with the crew, rooming with Andrew, another bellboy, and two younger seamen. Time passed rapidly, and Rupie learned more about the history of the *Lusitania* and its voyages from his shipmates.

On the return trip, another British theatre company, which had been performing *Charley's Aunt* in New York's Metropolitan Theatre for three months, came aboard. There were ten cast members and three stage administrators. During the voyage to England, the cast was preparing to open a short run of Oscar Wilde's *The Importance of Being Ernest,* booked at the Theatre Royal in London. Meeting with Mr. Moody to arrange for rehearsal space aboard the *Lusitania*, the company's manager, Mr. Burris, was happy to accept Moody's suggestion to use Rupie as a prompter.

Moody also convinced the manager that performing *Charley's Aunt* on the third night out at sea and the *The Importance of Being Ernest* on the sixth night would be good for passenger morale, especially with the constant fear of German submarines roaming the Atlantic Ocean. Because Moody was interested in as many passengers as possible enjoying the productions, he had convinced the captain that the first-class gallery should be used, even for lower-class passengers. This would enable the theatrical company to conduct two performances for each of the plays, a matinee and an evening performance.

Since there would be neither stage dressings nor costumes, Moody volunteered Rupie and the other two bellboys to assist in setting up the scenes as well as possible, using furniture and properties from various sections of the ship. Accordingly, the first night of the voyage required a long meeting with Mr. Burris and his assistants to determine what settings and articles would be needed by the actors.

With their lists in hand and the written permission of Mr. Moody, the bellboys scoured the ship for light and movable chairs, tables, lamps, urns, plants, plates and silverware, bringing them all to the bar adjacent to the first-class ballroom.

After their day of service for the Enquiries Office, Rupie and his colleagues reported to Mr. Burris. At five o'clock, he explained the various set-ups and properties to be used with the actors. At six, he began the first rehearsal of *The Importance of Being Earnest*. The actors gathered, as had the Bensonians, on two benches with the three administrators in front of them.

Rupie sat to the side, again serving as the prompter. He had heard of but never seen the Wilde play. The zany plot of an imaginary Ernest - the pursuit of suitors Algernon and Jack for Gwendolyn and Cecily; Jack's realization that he had been a foundling in a handbag; Algernon's deception as to the real Ernest; and final resolution with Jack turning out to be Algernon's older brother, originally named Ernest John – all captivated Rupie. After a week of intense, heavy Shakespeare, the more modern, dramatic work of Oscar Wilde's comedy, the twists and turns of character development always presenting the unexpected, furthered his desire to learn more about theatre in every way possible, as a reader of dramatic literature, as a playgoer, and, hopefully, as a participant.

The next evening, another *Earnest* rehearsal saw the performers rising from their seats and moving about the imaginary stage as directed by Mr. Burris, entering the stage area, exiting, rising and sitting on cue, discussing gestures and what Burris called "pieces of business." Rupie loved this next step in the process of play production, moving from play reading to the blocking aspect, creating, as Mr. Burris called it, "a series of stage pictures." He told Mr. Burris he planned to make the train trip from Bristol to see one of the cast's performances in London. "With sets and costumes, this will be a smashing production," he added.

On Wednesday, at two p.m., the first-class lounge was filled to capacity for the matinee of *Charley's Aunt.* Rupie and the other bell boys, who had been released for two hours from their cable delivery duties, had arranged two sofas, several small tables, and carpet-backed chairs to resemble a living room setting. Chairs had been provided for the audience so that a small theatre arrangement separated the audience from the actors. Over 200 were in attendance. Mr. Burris introduced the company, told of the roles the actors would be performing, briefly reviewed their successful run in New York, and mentioned that they had obtained their original costumes from the hold and would be wearing them for both the matinee and evening performances. The audience collectively applauded vigorously.

Charley's Aunt unfolded. As each actor entered the stage area, applause welcomed him. After their relatively long run in New York, the actors had perfect recall with their lines and on-stage movements. Beginning with the marriage pursuit of both Jack and Charley of solicitor Stephen Spettigue's wards, Kitty and Amy, to the anticipated arrival of millionairess Donna Lucia d'Alvadorez from Brazil (where the nuts come from), the play begins with hilarity. Convincing their classmate, Lord Fancourt Babberly, that he must impersonate a millionairess to impress the women, "Babbs'" performance was hysterical. His very masculine portrayal of a woman in a large uncomfortable dress is awkward, his attempts to lighten his cracking bass voice futile, and his obvious forgetting that he is a nice old lady of the Victorian era was plain old fun. Further complications arise with the girls confiding secrets to someone, whom with increasing familiarity they believe to be of the same sex. The identity deception continues successfully with Jack's father, Colonel Sir Francis Chesney, and Mr. Spettigue's awareness of Donna Lucia's wealth. Both contemplate proposals of marriage. The real millionairess arrives incognito, quickly recognizing the intrigue. Jack and Charley obtain their desired marriage engagements but must obtain Spettigue's permission as well. Spettigue, for monetary reasons, asks for the fake Donna Lucia's hand in marriage. Babbs accepts, pending his approval of his wards' betrothals. Jack's father proposes to the real Donna Lucia. After Spettigue formally announces his marriage plans and that of his wards, Babbs' deception is revealed and the play ends with a happy conclusion for all. Applause, applause. The matinee audience was enthralled; the evening's audience even more so. Theatrically, the *Lusitania* was flourishing as it headed home in calm seas.

Rehearsals of *Earnest* continued the fourth and fifth seagoing days, and the cast members all appeared to have memorized their parts. Burris suggested that they treat their two Thursday performances as "dress rehearsals," and even without costumes, properties and sets act out the play as if they were under "real stage" conditions. That afternoon, because the sea had become rougher, almost anything that could go wrong, did: missed cues, muffled lines, and forgetfulness by the actors. Rupie was very busy in the prompter's corner, whispering corrections and proper renderings as softly as possible and answering rapid questions as actors tended to move towards his side of the stage as they delivered their parts. Audience members readily felt the uneasiness as they noted the mistakes and miscues of the cast.

At the end of the first act, Mr. Burris, having first met briefly with the cast, spoke to the audience. "I'm sorry," he said. "It doesn't appear we're ready to give a full-fledged performance." He excused his cast from blame, suggesting that he, Mr. Burris, had rushed them through their various scenes and that this aspect of dramatic preparation, continuous rehearsal, had been unfulfilled. With their collective permission, he asked the assemblage if the play could proceed as script-reading theatre rather than a performance. Ascent was nodded. As a reading, the second and third acts were rendered and, as the sea calmed, so did the tension in the first-class drawing room. With the actors relaxed as they verbalized their roles, so did the audience members relax, using their imaginations as to what action would ordinarily be unfolding before them. The talent, the clever script, and the audience feeling almost as another cast member in the development of a real-life theatrical company made it all a mutual experience. At least, this was the way Rupie saw it. When things aren't going well, step back, collect yourselves, review the process, and try it another way. In this case, it worked.

His final day aboard the *Lusitania*, Rupie said his goodbyes to his fellow crew members and his new actor friends. He received several pounds from Mr. Burris for prompting, packed his gear, and awaited the Liverpool dock. He had been allowed to keep his two bellboy uniforms, and two shirts and the trousers that Mr. Moody had given him. He had also been able to keep two of the Shakespeare scripts, plus those of *Charley's Aunt* and *The Importance of Being Earnest* that Mr. Burris had presented to him at the final cast meeting after the Thursday night reading.

A fortnight after his Bristol departure, Rupie was escorted down the gangway in the Liverpool Harbor, First Officer Moody nudging him into the waiting arms of his sobbing mother. "Rupie, how could you have done this to us? I missed you so. Are you all right?" The senior Thronson placed his arms around both of them.

Captain Dow was at their heels. Rupert Senior

approached the rugged merchant sea captain, and, thanking him, set several pounds into his palm. Then, he turned to Rupie with controlled anger. "Son. You're incorrigible! Why did you run away?"

"Ahoy mate!" interrupted the captain. "I don't need your money. Yer son worked his own way aboard the *Lusitania*. He proved a most worthy crewman. The Cunard Lines will be returning yer check from Barclays. Don't be too hard on 'm. He's a good lad." And to Rupie he said, "Farewell, Rupert, m'lad. Let me know if ya ever want to take a little sail again?" He gave Rupie a mock military salute with a broad smile and handed the money back to his father.

"Goodbye, sir. And thank you for everything. You'll tell the crew how much I appreciate..." The captain had gone beyond hearing range, the noise of the waves lapping at the hull muffling Rupie's words. Starting to address Moody, Rupie paused and then embraced the young officer in a bear hug, confessing, "I'm going to really miss you, Mr. Moody. I'll never forget you. You're my mate for life."

Unfolding himself from Rupie's grasp, Moody said, "Perhaps, someday we'll sail again together, m'lad. Maybe you'll be an actor bound for New York." With an about face, he headed back towards the *Lusitania*.

"Rupert, How could you run away like that?" asked Rupert Senior.

"Father, I want to be an actor!" the boy stated emphatically.

"Your mother and I thought that might be the reason. We found the models of stage settings under your bed. We also discovered several playbooks. But why America?"

"Yes, why America, my dear?" echoed his mother.

"Richard told me I'd have a better chance to work in the theatre there than here. And I could have stayed with Aunt Valerie and Uncle Horace."

"You don't think they would have sent you back, Rupie?" his mother inquired.

"If they wanted to. I would have run away from them, too," Rupie said defiantly.

"Let's go home and discuss this as a family," the elder Thronson suggested, and they all stepped into a waiting motorcar. "The train station if you please," requested the grocer.

Chapter 10

The Water Wanderer Returns

Bristol, 1914-15

Back in Bristol, sipping tea and crunching crumpets around the dining table, Rupie shared his shipboard experiences on many occasions in answer to his parents' questions, Daisy lying at his feet.

"Where did you sleep?" "How was the food?" "What was it like to have been a bellboy on the *Lusitania*," they asked him.

Rupie was delighted to respond. "On the way back, when I had time, I read books the Cap'n lent me from his personal library, books like *Mutiny on the Bounty* about a cruel captain, name of Captain Bligh, and the mutineer, Fletcher Christian, and Richard Henry *Dana's Two Years Before the Mast.* I read Cooper's *A Life Before the Mast, Autobiography of a Seaman,* and *A Voyage Around the World.*"

He avoided information about his service as a prompter.

"Oh Rupie, those nasty books by those terrible pirates, how awful," gasped his mother, who, between meals prepared by a housekeeper, spent most of her time in bed.

"They're only stories, Mother," Rupie giggled. "Would you rather I read plays?"

"All right, Rupie," his father said reluctantly. "If you finish middle school at BSG, I won't stand in the way of your becoming an actor. But you must go about it in the right fashion. You must study it as you might a real profession. Learn about it. Go to the theatre, take acting lessons, read as many plays as you can. To start with, I'll allow you to attend one play each month, which your mother and I will select. You must earn your own money for tickets. And you can make models of stage settings if you desire. But that's all until you finish the Fifth Form."

"May I see Richard Bates, Father?"

"Yes, you may. But only at appropriate times."

"What's an appropriate time?" Rupie asked curiously.

"We'll see, Rupert. We'll see."

Several weeks after Rupie had returned, he was passing a newsstand, and a large headline caught his attention, "*Lusitania* Sunk By Germans." Hastily, he handed the nearby newspaperman two pence and anxiously read the tragic story of the first torpedoing of a British ship in the Great War. *Thank heavens,* he muttered to himself. *The captain listed is not Captain Dow.* He read aloud, "Captain William Turner, who was rescued, had just returned to take the helm of the *Lusitania* after a short leave." *But what of the other crewmen*, he pondered. *What's happened to them?*

During the next several weeks, his concerns were answered. His ship guardian, Lt. Moody, had perished. The body of his fellow bellboy, Andrew, was never found. Most of his former mates were still reported missing. In one of the Bristol newspapers, Rupie read a brief summary of the tragedy:

> On 7 May, the *Lusitania* entered the Irish Channel bound for the home port of Liverpool. Captain William Turner had slowed the ship from 20 down to 15 knots because of the fog. As a precaution against the submarine threat, he posted extra lookouts and swung the lifeboats out. At about 1:39 pm, lookout Leslie Morton, 18, saw a burst of bubbles beginning to approach the starboard (right) side of the ship at about 22 knots. He shouted, "Torpedoes coming on the starboard side." None of the officers heard him. Thirty seconds later, Thomas Quinn, a lookout high above in the crow's nest, saw the torpedo's wake and sounded the alarm. Captain Turner arrived on the navigating bridge just as the torpedo detonated. There was a large explosion similar to a crack of thunder at the side of the ship just ahead of the 2nd funnel. Then there was a second, larger, muffled explosion that seemed to come from the bottom of the ship. The power suddenly failed. Without power, the rudder and the engines did not respond, and the watertight doors could not be closed. The wireless room tapped out an S.O.S. on battery power.

Mentally, Rupie composed a picture of the confusion, the chaos, the catastrophe of the explosions. He read on:

> "Lifeboats on the port (left) side could not be launched. The starboard-side boats had to be swung out so far as a result of the listing ship, many passengers had to jump from the deck to the lifeboats, risking falling into the water many

> storeys below. Many crew members panicked and a few lifeboats were launched that contained only passengers and a few crew members. Other lifeboats capsized and two were damaged when the torpedo hit the ship. The *Lusitania* sank below the waves shortly before two p.m. The *Lusitania* was sunk by German submarine U-20, captained by Kapitanleutnant Walter Schwieger. One thousand two hundred and seventy-two passengers perished and 850 crewmen were killed."

Rupie was crushed with sorrow. He recalled the good times with Gustifson, how he admired Mr. Moody, and how much he had learned about ships and Shakespeare. He thought about the responsibilities Captain Dow had entrusted in him. *There was another captain mentioned. Dow wasn't on the ship. Oh, how I hope somehow the others might have been among the survivors,* he thought, wiping tears from his eyes.

After he returned home, he wrote a letter to Rosie in which he expressed his anger on the loss of so many of the friends he had made aboard the ship, and how he hated the Germans for starting the terrible "Great War." Of the good news, he wrote about several of the recent films he had seen and that he was planning a trip to London to see *The Importance of Being Ernest*, featuring his seagoing friends. "First," he wrote I have to earn some money at the greengrocer's store this summer." He posted the letter the following morning on his way to school.

Once his next year at Bristol Grammar School began in October, Rupie took a keener interest in his studies. His teacher, Mr. Percy Whittington, a mathematician, emphasized approximations, interest, logarithms, factors, and factors in algebra and area and circumference calculations in geometry. Though sometimes lost in the mire of formulas and graphics, Rupie performed somewhere in the middle of his class of twenty-two in studying mathematical formulas. "Psalms," "St. Mark," and the Old Testament were covered in religion. Caesar, the Roman and Norman invasions, and the nineteenth-century were all included in history. In science, his class studied graphing, specific gravities, pressures of liquids, and hydrometers and barometers.

Rupie rose to the top of the class in the latter because of his unanticipated apprenticeship as a bellboy aboard ship. He used his newly acquired knowledge with a heavy dosage of meters and measuring equipment for pressures and temperatures, enlightening his admiring teacher and fascinated and envious classmates with practical lessons transported from the unbearably hot engine room of the *Lusitania*.

French and English grammar and composition, and oral recitation and composition fulfilled his language requirements. His favorite subject, drawing, enabled him to challenge himself with more difficult subjects to sketch, and more varied color combinations. He especially enjoyed sketching landscapes and detailing the architecture of selected Bristol buildings. In his English lessons, besides writing essays on assigned topics such as "The Future of Transportation in Britain," "Monarchy or Democracy?" and "My Favorite Commonwealth Nation and Why," he and his classmates enjoyed reading stories from Dickens aloud. His classmates were also memorizing their parts for William Shakespeare's *The Merchant of Venice*, the play the middle school was to perform as a May class project. Rupie knew all the lines but didn't say a word. He didn't want to be a showoff and know-it-all.

Rupie also loved the cinema. By early 1915, there were over thirty theatres showing moving pictures in Bristol alone. Throughout England, over 3,000 cinemas had been established, mostly in converted stage houses, meeting halls, and pubs. Cinema was the bolt of new popularity penetrating the previous sole domain of live theatre, musical reviews, sports, and classical entertainment. Initially, there were a myriad of names for this newest of novelties: moving pictures, the Bioscope, Eragraph, Kinima, Theatrograph, Edisonograph, Orthograph, Edison's Concertophone, and Cinematographe. Eventually, "cinema" became the most common reference. By 1911, Bristol had such movie houses as Colston Hall and the Bedminster Hippodrome on East Street. Nineteen twelve saw the Ashton Cinema opening on North Street, the Prince's Theatre on Park Row, and the Coliseum Picture House. Hamilton Barnes, managing director for the owners of the Tivoli Theatre, even compromised his love of the living stage for celluloid, turning the Tivoli into a palace for the new moving pictures.

For Rupie, Whiteladies Cinema on Whiteladies Road was the most convenient picture house. At the Saturday afternoon children's matinee, the first box office was a large fire bucket by the entrance door. It required one penny for admission. When Mrs. Alice Tucker, a neighborhood fixture for years who knew all the children, would let you in, she'd wait until she heard the plunk of the coin, grab an arm and pull a young body into the theatre foyer. Rupie, Phillip, and Peter collected scrap washers next door at the wrecking yard and always threw them into the bucket when Mrs. Tucker's head was turned. Inside Whiteladies, the two long sidewalls of the theatre were beautifully hand-painted, rectangular murals depicting the Great Fire of London. Colorful murals representing various periods of England's history were popular cinema theatre decor. The owner of the Whiteladies theatre, Mr. Easton, when asked how his proud possession theatre with its many murals was doing, always answered, "I'd like to see it after it was burned down!" This was always good for a laugh. Mr. Easton was blind!

One Saturday morning, Mrs. Tucker caught Rupie cold, right in the act of tossing a slug into the bucket. Taking him by his right ear lobe, she locked the theatre door and deposited him across the street to the delight of the other snickering children standing in the queue. She announced loudly, "Rupert, you can't come to the cinema for two weeks!" However, the three friends had been prepared for exactly this type of punishment. After the projector noisily started, Phillip let Rupie into the theatre through a side entrance. Peter stood watch.

The cinema added many diversions to young people's experiences. Some of the smaller children snuck into the cinema under the long skirts of an older sister. When Mary Morris didn't have enough pennies for her eight brothers and sisters, she made four trips to the entrance with the excuse, "I have to see if Bernard (or Cecil) (or Sidney) is waiting outside." Rupie was too big for this ploy, but it was tempting.

Every twenty minutes, the film wound about the projector reel had to be changed. It usually took five minutes for the projectionist to make the switch, to place a new reel on the camera spool. During this interval, children threw monkey nuts, orange peels, and apple cores at one another and across the theatre. Mrs. Tucker regularly made announcements from the front of the theatre for them to stop, or she said, "I'll halt the motion picture!" But that never happened. The staff couldn't afford to lose their audiences. The projectionist counted on his fifteen shillings a week, and Mrs. Tucker and the pianist also needed the income. As the Bristol theatres became more popular, paid advertisements were flashed on the screen between shows announcing the next film as well as goods that could be purchased locally.

In theatres in the poorer areas, people brought in fish and chips, pork bones, ale, and beer. There wasn't much throwing of items in those theatres. The patrons ate everything chewable. Other theatres used ropes to separate different sections for different prices: front, two pence; middle, four pence; and back. six pence. The rear of the theatre offered the best overall perspective for viewing and was the most desirable seating area. Cinema audiences sometimes resembled waves bursting in the ocean with the movement under the ropes seeking a better seat or heading for the loo.

All the films were silent. The ever-present pianist supplied his choice of mood music to help the plot along. Certainly, his contribution was far better after he had seen a film several times than the first time, which often could be a disaster of mixed messages. A cinematic character lost much of his heroism when stalking a murderer with a soft waltz sounding in the background and titters in the crowd were emitted if two lovers cuddled accompanied by heavy Wagnerian melodies.

Rupie and his friends had many film favorites. *Perils of Pauline* was one. Their tongues were sore from biting every time Pearl White was tied to a railroad track or lowered into a pot of boiling oil. Rupie was always reminded of seeing Charlie Chaplain live in *The Football Match* and treasured every moment watching the vagrant hobo with his standard bowler hat, oversized boots, baggy trousers, tight jacket, and pendulum-singing cane. They watched *Shoulder Arms* and *The Kid* with Jackie Coogan when they had saved up the admission fee. Rupie liked westerns and the comedies the most. Besides Chaplin, his film idols were American actors Tom Mix, Buck Jones, Harold Lloyd, and Fatty Arbuckle.

Rupie would often mix his imaginary world with the real one. On a Monday morning at school, he would usually entertain his classmates with a running commentary borrowed from the last film he had seen. Telling his schoolmates about his most recent errand for his mother would be re-interpreted as "So I gets on me 'orse and gallops to the butcher's. On the way, I shoot Fatty Arbuckle. He's a teacher's pet and a sneak. He goes for his gun, but I beat him. I'm the fastest gun on Melrose Place. Hitchin' me nag to a light post, I enters the bar. 'Gimmie a shot o' rye!' I orders." With his whole body into the act, he had his audience where he wanted them - laughing uproariously. "The butcher says, 'What! Auf a pound o' sausages,' wraps up the dogs, gives 'em ta me, and holds out 'is hand. 'That'll be a trupence,' he says. I shoot him. 'The kid's bonkers,' the lady customer says. 'They all are,' says the dead butcher. I shoot the lady, too."

Recalling the most recent film he'd seen helped Rupie fall asleep at night. He often dreamed that Mr. Easton had granted him a free pass to the movies for life, until he woke up.

To their patrons, these new cinemas were cheap, and the length of the performance, the comfortable seats, and the veil of darkness had great appeal. If it were a race, live entertainment would be the loser. In Bristol and in other provincial cities, every week, great actors performing in their original London roles were brought to local theatres. Audiences preferred originals to the second companies that predominated the touring circuit. But, in cinema, there were no delays for scene changes. Films were cheaper to attend, easier to watch, and had more to offer than live theatre. Exciting comedy action, spectacular scenery, crowd scenes, and battles, which could never be re-created on a curtained stage, were unveiled. Even the appearance of a person could change before your eyes.

Prominent British performers like Seymour Hicks,

Matheson Lang, Martin Harvey, and Frank Benson found it increasingly difficult to hold their audiences with the overwhelming competition of the silent film. Stage actors gave up their pistols, swashbuckling, and daggers to film stars such as Douglas Fairbanks, Rudolph Valentino, and Ramon Navarro.

Movies had seen the first light of day in the form of peepshow arcades. Kinetoscope parlors became a habit with their introduction of screens and projectors in off-the-side vestibules. In England, a regular "Daily Bioscope" was first operating in Bishopsgate, London, in 1904. From that time on, Rupie learned that permanent cinemas began to mushroom throughout the world. Nickelodeons became a generic name for the first movie houses. Audiences were willing to patronize one or two or even seven changes of programmes in a week. Enthusiastic amateur photographers and ingenious inventors created little films at the cost of a pound or so in their own backyards and were astonished at the profits they could accrue from their local cinemas.

At first, French films were popular, until Americans began distributing countless films in England through the Motion Picture Patents Company. French filmmakers had begun to film celebrated artists of the theatre and music hall. They used famous names to sell cinema seats.

By 1909, Hollywood, California, had become the center of film production because of good climate, cheap labour and real estate, and reliable sunshine. The jerking film and speeding slides became more organized with time. For several years, long after the discovery of story cinema, filmmakers preferred using the screen like a stage proscenium. The entire scene was viewed from a fixed, head-on position. All figures were shown in full length, from head to feet. Characters entered and left the screen as they would on a stage. They followed the trend of still photography. The first films were literally animated photographs. Film trickery grew, and the beheading scene in *The Execution of Mary Stuart* was in the news throughout England. In America's *The Great Train Robbery*, released in 1903, the idea of parallel and overlapping action in a story was introduced. One scene shows the bandits making off towards their planned crime; the next shows the telegraph operator, left bound and gagged, rescued by his little daughter. The following scene is a dance hall into which the exhausted but now free operator suddenly bursts with news of the impending robbery. Finally, there was the robbery, the capture, and the favorable ending. Audiences were enthusiastic. Films stirred them more than theatre drama, and they were less expensive to attend. Cinema discovered itself as an art, a new medium of performance. Rupie was in a movie theatre almost all his waking hours when he wasn't in school or at the greengrocers.

Favorite plots involved crime, the penalties and romantically ennobling effects of poverty, the horrors of dying, the roles of women, and other themes derived from the realities of urban life. In English films, stage tricks occurring in natural locations - a front garden, the countryside near Brighton, and side streets in familiar provincial suburbias - were most popular. The chase was featured in such early films as *The Runaway Match, Marriage by Motor, Welshed, A Derby Day Incident, Daring Daylight Burglary,* and *Fire, Stop Thief.* Also, a British actor, Max Linder, shaped the whole future of film comedy in the country. He developed his own screen character: the elegant young boulevardier with sleek hair, neatly rakish moustache, elegant cutaway, beautifully crafted splendid silk hat, and a trim walking cane. He continuously was in and out of scrapes into which his roving eye invariably had led him.

Rupie began to look at film in the same fashion he

had observed Mr. Franklin Benson discussing a stage play. He was fascinated by the different photographic techniques and the manner that plots unraveled. Accordingly, he was not surprised when reading that the prominent Charles Frohman, the eminent London and Broadway theatre impresario had also begun producing films. Another name he took notice of was that of American D.W. Griffith who first had directed the *Adventures of Dollie*, a nine-minute melodrama, which Rupie had thoroughly enjoyed. He loved Griffith's *Birth of a Nation* about the American Civil War, which was to become the most influential picture in film history.

Rupie was also attracted to suspense films such as *The London Villa*, which appealed to young audiences. He was especially taken with the development of suspense and speed and excitement by the accelerated pace and rhythm of cutting from shot to shot between two actions. He was also intrigued by the use of flashback in the *New York Hat.*

Another of Rupie's favorite filmmakers was Mack Sennett who had founded Keystone Studios in Hollywood and employed an entire company of players, much like a theatre group. Sennett produced all the elements of comedy - vaudeville, circus, pantomime, commedia dell'arte, and old French comic films - yet his genre were distinct and unique. Sennett revealed the real world of America. He transformed his short films into long reels and familiarized his audiences with men in bowlers and large whiskers, ladies in harem skirts and huge hats, horses and buggies, and, especially, funny policemen. When Hollywood films first introduced former Britisher Charlie Chaplin, Rupie realized this comedian would become the first universal legend. He read that Chaplin's unique technique and acting styles were derived from his early training in English music halls. Even his costume added to his fame: a too-tight jacket and too-loose pants held up with strings, oversized boots and the undersized bowler hat, holey gloves, a little cane, a tie and wing collar, all indicated vain aspirations to gentility.

Rupie found that moving pictures were becoming longer and more sophisticated in their technique and content. Cinemas had also acquired new economic and social status. Most of the American films he saw depicted the country as the land of opportunity. They appealed to every age group, every walk of life, even immigrant groups who used them to learn the English language. *I must go there,* Rupie ruminated. *I must go there.*

His interest in film started him on a new paying project. He began drawing advertisements for several local businesses on Whiteladies Road. One of his schoolmates, Lawrence McGilvery, was a talented photographer. Rupie persuaded him to take photographs of his drawings of storefronts, of customers buying items, and of tempting merchandise such as bananas or oranges at the greengrocers'; men's hats for the haberdashery; and furniture for Maggs' store. In a short time, business flourished and Rupie soon earned enough money for his long awaited trip to London.

One of his most popular advertisements, which began to be used by several cinemas besides Rupie's familiar Whiteladies Cinema, claimed, "Motion pictures will bring you more enjoyment than ever." To go with his lettering, he had drawn a comical picture of a movie projector with film unwinding all over a projectionist. Mr. Eaton gave him a lifetime pass to his cinema.

Chapter 11
The End of Formal Education

Bristol, 1915-16

Rupie made one major decision during his last term at BGS. He changed his name.

There were a number of reasons for this. He'd outgrown the name "Rupie." It was a child's name, and his schoolmates would often use baby talk to raise his ire, teasing him with such expressions as: "Iddy bitty widdle Rupie," "Coo, coo, Woopy," or "There was a young lad named Rupie; his backside was so large they called him 'Poopy,'" among other insults that children create for purposes of annoyance.

The name "Rupert," to his friends, was too formal, a bit snobbish for their popular impish friend who was always joking or deeply engaged in planning still another act of defiance to authority, tradition, or morality. Butlers, chauffeurs, the King's dresser, the Duke of wherever, the son of a Member of Parliament, they were "Ruperts." Who else would want to be called Rupert? It was like Weddington or

Abraham or Alphonse, far too dignified and stuffy a name for a cut-up. It was also the name of his father, confusing as he matured as to which Rupert was being referred to whether at home or at the store.

"Rupert, come here!" brought them both away from what they were doing. "Junior" wasn't an answer, either. He wasn't actually a full-fledged junior because he had a middle name and his father didn't. Besides, he preferred not to carry his father's name on to the future fame he would gain in the theatre. *Father wouldn't approve of it*, he mused. In reality, he hated the name and vowed he would never use it. He declared to himself, *I'll try R. Ashley Thronson.* He practiced writing his newly discovered nom de plume in an exercise book. He liked it.

"Call me Ashley," he advised his mates. "That's the name you'll see transfixed on the marquee of London's Theatre Royal. Ashley Thronson now appearing." It took a while, but after the newly anointed "Ashley" began charging his mates a trupence every time they called him Rupert or Rupie, they complied. He had assigned Robert Adams, the biggest, strongest boy in the class, as his purser, and no one on record had ever argued with Robert. Ashley gave him half of all the money collected, so he proved to be a reliable watchdog.

He continued corresponding with Rosie St. John who was now touring Canada with the Bensonians, sharing his new name.

His final term swept by rapidly, and he looked forward to bidding farewell to BGS. Coincidentally, it was also the last term for the school's popular headmaster, Dr. Cyril Haywood, who had accepted a similar post at the more prominent Marlborough Grammar School. There were a number of receptions for the departing Haywoods, and Ashley used them to perfect his "Haywood Act" in which he would recapture the headmaster's words, deeds, and mannerisms with a remarkable flair for imitation. His own favorite was miming Dr. Haywood as commandant of the BGS military cadets

"Now men, the Krauts are just over that hill. Our strategy is the same that lost us the Revolutionary War. We'll march in straight lines heading directly at the enemy." Crossing his arms and looking kingly for effect, Ashley would scan his listeners with squinted eyes and add, "Now are you certain you have no ammunition in your rifles? We wouldn't want to hurt anyone, would we?" He would then march off with an exaggerated, stiff-legged high-step to the laughter and applause of his mates.

Another running monologue took place in Haywood's imaginary office. Ashley would set two chairs apart from one another, and moving hurriedly from one to the other, carry on a dialogue between the headmaster and a pupil who had burned his master's teaching notes, rendering him helpless to conduct his classes without them. The former Rupie also had his mates in hysterics when he performed what he termed "The Haywood Bedroom Scene," in which he also played both roles. His plot was simple. Dr. Haywood cuckolded his wife. He had bedded down with a dockside prostitute. A friend of Mrs. Haywood had seen him leaving the house of ill fame. In a high falsetto, Ashley would chastise the unfaithful husband unmercifully, finally chasing him away with a broom screaming, "Out, damned sot."

Dr. Haywood made a number of departure speeches that Ashley happily added to his repertoire, but he was moved one day in the Great Hall. The entire school, students and masters, was assembled for what was to be the school leader's final address. Tears filled Ashley's eyes when the highly regarded educator said, as part of his speech:

"What has been done could not have been done if far the greater part of boys of each school generation had not supported me with all their hearts. For, in the end, you boys yourselves make the School and shape it to good and to evil. It is what it is because of the loyalty of boys past, of whom not a few have shown themselves loyal to death on a greater field, and it will be what you, the boys of the present, make it." Thirty-five of the many former members having given their lives for the British war cause.

The incoming headmaster, Mr. Joseph E. Bartow, was well qualified academically, having received his highest degree from Oxford. He had also served as headmaster for two grammar schools in smaller cities than Bristol, Crypt Grammar School at Gloucester and Queen Elizabeth Grammar School in Wakefield. The BGS boys had learned his greatest attribute was his uncanny ability on the golf course.

On his graduation day, 20 June 1916, when the awards and scholarships were announced, the fifteen-year-old Ashley, still referred to as "Rupert" by his teachers, received his third formal acknowledgment of "honors in drawing and manual training." His mother and father acknowledged the friendly nods of the other parents with polite nods of their own. However, his mother, who had been quite ill of late, cried softly, and his father disguised his envy when perhaps half the class was commended for being accepted to Oxford, Cambridge, or for further religious education. When Rupert Ashley Thronson crossed the platform to receive his BGS diploma, his new profession was proclaimed by the Assistant Headmaster as "Clerk to a Chartered Accountant." His teacher, Mr. White, had arranged the position through the "Old Boy" network.

On the first Monday of July, dressed in his new gray suit, a derby, a striped BGS tie, and too tight-black shoes, R. Ashley Thronson, now a slightly chubby, medium tall, handsome adult, reported for duty at Hastings, Furbershim, and Shaw, Chartered Accountants, at 77 Kingsland Road in Central Bristol.

"Thronson, my boy," said Mr. Furbershim, an enormous red-faced man of sixty, after Ashley had been provided a tour of the stately premises, "we're pleased to have you with us at H, F, and S. You're to apprentice under one of our newer accountants, my son Richard Furbershim. Report to him on the second floor! And, Thronson," he smiled, "good fortune to you."

Agonizing under the almost unbearable pressure the too-firm leather was administering to his feet, Ashley slowly made his way down the stairs and entered the door marked "Mr. R. Furbershim." The son was totally unlike his father. Ashley stared at him in disbelief.

"Oh, I know what you're thinking," said the thin, pale, sandy-haired accountant, 'He can't be Mr. Winston Furbershim's son. They don't look like they're from the same genetic pool.' Obviously, I favor my mother." He extended his hand and added, "Welcome to H, F, and S." With that, he explained Ashley's duties to him. He would receive and organize the daily post, delivering letters to the proper addressees. He would be assigned a few clients and would mark only expenditures, for no professional accountant could be entrusted to handle both credits and debits. He would serve as a messenger in collecting and delivering accountancy records to H, F, and S. He would make inventories of stock for clients, and, on occasion, he would double check accountancy records for errors. He would also be responsible for serving tea, in both the mornings and afternoons, to all the eighteen employees on the second floor. At least part of his responsibilities reminded him of the *Lusitania*.

"I hate it!" Ashley reported to his friend Phillip Maggs, meeting him in the Bristol Main Library some two weeks after he had begun his new job. "I can't stand numbers. How can anyone record numbers and add and subtract them for an entire lifetime?"

"Someone has to do it, doesn't he?" replied Phillip.

"Yes, but why me?" responded Ashley dejectedly.

"How else can you pay the piper?"

"I want to be an actor," Ashley informed Phillip for perhaps the hundredth time in their relationship.

"I know that, Ash, but you're going to have to wait. You can't just 'be an actor,' you've got to approach the art through the craft. You need lessons, for a start."

"You're right, but lessons are pricey."

"They're the pipers you have to pay, aren't they?"

Ashley was silent, knowing Phillip was right.

"And another way is to watch actors perform, isn't it?" Waiting for Ashley's nodded response, he added, "It just so happens that my father has two tickets to The Prince's tomorrow night and asked if I wanted to use them. Do you want to see *It's a Long Way to Tipperary,* a war play?"

On Thursday evening promptly at 8:30 p.m., the two boys sat comfortably in the stalls of the Prince's' Theatre. Watching the unfolding of dramatic intrigue, they became so involved with the drama they readily forgot the thunderous rain that had continued to fall on Bristol that week. It was a play about a military unit's experiences in France. It concentrated on the loyalty, love, and sacrifices of those who had been called upon to serve their country. Ashley and Phillip weren't sure the sacrifice was worth it. Ashley's old friend, Richard Bates, played the character of a young soldier and had several good moments in the play. The star, John Martin-Harvey, a prominent actor-manager, had played Bristol before. He was a local favorite. The audience stopped the progress of the play several times with patriotic applause and tribute to the splendid Thespian.

"Let's go backstage and visit Richard," Ashley requested of Phillip after the applause had died down and the audience began to disperse. Ashley fetched their rain gear from the coat stall and led his friend back into the auditorium and up the stairs to the stage, entering the backstage area through the front curtain.

They found Richard in a crowded dressing room with several other actors, and he immediately said, "Mates, join me at the Duke's Dragoon right now. We'll celebrate tonight's success."

"We can't go into a pub," said Phillip. "We're too bloody young."

"Don't worry, some of the soldiers are so young these days, the server won't even ask your age," Richard countered.

The threesome entered the teeming, noisy Duke's Dragoon, a centuries old public house, making their way to the darkened rear wall. A weathered, brash barmaid asked them, "What'll ya 'ave?"

Ashley, round-billed hat lowered over his eyes, replied in his deepest, most masculine voice, "'Alf a Bass, please," adding, with a look at Richard, "And that handsome actor there'll give you the biggest tip you'll ever receive."

Richard, ordering for himself and Phillip, suggested meekly, "He's a real wag, he is."

After the ales were brought forth, and Ashley and Phillip toasted their friend's Thespian triumph, he told his admiring listeners about John Martin-Harvey. "He's an actor from the old school. I'm sure you noticed," Richard began. "You can see his training by Henry Irving. He can't be anything else but an actor whether he's dancing in a ballroom, serving on the tennis court, or speaking at a morning reception. He has an actor's presence."

"What do you mean, an actor's presence?" asked Ashley.

"He's always playing a part, on stage or off. You can't miss him in any crowd of notables." Continuing enthusiastically, Richard said, "He's never perfectly natural or genial in mood. He expects a great deal from his fellow actors, constantly saying, 'I give the public my best; it is their due, and my prerogative.' He encourages us to do the same."

Richard told them about Martin-Harvey's early start in the theatre at nineteen, when, as a young actor with Henry Irving at London's Lyceum Theatre, he did "walker-ons," moving into occasional speaking parts when the play required additional actors, always under the commanding shadow of his idol, Irving. "He was at the Lyceum for fourteen years. Then he got his big break."

"I know," interrupted Ashley. "*The Only Way*. He played the Sydney Carton role."

"Right-o," acknowledged Richard.

"What's *The Only Way*?" inquired Phillip.

Richard explained that it was the dramatic version of Dickens's *A Tale of Two Cities* and summarized the basic plot. He told the pair how Harvey had a clergyman write the dialogue and how he had produced the first version at the Lyceum in 1899 while Irving was off on tour. "He lost a considerable amount of money," Richard professed. "Not only did the play fail in London, he almost went penniless on a short tour of the provinces. One person in the cast told me Harvey even pawned his expensive watch to pay a manager for one performance."

"Then what happened?" Ashley inquired.

"He tried a second tour as a last hope. This time, he was enormously successful. In the past seventeen years, he's played the Carton part hundreds of times, always to sell-out crowds. I've heard the *The Only Way's* the most successful adaptation of a book in Britain's theatrical history."

Richard related how Harvey had accidentally met

two American ladies who, under the dual pseudonym of "John Rutherford" had written a play specifically to feature the aspiring matinee idol. "Women aren't allowed to be playwrights," he said. It was called *The Breed of the Treshams.* Triumphant in London and through a brief tour of England's major cities, Harvey had taken the production to America where he performed on the grand circuit as England's newest and brightest theatrical hero.

"America…that's where I want to go," said Ashley dreamily.

Richard continued, "Max Reinhardt, the great German producer, came to London to direct Gilbert Murray's new translation of *Oedipus Rex* at Covent Garden. Reinhardt convinced Harvey to play the lead. He would be the first person to do so for over two centuries since the great actor, Betterton. It was more simply staged than a Tree extravaganza and much less expensive to produce. It was a record-breaker in nightly receipts."

"What do you mean, a record-breaker?" asked the newly groomed junior accountant, already on the mental alert of costing sales of products.

"In London, the average nightly receipts were forty-one pounds. When the play was on tour, they made over 152 pounds a night," responded Richard. "That's one of the reasons we have so many theatre companies on the touring circuits."

Richard added that John Martin-Harvey was widely known among his stage contemporaries as a "ham" actor. The broad histrionic over-exaggeration of actors in the past was, during Martin-Harvey's theatrical lifetime, changing to a more naturalistic and believable style. The long rhetorical speeches of both Shakespeare and Shaw were ideal performance mechanisms for so-called hams. It was traditional stage fare for the actor to act, to make the audience feel that something sinister was behind the make-believe cut-up of a castle with just an over-the-shoulder glance, to create tension with a slight movement of his hands, to generate fear or sympathy or sorrow or romance, or any other emotion, with only an infliction of voice. Actors like Harvey found many of Shakespeare's leading roles disappointing because there was too much mystery and not enough heroism. Actors of his ilk could never impersonate a perfectly ordinary human being. That wasn't theatrical.

"This is why I'm changing my own acting technique," Richard confessed. "The newer plays about the war and those being written by provincial playwrights and translated from German, Norwegian, and French are all naturalistic. They're about real people in real life situations. But let's not talk about me. "How are you getting on as a chartered accountant, Rupie?" asked Richard.

"His name's Ashley. Want to be fined a penny?" corrected Phillip.

"Ashley? What's Ashley? What happened to Rupert?" a surprised Richard retorted.

"It's going to be my stage name, R. Ashley Thronson," Ashley announced.

"Richard said jokingly, "Someone will certainly shorten it to Rashley."

The boys giggled.

"Are you still taking acting lessons?" Ashley inquired of Richard.

"Oh, yes!" was the response. "I'm studying with Miss Joyce Russell. Every week, we practice scenes from plays she chooses, and we perform them before the class. After each scene, Miss Russell and the other students offer critiques. It's been most helpful to me. I heartily believe I'm improving. You should go, Rup... I mean, Ashley. I'm not going to get used to that name too easily."

"I'd like to. What does it cost?" requested the young accountant.

"Five shillings a week for three nights. Besides the scenes, we practice dancing and calisthenics. Next week, we're going to start fencing lessons. I had to buy my own foil." Richard responded.

"I only make six shillings a week in my job. My father's charging me two bob for room and board now. I just can't afford it!"

"What if I go with you, Ash?" asked Phillip.

"Do you think Miss Russell would give us a reduction, Richard?"

"Two for the price of one?" Phillip asked.

"Let me ask Miss Russell," Richard responded.

"I've been given the part of Romeo at school," Phillip announced. "Not that I like to act really. But I don't want to disappoint my father. I think he'd like me to engage in theatrics. He always says he has to play all sorts of roles in the furniture store, just like a stage performer. He's one personality to the sales personnel, another to the cabinetmakers he hires, and he plays the part of a trusted advisor to his customers."

"As the bard said - 'All the world's a stage,'" intoned Richard to the muffled grunts of his friends offended by the too-oft-quoted phrase.

After a second round of ales, then a third, the trio left the thickly populated pub, with Richard wobbling in one direction, and his more than slightly inebriated friends heading towards Clifton by foot. Fortunately for Ashley, his parents slept soundly as he cautiously, but unstably, made his clumsy way up the stairs to his room.

The next day, Ashley was certain a large axe was solidly embedded in the center of his head.

Chapter 12
The Acting School

Bristol, 1916

Richard did obtain a lower rate for the two newcomers to Miss Russell's dramatic school. Phillip was also successful in convincing his father of its benefit, and, the payment of months in advance for a fledgling school of the arts, always on wobbly financial grounds, was certainly beneficial to the school head's many creditors.

Thus began Ashley's real entry into the world of Thespians. By day, he performed his apprentice accountant's duties faithfully, quietly, accomplishing barely enough to fulfill the responsibilities given him, with no effort to accomplish them more hastily, more fully, or more professionally. This was not a boat he wanted rock; he merely wanted to maintain a steady course to sustain his growing adoration and devotion to things theatrical.

His father had given grudging permission to attend "dramatic night school," as he called it, adding, "It's a great waste of time." Believing that his son, to whom he still referred as "Rupert" was using a portion of his wages at H, F, and S for his acting lessons, he had no idea that Phillip Maggs had picked up the tuition for them both, enabling Ashley to place all his monetary eggs in one savings basket.

Phillip and Ashley attended their first session at Miss Russell's school, which she called her "dramatic institute." Twenty-four aspiring actors, equally divided into males and females, all between the ages of fifteen and twenty-five, comprised the institute. Richard Bates was the only one who could be termed "professional," since he had been making regular appearances both in the circus and on several Bristol stages for eight years. He was also the institute head's pet and chief assistant.

Miss Joyce Russell, an attractive, blond-haired woman, had grown up in London, the only daughter of two actors, both of whom had been in the theatrical company of one of the earliest of actor-managers, Johnston Forbes-Robertson. They had joined a touring company of *Romeo and Juliet*, and, unlike Shakespeare's star-crossed lovers, had married and lived happily thereafter. Miss Joyce, after her arrival in the proverbial theatrical trunk, had grown up in dressing rooms, actors' digs, and train cars, touring back and forth across the English countryside. Her first part came at six, her singing and dancing lessons provided by members of whichever ensemble her parents performed with, and, by the time she was twenty, she was performing in Harry Irving's London production of Barrie's *The Admirable Crichton*.

Reaching thirty, Miss Joyce found herself no longer able to play ingénue roles. She had delicate facial features, a slight tendency towards plumpness, but maintained her attractiveness, dramatic bearing, and theatrical voice. What set Miss Joyce apart from her usually serious instructional peers was her genuine sense of humor. She had a wry and quick wit and always saw the sunnier side of every issue or situation. As an actress, she had been known to have a knack for timing. She could always elicit a laugh by merely raising her eyebrows to show suspicion or lowering them to show disdain. Often, she would repeat the last line of another actor's to gain emphasis for her own delivery. Her personality was so contagious to an audience, that even walking across the stage, she could recreate the royal gait of a queen, the sensuous strut of a confident prostitute, or the hunched shuffle of a beggar.

"When I was with Harry..." she would often begin a sentence, and the classroom always quieted down. Invariably, a pearl of theatrical wisdom was about to come forth. Harry Irving, the younger actor-manager son of Henry, the greatest Irving of them all, would be imitated as only the accomplished Miss Joyce could mimic with total believability. "When I was with Harry in *Hamlet*, he could be muttering along with a monotone and then surprise the trousers off the audience when he delivered a smashingly forceful line. It was like telling a joke and lulling your listeners before the surprising punch line."

Or "When I was with Harry, and he was playing Iago to Waller's Othello, he performed just as if he were Mr. Hyde. He was the most frightening villain you could imagine. He glowered at you with slanted eye, viciously curved upper lip, and spoke his dialogue like the meanest thug in the universe. And do you know why? He spent half his life at the Old Bailey watching the trials of notorious criminals. He loved crime! He studied murderers to be able to depict them onstage. He always kept a picture of his character in his mind's eye and never veered from his course." She noted that Harry Irving had excelled in melodramas because he always played the villain. Other actors were sometimes intimidated by his being so sinister and secretive all the time. Not only had he founded the famous Crimes Club in London, but he had also written four books dealing with eminent murderers and burglars.

"Remember, students, every play must have a villain, and actors have to make a living. Dear old Harry did, even though he was never a rival of his father's reputation."

Additionally, Miss Joyce had known Harry Irving's brother, Lawrence, an actor-manager who also never quite shared the fame of his illustrious father. Preparing for a career in the British Foreign Service, including studies in the Russian language and literature in St. Petersburg for three years, Lawrence's intentions to become a British diplomat were short-lived when his father, suffering the employment draught that even causes successful actors to succumb, could not afford to pay tuition. At twenty, the youthful Lawrence joined the Benson Company, helped by his father's intervention. Relegated to walk-about and supernumerary roles, despondent about his limited acting abilities, he attempted suicide. Afterwards, Lawrence claimed he'd had an accident with a pistol. In any case, the bullet was removed; it had been extremely close to his heart. His father took him under his wing. Though the younger Irving was an uneven actor, neither very good nor very bad, his boyishness and good nature attracted Lady Ellen Terry's professional attention. Lawrence had more of an intellectual's approach to interpreting a character than an emotional one. He loved to perform Shaw and such foreign playwrights as Ibsen, Dostievsky, Brieux, and Tolstoy.

"He was wonderful in the *Crime and Punishment* translation, re-entitled *The Unwritten Law* for the stage," Miss Joyce claimed. "In an Hungarian drama of Japanese life called *Typhoon*, he was utterly magnificent," she said adoringly. "He played the oriental lead over 200 times in four different London theatres." Then, with teared regret, she sadly announced, "Poor dear, he and his wife perished in the sea after their ship *The Empress of Ireland* was accidentally rammed by a Norwegian collier in a dense fog. It sank in ten minutes. That was two years ago." She strocked her cheek gently, remembering her lost friend.

"Now, Phillip and Ashley," Miss Joyce told the two friends during the first week, "since you've just joined us, I'm going to make Richard responsible for each of you preparing a primer on acting. He's not starting on a new play for several months, so he can help you. You must write down everything important and memorize it. Then I will examine you just as a master would an apprentice. That means you'll both have to be here on Monday evenings. The rest of the class has already prepared primers, and I don't want them to have to wait for you two to catch up."

So, faithfully for the next six Mondays, with the acting-out scenes on Tuesdays, Wednesdays, and Thursdays, Phillip and Ashley met privately with Richard at Miss Joyce's institute with the former actress wandering in and out from time to time, insuring her pre-paid pupils were receiving the proper instruction. Seated in three tattered arm chairs that had seen far better days in what Miss Joyce referred to as the "Green Room," the two boys, scratch books and pencils in hand, with their more adult mentor, began their theatre education.

"I'm not going to teach you just about acting," Richard promised. "It's important that you know all aspects of running a theatre: producing, directing, stage managing, and the technical aspects, as well as acting."

He started by pointing out the importance of the producer, the position that the two youngsters knew as actor-managers. "Most of the great actor-managers are still alive," reported their stage instructor. "Lewis Waller and Lawrence Irving are dead. Johnston Forbes-Robertson, Herbert Beerbohm

Tree, and George Alexander have retired. Frank Benson is producing Shakespeare at Stratford-upon-Avon. John Martin-Harvey is doing a new version of *Richard II* in London. Oscar Asche is very active. He found a play about Zulu life called *Mameena,* introducing a new German lighting system, but the war has caused so many restrictions he couldn't use his new toy. Now, he's got a rousing success on his hands with his new show, *Chu Chin Chow*, at His Majesty's Theatre in London. It's a real favorite of soldiers and sailors. Harley Granville-Barker's serving in intelligence for the War Office. And the *Stage* magazine, which you know is the actor's Bible, just announced that Harry Irving opened in *Dr. Jekyll and Mr. Hyde*. He still relishes playing dual roles."

"I know of the others, but who was the first one?" asked Phillip, looking at his notes, "Johnston Forbes-Robertson?" Ashley suppressed the urge to respond with information he had gained from Richard.

"He was an excellent Hamlet," responded Richard. "He could recite Shakespeare as if he were the bard himself. It was as if the words were written in his own idiom. Shaw was so impressed, he wrote *Caesar and Cleopatra* especially for Forbes-Robertson."

"Was he good as Cleopatra?" Ashley asked with a wide grin on his face.

Ignoring him, Richard continued, "He was very successful several years ago in *The Light That Failed.* He was one of the first to tour America with an English company. I heard an entire audience collapsed with the funniest line he ever uttered. That was three years ago in a Liverpool theatre. A carpenter had dropped a hammer from the grid just missing Forbes-Robertson in the middle of the stage. Stopping his Caesar speech abruptly, he looked up and said, 'Please don't do that again,' and went right back into the scene. The audience was flabbergasted."

"What's a grid?" asked Ashley.

"That's what the stage curtains and drops hang from over the stage," responded Richard. "You know, the steel beams underneath the ceiling of the stage house."

Continuing, Richard insisted that producers should first have been actors. "It's like a general commanding when he's never been a soldier. Producers have to know their plays thoroughly, from every point of view. They have to memorize the entire script. They mark the script scene by scene, the actors' movements on the stage, how they deliver their lines. If the actors' attention focuses on the leading player, they turn their heads towards him. The audience follows suit. Some producers ask a designer to build a scale model of the settings to better visualize where to move their actors.

"I can do that," reminded Ashley. "Then you have a better idea of entrances and exits, the lighting needed, what furniture's on stage."

"Right-o, Ashley," Richard confirmed. "The best-rehearsed play takes over a one-month's period, three rehearsals a week for the first three weeks, then every day the fourth week." Challenging his friend, Richard asked, "Phillip, what should the producer do at the first meeting with the cast?"

"Well, our master at school, Mr. Wellesley, gave us a full account as to how he'd like to have *The Admirable Crichton* performed at our first meeting," Phillip responded. "He also outlined each of the parts and showed us a ground plan of the sets. Then we had what he called 'a read-through' of the play."

"Good, Phillip. That's exactly right! Then, with a three-act play, you rehearse one act each week, walking cast members through the action. That's called 'blocking the moves.' Now write that down! It's important! Actors have to know where they're supposed to be on a stage at all times."

"What's the best way to memorize lines?" Ashley asked intently.

"We'll get to that when we talk about acting," answered Richard. "Listen carefully. Now, the items an actor handles whilst he's onstage are called 'props.' That's short for 'properties.' If the actors are having a tea party, it's necessary that they have real cups and saucers. You can avoid a number of problems if the cook has practiced making strudel onstage before the play opens rather than the first night. It's the same with wearing costumes or beards or swords. Once I had a part where I was supposed to drink grog through a beard. I'd never rehearsed that before opening night. It was terrible. I could never find my mouth," as he pretended searching for it with a cupped hand holding an imaginary mug.

The first lesson on theatre ended with a serious discussion on why producers selected particular plays. Ashley and Phillip decided that most plays, during the past several decades, both in London and on tour, were chosen to enable the actor-managers to play the best leading roles. Richard Bates complimented the fifteen-year-olds on their knowledge of Shakespeare and Shaw, but found they didn't know much about other prominent English and European playwrights. "You'll have to do some home lessons in the library on Pinero and Gallsworthy and writers like that," he insisted. "Actors must know plays as well as an aviator knows his plane; their lives depend on them."

Tuesday and Thursday evenings, Ashley and Phillip joined their fellow students in pairing off and rehearsing two-person scenes together. Phillip was given the part of Othello opposite Desdemona, which was played by a winsome young woman of eighteen. Ashley was cast as Falstaff in

King Henry IV and rehearsed with a taller older lad who was rather miscast as the king.

The first couple to perform before the class was Richard Bates as Romeo and the most beautiful girl in the class, who was a natural for Juliet, in the balcony scene. She had delicate, finely honed features, and raven- black hair hung below her tiny waist. As far as Richard was concerned, she could be his real Juliet the rest of their lives. However, the girl, Anne Lavell, was somewhat aloof when out of an acting role, rather shy and seemingly unsure of herself.

When all of the students had taken their seats in the Green Room, Miss Joyce insisted on their complete, unadulterated attention. "Now, consider yourselves as producers," she requested. "Determine if you would cast the performers in the roles they're playing and note what they did well or poorly. When you critique a performance, it is not for criticism, but an analysis. It is not the deed itself that's important; it's why the deed was done. You must look for the meanings. Now, Romeo, please begin!" she ordered.

Richard had set two high-backed wooden chairs some distance apart in front of his gathered peers. Anne Lavell sat in one of them, as Richard, strolling to the center of the area, which served as the stage, began.

"But, soft! What light through yonder window breaks?" Turning towards Anne, he continued, "It is the east, and Juliet is the sun! Arise, fair sun, and kill the envious moon, who is already sick and pale with grief, that thou her maid art far more fair than she."

As he recited the familiar words, the handsome young actor assumed a presence not his own. To the attentive onlookers, Richard was totally believable as Romeo proclaiming his love for the beautiful Juliet. She, too, when responding with total unfolding, was riveting.

"O Romeo, Romeo! Wherefore art thou Romeo? Deny

thy father and refuse thy name. Or, it though wilt not be but sworn my love," pausing, "and I'll no longer be a Capulet."

Pens held firmly in their hands, the classroom group of aspiring actors as a whole was entirely captivated. Not one was able to write a note, so engrossed with the sterling performances were they, collectively.

"Good-night, good-night! Parting is such sweet sorrow that I shall say good-night until it be morrow," said Anne, gracefully rising from her chair. She walked to the side of the room as Richard completed Romeo's final four lines of the scene.

For a moment, the tribute was complete silence until Miss Joyce led the enthusiastic applause with "Bravo. Bravo. That was just wonderful, you two. A superb performance!" Excitedly, she pointed out to her brood how important it was to establish a mood early in the dialogue and how Richard, with gesture and intonation, had captured the essence of Romeo's brooding character. "And, Juliet. Did you notice how Anne represented total love both with her facial expressions and the gentle, heartfelt manner in which she delivered her lines?" Anne blushed with embarrassment.

Next up, was Ashley.

Chapter 13
The Actor Prepares

Bristol, 1916

Ashley's performance as Falstaff went poorly from the outset. His opening line to Prince Henry, "Now, Hal, what time of day is it, lad?" sounded to the student audience like one long monotone word without a change of pitch or tone.

When Robert Robinson, as the prince, gave a rather long, but well-delivered speech ending with, "I see no reason why thou shouldst be so superfluous to demand the time of day," Ashley didn't pick up the cue.

Robert tried to help him, repeating, "So superfluous to demand the time of day."

Ashley, after a long pause, asked for a prompt.

Percy Thompson, following the scene in his own Shakespeare text, gave a loud stage whisper, "Indeed, you can come near me now, Hal."

Ashley repeated the line aloud, then looked up and asked to no one in particular, "What comes next? I forgot."

Reciting Falstaff's lines with great seriousness, as if they were the litany in a church, Ashley was totally humorless as Shakespeare's favorite comic. Several times, during the short exchange between the monarch and Falstaff, supposedly the witty friend, he stopped to silently ponder what his character was to say next. More than three times during their dialogue exchange Ashley requested a prompt.

Finally, stopping in midsentence, he stepped right out of his character. Standing stiffly in the center of the stage area, he removed his written speeches from a back pocket, and, to the astonishment of those assembled, read Falstaff's final lines to the student audience. It was impossible for the frustrated Robert, trying as hard as he could to play the character, to be a convincing Prince Hal.

After a silent phase at the end of the act, everyone critiqued Ashley's performance all at once. As the din of noise arose, Miss Joyce asked for silence. She told Ashley, as tactfully as she could, that he was ill prepared. She pointed out that even his short portrayal of Falstaff, before he had to use the script as a crutch, was rather "wooden," and he was "tedious" with the spoken word.

"Shakespeare is meant to be spoken; his writing is lyrical and flowing. You, Ashley Thronson, make him sound dull and long-winded. And," pointing to his partner, "you didn't give Robert any support at all with his role!"

Ashley was crestfallen but took the criticism courageously, responding with, "Next time, I'll be better, Miss Joyce. I assure you." To his classmates, he said, "I'm sorry, mates."

"And Ashley, please apologize to Mr. Robinson!" Miss Joyce said angrily. "Actors must work with one another, not create barriers for others' performances."

"I apologize, Robert," Ashley told him regretfully. The older boy nodded his acceptance while the other students whispered among themselves, not looking forward to a similar reproach from their teacher.

"Now, Thespians," Miss Joyce addressed them, "Phillip and Judith will perform a scene from J. B. Shaw's *Anthony and Cleopatra*. Let's come forward, darlings."

Phillip, just the opposite of Ashley, was natural, convincing, and quite at ease in his role as Antony. His mother had insisted he have a tailored costume, so he was dressed as a British lord. His dashing red cape and a black periwig made him look quite authentic. Unlike Ashley, Phillip was also very attentive to the speeches of his counterpart, and, with innate ability, reacted to her lines with reassuring nods, smiles, frowns, and "ah-hahs" as the dialogue instinctively suggested to him.

After Judith's final lines, "And all the Gods go with you! Upon your sword sit laurel victory and smooth success be strewn before your feet!" Phillip rushed to her.

In his response and scene-ending speech, he made pertinent gestures. "Let us go," shrugging his shoulders, he took her hand. "Come! Our separation so abides," placing his hand over his heart; "and flies," casually waving his hand; "that thou, residing here," pointing to his heart, "goes yet with me," Bowing; "And I, hence fleeting," throwing his partner a kiss, "here remain with thee," with outstretched arms. "Away!" He swept his cape in a broad flourish and left the stage area.

As one, the entire class rose, applauding enthusiastically, while Phillip's female partner complimented him with a heartfelt hug and a warm kiss on the cheek before the appreciative audience. "Oh, Phillip, you were so much fun to work with," she said.

"Ripping," "Delightful," "Keen," were some of the other overt remarks from the group.

Miss Joyce took great pains to point out why Phillip

was so effective in pretending he was an important military figure and lover in an historical period with which he was unfamiliar. He had approached his character in a fashion by which he had captured some of the skills of "real pretending."

"Actors must try to get into the skins of their characters," the school director insisted, scanning the faces of her attentive flock. "You want to try to be the person. The Victorian techniques of overacting, of being larger than life, and of crowing and prancing around the stage, rather than imagining you're another's self, are old-fashioned. Melodramas, Shakespeare, and Shaw may still require Irving-like performances, but the newer, more popular playwrights, especially the translations from Europe, Ibsen, Strindberg, and Chekov, are plays about real people, not aristocrats, kings, and strutting poppycocks."

"Should you play a Shakespearean role like a Victorian actor or like Phillip just portrayed Antony?" asked a portly, ruddy-faced 20-year-old.

"That's a grand question, Percy," Miss Joyce responded. "It depends. It depends on the producer or director, the audience, the scenery, and the abilities of the actors. The producer must firmly state what type of performance he's expecting. If you're in a cast with Benson, for example, you can't play the part of Mercutio in a quiet, realistic way when Benson is bellowing and bouncing all over the stage showing off all his athletic talents. London is known as having intellectual audiences that accept different interpretations of Shakespeare or Shaw. While in the provinces, actors are expected to be larger than life while onstage. Repertory companies, 'fit-ups,' melo groups, and musical reviews all require different styles of acting."

Memories of his experiences with the Bensonians raced through Ashley's head.

"Could you explain the differences, Miss Joyce? I'm rather confused," asked one of the young women, a serving girl in a pub who wanted to perform in reviews.

"Haven't I told you about the various types of acting companies? Forgive me. I thought I'd covered that before," Miss Joyce replied. "Most of the famous actor-managers such as Forbes-Robinson, with whom my parents performed, and Harry Irving, whose touring company I joined, Benson, Asche, and others performed five to eight plays, which they changed nightly. This was economical. It enabled a company to stay in one place longer, alternating casts and plays. Often, you can use the same scenery for all the productions, changing only the costumes and stage furniture. It also gave the audiences opportunities to see their theatrical favorites in their most successful roles."

Her student audience was attentive, all aware she was sharing the secrets of a professional.

"You, as actors, have one or more roles to play for each of the productions; you're also expected to understudy others. Playing relatively long runs is the method of most of the theatres with large resident companies in London, here in Bristol, Manchester, Brighton, and elsewhere, as well as fit-ups. The Stratford and the Alwich theatres in London would be good examples of nightly exchanges."

"What's a 'fit-up?'" asked Miss Collins. Several eyebrows were raised with surprise at such a naïve question.

"You tell them, Richard? Aren't you auditioning for a fit-up company next week?" Miss Joyce asked.

Richard Bates rose, replacing Miss Joyce in front of the group. "Yes, I've a good possibility with a touring company of *Raffles*. The juvenile lead's leaving the tour for a part in a new London play. A fit-up," he explained with his arms outspread demonstratively, "is a collapsible touring company. It carries its own portable stage, proscenium arch, and full lighting equipment. A fit-up doesn't need a theatre. It can play anywhere - a barn, a large public house, or a church vestibule, even out-of-doors. It's always travelling, usually in smaller villages and towns where it's the only entertainment around. Now, with the cinema becoming so popular, there are fewer fit-up companies, but in some places it's the only way a young actor can learn his trade."

"Is it a repertory company, too?" asked Teddy Barrett, a leading-man hopeful.

"No, usually, you're touring only one play. You can perform it from one night up to a week," Richard responded.

"And a melo?" Miss Collins asked. Richard looked to Miss Joyce for help.

"A melodrama! You don't know?" A somewhat astonished Miss Joyce commented. "The only plays melo companies perform are melodramas. There are several of them touring out there," broadly gesturing with her arm. "They're known as 'blood and thunders.' A good melo actor can work all year round. More actors are in melodramas today than in any other form of theatre. The plots are always wild, and, usually, you're only touring one play. The casts are sufficiently small; usually, they have a hero, a heroine, a villain, and several minor roles. People in our rural villages love them. Audiences can cheer for the good characters, hiss and boo at the villains, yelling their support or disdain at the top of their lungs without penance. Everyone, including the actors, has a jolly good time. Every two months or so, you rehearse a new melodrama, change characters, and start the tour again. Melos are a good place for a young actor to start," she added.

"I think we all know what musical reviews are," offered one of the older boys in the group. "That's about all we see here in Bristol."

"True, Ronald," responded Miss Joyce. "Besides the cinema, they're what our Bristol audiences like most of all: singing, dancing, acrobats, comedians, jugglers, wild animals, and magicians. They don't want to think. They just want to be entertained."

"Rupie... I mean Ashley, did an act with a magician once," Phillip contributed. "Tell them about it, Ash!"

Ashley, pleased that he might somehow redeem himself from earlier embarrassment, rose before the group. He asked Richard to join him in explaining what it was like to be sawed in half by Martin the Magician. The evening ended happily for all, with Ashley also demonstrating a card trick Martin had taught him.

The next weeks sprinted by. However, his mother had been driven to her bed by consumption. Doctors admitted there was little they could do to help her. Rupert Senior had employed a full-time nurse to tend to her needs. He feared the worst. Also concerned about his mother's poor health, Ashley allowed his job to fall into a routine, almost the same tasks at the same times every day.

Richard had received a five-month contract with the touring fit-up company and was already in northern England. But, before he departed, a class party was held at the school to celebrate his good fortune as the first student of Miss Joyce Russell's drama school to be employed in the theatre. He ably finished his orientation to the theatre for Ashley and Phillip. Miss Joyce gave them their oral examination by themselves on a Monday evening after class was over. They met in the Green Room with their exercise books in hand.

"Now boys, I'd prefer that you not look at your notes but answer my questions from memory. Actors are like soldiers. They have to know the territory where they're going to fight.

On the battlefield, you can be killed. On the stage, worse yet, you can be embarrassed, and you're still living to be told about it," she said with a broad smile.

"Phillip, why does a theatrical company have a stage manager?" she addressed him while raising her eyebrows with theatrical emphasis.

After a thought-gathering pause, Phillip responded, "A stage manager is of paramount importance to a theatre company. He has to attend all the rehearsals and note what the producer tells the actors, recording every move, every sound effect."

"And every item the actor has to carry or use," interrupted Ashley.

"He has to record cues for gunshots, footsteps, door knocks. He has to sketch out where every actor is standing or moving on stage,"

Phillip continued. "He's the prompter when no one else is doing it."

"It's a thankless job, too," Ashley intruded. "Everyone else gets the credit when the play goes well, and he's blamed if it turns out poorly."

"That's correct, Ashley," said Miss Joyce. "Anything else, Phillip?"

"Well, he's always the first to arrive, the last to leave. He has to prepare the stage for the actors, put props where they're supposed to be. He must have the ones actors will carry on the property table."

Ashley burst in, "He also has to let the cast know how much time they have before opening curtain."

"Ashley, stop interrupting. I'm asking Phillip. You'll get the next question. All right?" Miss Joyce affirmed.

"Yes'm," said a quickly subdued Ashley.

"Phillip, what are the normal calls to the cast in dressing rooms?"

Phillip answered cautiously. He wasn't quite certain of the answer. "I think there're four. Yes, four," gaining confidence. "The first is "half an hour,' the second 'quarter of an hour,' and the third is 'five minutes.' 'Places' is called when the actors must report on stage or 'overture and beginners, please' if you've got music."

"Good, Phillip. Now, do all the actors have to be in theatre even if they're not used until later scenes?"

"Of course. The stage manager has to have everyone on board before he can launch the ship."

Ashley waved his hand for attention. Miss Joyce nodded to him to speak. "H-H-He forgot something," he announced.

"What is it, Ashley?"

"He's got to give notice to the front of the house. If he's doesn't, the audience won't be in the theatre when the curtain opens."

"Good thinking, young man. You're right. Now, that takes care of the stage manager, doesn't it?" she stated.

"There is one more important duty of the stage manager," Phillip reported.

"And that is?" asked Miss Joyce.

"After the play opens, whether it's on tour or in a theatre, the stage manager's in complete charge."

"Is he now?" asked Miss Joyce. "What do you think, Ashley?"

"Well, I believe that when you're rehearsing a play with someone like Harley Granville-Barker, Barker is in total control. No one would challenge his authority."

"Exactly, Ashley. When you have an actor-manager, it's like taking the producer on the road. When you don't, such as with a resident company in a resident theatre, the stage manager moves up as next in the command chain. Remember that!" Continuing, "There are three entities an actor must please. Do you know what they are?"

Simultaneously, the boys turned their heads slowly from side to side.

"The actor-manager or producer, the audience, and yourself. Remember that, gentlemen!" Turning to Ashley, she asked, "What are the stage positions?"

"I know that, Miss Joyce, I know that," he responded eagerly. "Upstage, downstage, and cross. All the positions extend from the actor standing in the center of the stage facing the audience. To his right is stage right, to his left is stage left." Miss Joyce beckoned for him to continue. "In back of the actor is upstage, in front of him is downstage."

"Good, Ashley." Turning to Phillip, she asked, "How many positions are there?

"Fifteen," he said quickly.

"So, this is the stage; I'm standing over here to your right. Where am I?

"You're down right center," Phillip responded.

"And where is Ashley?" Miss Joyce requested.

"Right now, he's up left center."

"Excellent," the teacher complimented. "Now let's talk about actors, shall we?"

As before, Miss Joyce questioned each of the boys about the acting profession, encouraging them to help one another with their responses. She was pleased with the results. Richard had provided them with a fine foundation.

Phillip and Ashley demonstrated that they had learned there are several, rather than one approach to acting: some actors try to 'live' a part; others simulate a character with utter conviction; while some approach a role rather scientifically, and mentally stand apart observing themselves in performance, as if manipulating their bodies and voices as puppets, with their minds serving as puppet masters. For rehearsals, they had learned that an actor should know all his lines by the third meeting, that he should have read and reread the play at least six times, trying to understand everyone's part in relationship to the character he was playing. Phillip, especially, seemed to have sensitivity as to how an actor should prepare for a part and demonstrated this knack in acting out scenes in front of the class.

When asked how an actor could bring realism to dialogue, Phillip showed knowledge beyond his young and tender years. "He should vary the tone of his voice. Otherwise, he'll sound dull and monotonous. He should listen well and act like he's listening when other actors speak. He should slow down to emphasize main points and learn pitches so, when he has a line, he'll come in at a different tone than the last speaker. Richard told us that if we all speak in the same tone, it would sound like an orchestra instead of individual soloists. Another piece of advice he gave us was to learn the meaning behind the lines, not just the lines. Your speeches should sound spontaneous rather than as if you're parroting someone else."

In praising Phillip, while insuring that Ashley understood, Miss Joyce reviewed thoroughly that an actor must provide an audience with thoughts rather than just words. She also gave them a number of suggestions on memorizing their lines, that constant reading and practice with another person without the script were helpful. "Writing down your lines without crib sheets is another way to test your memory, or jot down the cues and recite your own speeches after reading them," she told them.

The Tuesday and Thursday acting classes continued. Every student was showing improvement, even young Ashley. Miss Joyce found him better at playing the roles for boys in his own age category. He had great trouble pretending he was anyone but himself.

She tried group scenes with more than two parts,

insisting that students use props: bottles, glasses, cups and saucers, emphasizing her point that humans weren't the only actors in a play, that a glass could hold poison, a pistol could contain only one bullet, or a suitcase might be full of money, and the audience might place more importance on them than the character the playwright had invented.

Eight of the students had a wonderful time with a tea-pouring scene in *The Admirable Creighton.* By the time, they had rehearsed it several times, while engaged in dialogue, the Green Room floor was covered with green tea that had missed the cups or overflowed while the amateurs tried to pour it from the teapot into shaking dishware. Ashley, reminded of his shipboard experiences, manned the mop on several occasions.

Miss Joyce had the girls bring full-length skirts to class if they were in a period scene. The boys often donned a belt, sheath, and sword, which Miss Joyce kept in inventory for a swashbuckling act, or they used one of her several beards, wigs, or moustaches to add believability to a character.

Occasionally, she would have her students practice "improvisations," in which class members pretended they were in whatever situation she described.

Miss Joyce closed her eyes and pointed her finger at Miss Collins, "You're on a beach, sunning yourself. You're alone. You're a vain and conceited person. Think now," she added. "You hate cold water, but swimming is the current fad. You're at the beach in Weston. The water is very cold, it's freezing, and it's shallow. You must show your pluck! You must be heroic! Even the brave can't keep their feet in the water too long. A huge wave arrives and soaks you. You lose your self-control. Now, do it, Rosalyn!"

And the diligent drama pupil, as best she could, tried to recreate the actions, by expression, gesture, and bodily movement, of a snob making a fool of herself at the ocean side.

Phillip excelled at the improvisations. He was particularly apt with facial expressions, and he had his classmates in hysterics when he played the part of an overweight, stuffy banker attempting to enter the tube-train during rush hour. He pretended to stand impatiently in line, creating the impression that he was suffering from heat and anxiety by constantly wiping his brow and wringing his hankie. He was funniest when he feigned getting on the train. He missed the door, bounced off the car, and painfully watched it move off without him.

"How did you think up all that stuff?" asked Ashley with some envy.

"Watching W.C. Fields in the cinema," was Phillip's instantaneous response.

Ashley, because of his creative imagination, was better at improvisation than acting in scenes with dialogue. His classmates applauded and complimented him when he pretended he was a thief in a hotel. He looked very sinister and cruel as he softly padded across the stage of the Green Room, and, using a set of imaginary keys, he convinced his audience of classmates that he had opened a hotel guest room and was searching for something to steal. Discovering a chest of drawers in what was assumed to be a dark room, he found a jewelry box, and, with an over-acted sense of accomplishment, snuck out of the room without detection.

"You're a natural for melodrama," Charles announced, with "Right-o" from other students. That made Ashley feel warm all over.

Miss Joyce then announced that classes would be suspended for the summer as she'd been cast in a small part in a touring company playing the beach resorts in southern England.

In June, the whole of Miss Joyce's class turned out to see Phillip in Bristol Grammar School's Upper Form's production of *A Midsummer Night's Dream*. After graduation, he had visited America with his father and, upon his return, had been asked to play the lead in the school play. As in the case of boys' schools, BGS students played all of the parts with the utmost sincerity. Mr. White had successfully drilled into their minds that William Shakespeare originally wrote female parts for male actors and that make-up, costume, and, even more important, voice and mannerisms should be convincingly womanlike.

Sixteen-year-old Phillip Maggs was perfectly cast as the delightful fairy Puck, and Ashley's other schoolmate, Peter , was a delightful comic as Bottom, the weaver. Others, in the view of most of the audience, were underage and miscast as the male lovers, Lysander and Demetrius, and their female counterparts, Hermia and Helena, as well as the King and Queen of the Fairies, Oberon and Titania. In this surrealistic fantasy, the supernatural, the human, and the bestial worlds co-mingle. Puck's love juices change the objects of two pairs of lovers and cause the fairy queen to become enamored of a transformed Bottom, crowned with the head of an ass. Other players included Athenian tradesmen who gather in the magical forest to a "play within a play" to honor the forthcoming weddings.

The colorful scenery consisted of gaily conceived trees, leaves, and flowers, vaguely resembling an Athenian woodland, painted on white canvas and hung from the ceiling of the Great Hall. The costumes were homemade and very courtly. Many had been obtained from attics and rag discard bins and were embellished with brightly stained material in reds, greens, and yellows. Wigs, primarily cut from rope hemp were died black, brown, or white and pinned onto scalps that resembled either wild growing weed patches or carefully groomed lawns. Mustaches and beards were pasted on fuzzy or pimply cheeks and chins.

Phillip, as the mischievous fairy, was an athletic and charming Puck, also known as Robin Goodfellow. His first line, "Over hill, over dale, through bush, through brier, over park, over pale, through flood, through fire, I do wander everywhere, swifter than the moon's sphere," set the stage. His gestures and ballet-like movement, described by the dialogue, had almost everyone in attendance uttering admiration, all smiling with belief at the unbelievable. Admitting, as Robin Goodfellow, that he was the merry wanderer of the night, Phillip enchanted those assembled and reminded them of their own dreams in which reality was replaced by a pleasurable dream world.

By the time Bottom had donned his ass' head, and Puck promised to lead him "through bog, through bush, and through brake," onlookers had lost themselves in the comedy and seemed emotionally prepared to travel through wonderland with the cast.

At the play's end, Phillip, pretending his character to the hilt, said, "If you pardon, we will mend, and, as I'm an honest Puck; if we have unearned luck now to 'scope the serpent's tongue,' we will make amends ere long; else the Puck a liar call: So, good night unto you all. Give me your hands, if we be friends. And Robin shall restore amends."

As his hands stretched in a sweeping upward motion, his invitation to the audience brought them collectively up on their feet applauding. Phillip had clearly stolen the show!

As the exuberant cast made their way across the Great Hall, through the throng of parents, classmates, teachers, relatives, and friends, Phillip's wandering eyes sought out drama school colleagues, Ashley, and, especially, his revered mentor, Miss Joyce. As they found him, one by one, and either hugged him or enthusiastically shook his hand, their congratulatory comments boosted him into an unfamiliar, relaxed aura of satisfied relief. It was the same feeling of accomplishment experienced by the runner who first crossed the finish line, the kicker who scored the goal, the MP who finally realized victory.

At last, he saw Ashley and Miss Joyce together, and rushed towards them. His proud, beaming drama teacher held out her arms affectionately and drew Phillip into them. Clasping him tightly, she whispered in his ear, "Phillip, you were splendid. I'm so proud of you I could cry." And tears actually welled on the edges of her eyes.

Ashley grabbed his friend's arm and turned him for a manlier hug, crying out happily, "Mate. You were great! You were just marvelous."

"Phillip, come here for a minute," Miss Joyce beckoned to Phillip. "I want to tell you something privately. Excuse us, Ashley." They stepped a few steps from the milling crowd. With Phillip in front of her, she faced him, and with a serious voice, she said admiringly, "Phillip, you are an actor! You have more talent than anyone I've ever seen at your age. And I want to help you even though I'm off on tour."

Phillip, hypnotized by her words, mumbled softly, "Yes, but how?"

She asked him to promise to read every one of Shakespeare's works at least four times and to memorize the major speeches of the Big Four: *Hamlet, Macbeth, King Lear,* and *Othello*. She also asked him to read Shaw's *Candida* and *Pygmalion,* and Pinero's *The Second Mrs. Tanqueray.*

Phillip promised.

"I must go now," Miss Joyce said, leaning close to Phillip and kissing him softly on the cheek. "I'll miss you, my young darling. But I'll see you in September. Don't forget to read what I told you to." Turning and hurrying off, she didn't see the unhappy expression sweeping across Phillip's face or hear his whisper, "I'll miss you too, my dear friend."

Phillip began his summer apprenticeship in his father's Bristol furniture store and purchased a book of Shakespeare's folios. He had also obtained permission from his father to spend a fortnight or so in London, seeing plays. He had asked Ashley to accompany him.

As for Ashley, his sixteenth birthday was approaching. His mother, facing almost immediate death, wanted to reward Ashley for working so hard at bookkeeping with a trip to London with Phillip where they could also stay with one of her married sisters. Mrs. Thronson whispered weakly to her grieving husband, "I don't want him to be here when I pass on."

Later, when they were alone, Ashley at her bedside, she said softly, "I've saved some money so you can attend a few plays as well. But don't tell your father about the money. He might become angry. You know how he is about the theatre. Too much will encourage you."

And so it was, in November of 1916, R. Ashley Thronson and Phillip Maggs took their first train ride to London.

Chapter 14
The London Theatre Invasion

London, 1916

Ashley felt like a wide-eyed rural farmhand as he and Phillip walked his country's capital from one end to the other. Arriving at Paddington Railway Station, the boys were met by Ashley's aunt Sophie and her husband, who picked them up in their shiny new Rolls Royce motorcar. They were delivered to an attractive home in Chelsea where they were given their own private bedroom. It was decorated all in pink, once being the domain of Sophie's long-departed daughter, who had moved to France with her Parisian husband.

For the first three days of their holiday, by day, the boys, who had never seen London before, visited all of the famous places they had heard of throughout their youth: the impressive stately buildings of Parliament; the almost endless green lawns of Hyde Park; the flowers of Kensington

Gardens; Westminster Abbey; Kensington Palace, which had been occupied by Queen Victoria; St. Paul's Cathedral; and Victoria and Albert Museum, which appeared to contain the entire history of the kingdom. They marveled at the number of automobiles, horse-drawn carriages, subway trains; the crowds of people at Piccadilly and Oxford circuses; the ever-present street vendors and street performers, called "buskers," frequenting Covent Gardens; the ancient fortress known as the Tower of London, rumored to house more ghosts than any other building in Britannia. They cherished the efficiency of the underground railway system, which became their major form of transportation.

They stopped at the front of 10 Downing Street, hoping to see the Prime Minister or another British executive. They didn't. They toured Sherlock Holmes' supposed residence at 212B Baker Street, and purchased fresh fruit from the venders on Petticoat Lane. They listened to the hurdy gurdy man grinding his organ. They bought snacks from the "lobster mongers," watched the giraffes and other animals glare back at spectators and devour their unsavory meals at the zoo. Ashley pretended he was a paying guest when strutting through the posh hotel lobbies of the Carriage, Savoy, and Hyde Park hotels. The shyer Phillip enjoyed Ashley's antics from afar, always hiding behind a newspaper. Ashley would ask if any messages had been left for him. He previewed several rooms for future booking just to see what they looked like. He managed a personal tour of the entire Savoy premises for both of them. One day, he bartered for the lowest possible price on a tarnished silver pocket watch at a hock shop in the East End slums and took pleasure in his new timepiece. The boys wandered through the vastness of the huge store an American, Gordon Selfridge, had opened. Selfridges, in one large shopping structure, combined on four floors all the singular small shops with which he was familiar in Bristol - the chemist and pharmacy; the drapers selling curtains, clothing, mourning, and wedding dress; kitchen ware; personal care goods; and gift items – all in one place.

From the beginning of their stay, in the evenings and when theatres offered afternoon matinees, the boys concentrated on what they referred to as their "London Theatre Invasion." They also talked their way into several rehearsals. Unfortunately, the one play and company Ashley most wanted to see, *The Importance of Being Ernest*, had closed after two months of performances. The boys planned to attend as many plays as possible over a fourteen-day period.

Ashley wanted to see with his own eyes all the theatres in which he imagined he might play as one of England's future leading actors. They walked the West End's theatre district, Shaftsbury Avenue, West Street, Piccadilly Circus, Drury Lane, The Strand, and Charring Cross. Miss Joyce had advised them that if they told the stage doorkeepers they might be auditioning for the cast of a coming attraction, they would allow them entry to the backstage area. In most cases, the ploy worked. They toured the new Ambassador's; the Alwych; the enormous Coliseum, inspecting the first revolving stage ever built in London; the Cockpit; the ancient but still attractive Covent Garden Theatre; the Duke of York's; the London Hippodrome; the Palladium, a popular home for variety shows and reviews; the Lyceum, which Sir Henry Irving had managed for so many years; the Palace; Drury Lane; the Old Vic; the Royal Court Theatre; but, of all the grand theatrical houses they admired, none could compare with the Theatre Royal.

In the Royal's gallery, by the auditorium entrances from the King's side and the Prince's side, they carefully studied the statues of the great actors Garrick, Balfe, and Kean; the legendary Shakespeare; and the handsome bust of Henry Irving. The boys wondered what enabled them to succeed to immortality. They peeked into the Royalty Retiring Room where monarchs, past and present, sipped champagne between acts under the Waterford crystal chandelier. It was there, the stage door man told them, "Nell Guinn, then an usherette, was probably induced to become the King's mistress." The boys ascended the large curved staircase to the highest balcony to view the stage from afar. Backstage, behind the curtains, they wandered through the dressing rooms where the greats of drama throughout the ages had applied their make-up; they examined and admired the thick, iron safety curtain and inspected the painting dock where canvas curtains could be raised and lowered to sketch the forests, palaces, or mountains they represented. They descended the stairs taking them under the stage where they observed the water tanks, the trap doors, and the mechanisms to lift and drop parts of the wooden stage floor overhead to allow a wizard to disappear, a prince charming to arise to stage level, or a ship to cross the stage behind the footlights.

At night, despite the war's restriction on streetlights, and illumination from buildings and residences being curtained off, the curfew laws were not widely enforced. There had been some German aircraft invading the British skys, but it was only occasional and unsuccessful. Theatre, especially with war-related themes, flourished. The boys noted that many of those walking the streets in both the day and night wore some type of uniform: soldiers; sailors; chippies; women who had replaced men in many of the military's non-combat jobs; nurses; and pilots, who were distinctive because of their flamboyant outfits. Limps, canes, absent limbs, and eye patches were constant reminders that a war was being conducted. At night, the streets were dark, and there was limited transportation above ground.

Thank God, said Ashley to himself, *the tube was built so long ago and operates so well below ground.*

The London Daily, The Mail, The Fleet Street, and the *Daily Express* kept the city's populace well informed on the activities of the allies in the war. The news constantly was bad. For almost eighteen months, little progress had been made by either side, and Ashley felt that the entire battle between the two non-advancing, opposing front lines was being held in France's "No-Man's Land." During the previous year, General John French's British Expeditionary Forces had fought effectively enough to establish a definite battlefront, extending along the Marne from near Dunkirk to the Swiss Frontier near Mulhouse. Until now, it had never varied more than fifty miles, even though immense losses were constantly reported by both sides and neither appeared to gain an advantage. This had been the worst period of the war. General Haig's troops had so many casualties that morale had sunk close to despair, and Kirtchener's new Army was so ill prepared for battle, they were described as proverbial lambs being led to slaughter. Compulsory military service for young men eighteen and older had created the lambs, and their masters, the war's lions, seemed bent on little other than their slaughter.

Their first night in London, Ashley and Phillip met Richard Bates in front of the Aldwich Theatre, where he was playing a small part in T.W. Richardson's *Caste*. The play dealt with an aristocrat in love with an actress. In the first act, his dignified friend points out that social law forbids a relationship with a "woman of the theatre." One of his lines read, "A giraffe cannot fall in love with a squirrel," or words to that effect. The comic in the play, with whom Ashley identified, was a drunk and a money grabber. Following every encounter, he would leave the stage "heading for a pub." Following the final act, Ashley and Phillip went to

Richard's shared dressing room, which he shared with four other actors. Recognizing one as the principal's aristocratic friend, Ashley told him, "That was a great twist in the play, when you, playing the snob, stopped the male lead from lighting his cigar in front of the actress whom you termed 'a lady.' You stole the show."

"Well, I appreciate your kind words, laddie," the actor responded. "But, as you noted, in the play, they married anyway. The lady had outclassed her class."

"Wouldn't it be marvelous if that could be true of all actors?" Phillip remarked.

Everyone in the dressing room nodded. In a few minutes, they had all left for the pub. While there, they mapped out a theatre itinerary for the rest of their stay.

The next afternoon, they could be found seated in the rear seats of the Criterion Theatre in Piccadilly Circus, watching a matinee performance of *London by Night* by the prominent actor-manager Dion Boucicault and others. Ashley had met the author's daughter Nina, an actress who had played the part of the mother in *Charley's Aunt* on the *Lusitania*.

This was a complicated mystery play about Henry Marchant, a naval officer, who had returned to London as a man who had made his fortune, seeking his former sweetheart. She, in turn, had "fallen into shame" and, unbeknownst to the former naval officer, had fallen in love with his own brother, a popular member of London's lower class of drunks and drop-outs. A wealthy banker's daughter has her eye on Marchant, and, at her request, her father draws up a contract of marriage. One of the members of the lower-depths group finds the document and, after kidnapping Marchant and leaving him for dead, attempts to substitute Marchant's brother as the potential groom. The brother, at first quite willing to substitute, refuses in the end, claiming his love for his sibling's former sweetheart. In the end, the brother gets the sweetheart, and the former naval officer gets the banker's daughter.

In discussing the play, Ashley claimed he should later be cast in the role of the sweetheart's father, while Phillip, with a heavy make-up job, could play the former naval officer. Phillip agreed, boasting that he would have performed especially well in the kissing scenes.

The following afternoon, they attended Edward Sheldon's play, *Romance*, at the Duke of York's theatre. The theatre's American producer, Charles Froman, was the featured profile of the program. Ashley was fascinated. "Phillip, look at this!" he said loudly before the curtain was to rise. "Charles Froman was the first producer of *Peter Pan* in England. It says so, right here. He was also the person most responsible for transferring British plays and musicals to New York."

"Why don't you ask him if you can go to America with one of his plays?" Phillip responded.

"I can't." Ashley muttered. "He's bloody dead. He drowned on the *Lusitania*. He never got off the ship. Didn't you know?"

Phillip shook his head.

During the entire performance, Ashley had trouble concentrating on *Romance*. His mind wandered, and he returned his thoughts to how close he had come to being in America, how much he wanted to see the vast land, how the current war struggles of England conflicted the freedoms he knew existed overseas in the so-called promised land. *I wish Charles Froman had been on the earlier voyage with me*, he thought.

The Edwin Sheldon play was about a bishop trying to persuade his son from marrying an actress. In so doing, the Bishop of Giles related his own story of youthful romance. It went back to a time when visiting New York, he, as a rector, had met and fallen rapidly in love with a young and beautiful American opera singer. At his climax of infatuation, he discovers she has an unsavory past and fights valiantly to save her soul. Unconvinced that either religion or a rector is suitable, she sails off to Europe. The Bishop's son gets the message.

Another play they thoroughly enjoyed was *Hobson's Choice* by Harold Brighouse at the Drury Lane Theatre. The plot revolves around Willie Mossop, a gifted, but unappreciated shoemaker employed by the domineering Henry Horatio Hobson. Semi-literate and content with his lot, Willie is bullied by Hobson's eldest daughter, Maggie, over the hill by Victorian terms at the ripe old age of thirty, into marrying her and setting up a shop of his own. Maggie and her two younger sisters, Alice and Vickie, have worked most of their lives in their father's store without wages. They're eager to be married and out of the shop. Alice is engaged to a young up-and-coming solicitor, Vickie to the son of a respectable corn merchant. Between Maggie's sales skill and Willie's shoemaking talent, the enterprise is very successful. Within a year, he's taken nearly all Hobson's trade. At Maggie's urging, her husband enters a partnership with Hobson, now an almost-bankrupt alcoholic, on condition that Hobson take no further part in the business. Marriage and success come to all and happiness to Hobson. Ashley and Phillip had long discussions about how they would play the roles of Willie and Hobson, respectively.

One of their favorite matinees was a performance of the comedy *Potash and Perlmutter* at the Alwych Theatre. The newspapers advertised it as a Jewish farce. The boys were eager to see it. The plot began with the failure of Potash's tailoring business. In desperation, he latches onto the wealthy Perlmutter as a partner. Their enterprise shows success, but they find they have an enemy in Feldman, a rich attorney. Feldman fancies Potash's daughter, which was the main reason he invested in the enterprise. However, Potash has picked out a husband for his daughter, Irma. She is already in love with Boris Andrieff, a starving musician who Potash employs in a low position. A murder is committed at the partner's establishment, and Andrieff is charged with the crime. Feldman shows his true colours by refusing to clear the young man's name. In the end, Andrieff is eventually found to be innocent and proves a suitable husband for Irma.

Both Ashley and Phillip claimed the future role of Andrieff for themselves. At dinner, between the afternoon's entertainment and their next evening's performance, they argued what make-up and costumes each would use to be convincing as the sad, young, but romantic, musician. Ashley eventually gave up and chose the part of Feldman for himself. "He's the kind of Jewish gentleman I'd really want to be. Rich and mean," he joked.

For four days in a row, they saw only war-related plays. *Home and Beauty* by Somerset Maugham, booked at the Palace Theatre, followed the success of his play, *Constant Wife*. It was the sixteenth of his plays, the only one set during The Great War. The main character was Victoria, a privileged widow of a soldier missing in action. She had married another hero, her dead husband's best friend. Surprisingly, the first husband returns from the dead. Ashley felt the real twist in the play was that Victoria actually wanted to marry a third man, Leicester Wagner, a Member of Parliament. Unbeknownst to her, both her husbands wanted to be free. The serious drama took on comedy in both the first two acts, with the two husbands making beds and cleaning house with no servants to help them because of the war. The final act found them working in the kitchen together as cooks, where a divorce attorney visits them to set up the required claim of adultery. A professional co-respondent stays with them all night playing cards. Victoria eventually gets her public servant. Her role was played over the top by actress Mary Jackson, who squeezed out every bit of comedic spice within extravagant settings. The boys concurred that the play was a serious social comment about divorce laws in England during serious economic and war situations.

Havoc by Harry Wall, also shown at the Duke of York Theatre, was sheer war-time realism. Produced at the Haymarket Theatre, it starred Richard Bird as a half-demented lad, the Babe, who had seen hand-to-hand fighting for the first time. The boys concurred that Henry Kendall played the blinded officer beautifully. The author and most of the actors had been at the front so the trench language and other military details were perfectly rendered, including the gramophone with the singing of "A Little Love, a Little Kiss" on all sorts of occasions. All the scenes took place in trenches, with one wall removed from the realism of an actual dirt dugout.

"It's not strictly a war play," said Ashley, as he and Phillip discussed it on a subway car on their way to their temporary lodging. "It's more a story of thwarted love, don't you think, Phillip?"

"Yes, I believe, you're right," Phillip responded. "A great deal of thwarted love. But it had haunting power and originality, didn't it?"

The main theme concerned a subaltern, Dick, who had fallen in love with a woman who, he wasn't aware, played the field of men pursuing her. Some soldiers were betrayed; some even died without knowing the miserable basis on which their loves had depended. Most of the unfaithfulness was realized through their trench talk in between raids from the enemy. The play's climax occurs after one of the soldiers has committed suicide over his ruined love life, and the curtain falls after Dick returns home to find Violet in the arms of another man.

Suspense, by Patrick McGill, playing at the Royal Court Theatre, told of a party of soldiers who took over a dugout under which the Germans could be heard mining. The trench jests, songs, and back-chatter mingled in telling fashion with the dramatic tap-tap-tap of the German miners, suggesting the possibility that this section of the front might explode at any time. Finally, it did "go up" as the German line had done in reality. Happily, the British soldiers had been transferred to another trench before the Germans met their horrible fate.

After the war stories, both boys wanted a change of entertainment and took in two variety shows where the acts consisted of magicians, dog trainers, comedians, dancers, singers, and acrobats. Two nights and one matinee gave them more of an assortment of different types of demonstrative activity then they'd ever seen. Discussing this array of presentational features in a pub after the second night, Ashley said to Phillip, "You know, mate, it might not be a bad idea to work up an act for variety to tide you over between acting jobs. What do you think?"

Pausing in thought, Phillip responded, "What are you thinking about? A dog act?"

"No, silly," Ashley replied, "A song-and-dance piece. If I could find a dandy-looking lady to work with me, I'll bet I could make up a quality act."

"Doesn't that girl you met on the ship heading for the States sing and dance?" asked Phillip.

"Right-o. That's a smashing idea, Phillip. I'll just have to find out where Rosie St. John is these days and give her a call."

Next, the boys attended a performance of the very

popular *Peter Pan* at the enormous Covent Garden Theatre. The fantasy opened with Peter Pan visiting the house of Mr. and Mrs. Darling, who have three children: Wendy and her brothers John and Michael. Peter has lost his shadow, but after Wendy finds it, needing a surrogate mother for his gang of Lost Boys, Peter convinces her that she and her brothers must leave with him for Neverland. Wendy agrees, and John and Michael go along.

The great dangerous and magical flight to Neverland is followed by numerous adventures. The children are blown out of the air by a cannon, and Wendy is nearly killed by the Lost Boys. Peter and the Lost Boys build a little house for Wendy to live in while she recuperates. Soon John and Michael adopt the ways of the Lost Boys, while Wendy plays the role of mothering them, all the while provoking the jealousy of Tinker Bell, Tiger Lily, and the mermaids. Peter is often oblivious, concentrating on real and make-believe adventures and on taunting the pirate, Captain Hook. There are additional encounters at the Mermaids' Lagoon, the near deaths of Tinker Bell and Peter, a violent pirate/Indian massacre, and a climactic confrontation with Peter's nemesis, the evil, but humorous, seagoing villain Hook. In the end, Wendy decides that her place is at home, much to the joy of her heartsick mother. Wendy brings all the boys, including the lost ones back to London. Peter remains in Neverland, promising to return and take Wendy back with him once a year to help him with his spring cleaning. However, Peter soon forgets all about Wendy. Years later, when he returns, she is a grown-up woman. Phillip and Ashley thoroughly enjoyed their theatrical journey into Neverland but didn't see themselves in any of the parts.

Ashley insisted that they see *Peg o' My Heart* at the Cockpit, "Because it's a rage in London." he said. A comedy by J. Hartley Manners, the play features Peg, a poor Irish girl living in New York, who becomes an heiress by the death of her uncle and returns to England to be raised by an aristocratic aunt. A duck out of water in these surroundings, she eventually wins her way, as well as a worthy Englishman named Jerry.

"Now this was a fine clean play with plenty of wit and fun," stated Phillip.

Next, they both thoroughly enjoyed *The Merry Widow* at the Ambassador's, an operetta with book and lyrics by Charles George and music by the highly regarded Franz Lehar.

"Here were all the world's famous songs in one show, with a dashing European prince romancing a beautiful American widow, who was both clever and wholesome," Ashley announced. "Maybe I can find one when I go to America," he added.

School for Wives by Moliere was Phillip's choice. "I've always wanted to see a Moliere play," Phillip admitted.

In this popular London Hippodrome offering, Arnolphe, a rich man of fifty years has been afraid of taking a wife because of the possibility of being cuckolded. He now plans to wed his own ward, Agnes, whom he has educated in French convents to keep her innocent of the ways of the world. However, the ward's innocence is his undoing. When a man tips his hat to her on the street, she responds politely. Since one can meet a lot of swains that way, it happens to Agnes. At length, she and Horace fall in love. Horace confides to his friend, Arnolphe, how he has pulled the hood over the eyes of her guardian. Instead of nipping this affair in the bud, her guardian is confounded by Agnes' continued innocence and naivety. At length, her father, thought to be dead, surprisingly returns, immediately announcing his intention to wed Agnes to a son of a longtime friend. The father has a celebration for Arnolphe to congratulate him for raising Agnes so well and avoiding matrimony himself. He introduces his daughter's new bridegroom. It's Horace.

"Moliere translates to English very well, don't you think?" stated Phillip to Ashley, who nodded his affirmation.

They found the Lyceum's production of *Dick Whittington* by Norman Robbins "fun and games" as Ashley commented. There were more female roles than usual, which they appreciated: especially the fairy, Alice, and Sultana, the woman slave. They found it a bright and bouncy, fast-moving pantomime with full sets and front-curtain scenes. It was a zany tale of a warmhearted girl who mistook a telephone repairman for a burglar. She earnestly tries to convert him from what she envisions as his life of crime. An unexpected interruption causes her to pretend the supposed burglar is her husband. This imagined union dismays her sister's evangelical and very religious fiancé causing hilarity that had critics and audiences cheering, according to the newspaper reviews. Phillip's personal review in a letter to his parents was that *Dick Whittington* was fast-moving and witty, had no smut, was light as feather, smooth as silk, a smash hit.

Another surprise was that Rosie St. John had a small role in the production. Ashley and Phillip went backstage after the performance and met her coming out of her dressing room. "Ashley, my lord, how you've grown. How marvelous to see you," the petite actress exclaimed excitedly.

After introducing Phillip, the trio visited the Old Shanty, a popular theatre-goer pub. Once their recent histories were exchanged, Ashley asked Rosie about the possibility of their becoming a song-and-dance team.

Despite Ashley's begging emotionally, Rosie responded, "Let me ponder the idea for a while, Ashley. My career's just getting a good start here in London. I want to see that through first. Give me your address in Bristol. I'll write my decision to you in a few weeks. There's a great deal to consider."

With an end to their enjoyable London visit looming shortly, they bought tickets to *Caesars' Wife* at the London Palladium. Both lads found the three-act comedy by Somerset Maugham "very dull." Just as Caesar had ruled Egypt, Sir Arthur Little has been sent by the British foreign office to represent the country in Cairo. Billie Baker, an American actress playing his young wife, has fallen in love with Little's male secretary, who wants to be transferred out of the situation. Sir Little says, "No!" needing the youngster in Cairo.

"Will he let his wife run away? No! Why not? She has to be faithful to the empire. England is never the slave. This happens all the time. We must be British. I saw this ending coming," Ashley remarked. "The wife would give in, and the secretary was interested in another woman."

Phillip nodded his assent.

The last four productions they attended were *When London Sleeps, Conquering Hero, Ace*, and London's most popular theatrical event, *Chu Chin Chow.*

When London Sleeps, seen at the Old Vic, was a melodrama about a slippery hoodlum, Rodney Hanes, who runs a high class gambling joint in Hamstead while elsewhere in London's Lamburty's Square is another gambling house on its last legs. The only link between Hanes and Lamburty is gambler Tommy Blyth, whose betting has put him in serious debt with Hanes. The twist is that he fancies Lamburty's adopted daughter. Lamburty pays off the debt by joining the two gambling worlds. "That one, I didn't believe," was Ashley's evaluation.

Monkhouse's *Conquering Hero* had played in Birmingham before being brought to the Royalty Theatre's London stage. It was laid out in England, but the theme concerned the war, with chief character, Chris Rokeby, who was the antithesis of everything that made a natural soldier. He was not a conscientious objector, serving his command with distinction, but he struggled against the facts of the war as he experienced them. This struggle gave the play its name, its unity, and its compelling power. His family viewed Chris as a shirker and a coward. Friends thought of him as an idealist and a dreamer. The tragedy was that he was immensely courageous, as well as honest, thus becoming a conquering hero. To patriotic Phillip and Ashley, the play was an eye-opener.

The *Ace* by German playwright Herman Rossman had been translated by Miles Malleson and played at the Lyric Theatre. It concerned a German war-time aviator with forty-nine victories in aerial combat who realized that the fiftieth must be a crucial struggle with an equally clever and courageous English "ace." The point of the play was that the German could win only if he could avoid thinking about the coming conflict. He failed. His real foe was a phantom Englishman, which had been created in his imagination. This was the first time the boys had seen the rising young actor, Raymond Massey, who played the fiery, fretful, dream-haunted German ace who was outwardly insolent but, internally, a victim of his ceaseless imaginings.

This experience finally caused both Phillip and Ashley to begin pondering aloud between them what this big war really meant. They could talk of little else for several days.

For their final London theatrical experience, they spent their last pounds on *Chu Chin Chow* at the Theatre Royal, publicized as a combination of musical comedy and pantomime. It was a big-budget spectacular costing £5,300, with over a dozen scene changes, fantastic sets, difficult dance routines, exotic costumes, and director Oscar Asche's well-known innovative lighting designs. According to the

London Daily, "The design for the show was influenced by the English taste for all things connected with Asia, popularly known as "orientalism," which had originated with Diaghilev's production of the ballet *Scheherazade*.

"Listen to this review in *The Post*," Ashley asked Phillip, reading the following item aloud:

> "Tickets to see *Chu Chin Chow* were eagerly sought after by troops on leave from the Western Front. One of the attractions for the on-leave soldiers is the chorus of pretty slave girls who are very scantily dressed. Complaints, not by the soldiers, resulted in the Lord Chamberlain (the British theatre censor) viewing the show and requiring "this naughtiness" to be stopped -- at least for a while. The cast was large and included a camel, a donkey, poultry and snakes. A total of two million people have already seen this show."

"I can hardly wait for this one. I hope we can get in," Phillip said, as they waited in front of the box office to learn if any tickets were still available. There were.

Once in their seats at the very top of the balcony, before the performance began, Ashley softly told Phillip what he had garnered from his short study of the *Chu Chin Chow* program. "It was the success of the Arabian Nights production of *Kismet*, a 1911 play written by Edward Knoblock, that inspired Oscar Asche to write and produce this one. He plays the lead role of Abu Hasan, who's the leader of the forty thieves. Chu Chin Chow is actually the robber chief himself, who's impersonating one of his victims."

As the complicated plot unfolded, the audience learned that the wealthy merchant Kasim Baba, brother of Ali Baba, was preparing to give a lavish banquet for a wealthy Chinese merchant, Chu Chin Chow, who is on his way from China. The robber chieftain, Abu Hasan, wished to add Kasim's property to his own riches. By holding her lover hostage, Abu Hasan forces his captive, the beautiful Zahrat Al-Kulub, to spy for him. She is nearly found out several times. She tells Hasan about the banquet, where he arrives at Kasim's palace disguised as Chu Chin Chow, whom Hasan's gang has robbed and murdered. He tries to glean information that will enable him to rob his host.

In the meantime, the slaves tell Ali Baba about Hasan's secret cave and the password, "Open, sesame." Ali Baba helps himself to some of the thieves' treasure. Kasim persuades his brother to tell him where his sudden wealth came from and slips out to see what he can find at Hasan's cave. Kasim finds the treasure but is captured by Abu Hasan and put to death. Finally, on the eve of an attack on Ali Baba's family planned by Abu Hasan, Zahrat gets her revenge on Hasan. Zahrat disposes of the forty thieves using traditional boiling oil, stabs Abu Hasan, and, generally, saves the day. The lovers are united, and all ends happily.

"Now that was great theatre," Ashley announced as the boys applauded during the third curtain call. "Oscar Asche was absolutely magnificent."

"I agree," Phillip said. "He's the finest actor I've ever seen. I'd really love to work with him."

"Let's go back stage and tell him," Ashley suggested. "I know he used to tour with the Bensonians. So did I. We're theatre mates, aren't we?"

Within a short while the boys had convinced the stage doorman they were both Bensonians who wanted to visit *Chu Chin Chow's* star. He escorted them to Asche's dressing room, which was crowded with members of both the audience and the play's company. The boys stood in a short line with each person in turn addressing Oscar Asche, seated royally in front of his dressing table. When Ashley arrived at the front of the queue, he told Asche of his shipboard experience with Benson. He also mentioned his meeting the Townsends whom Asche remembered fondly. The famed actor seemed delighted to have met Ashley who, in turn, introduced him to Phillip.

"Sir," Phillip said earnestly, "You're the finest actor I've ever seen. Thank you for a marvelous performance." He paused, adding, "Incidentally, I'm an actor, too." Handing Asche his program, he asked, "May I have your autograph?"

"Of course, young man," Asche said, signing his name, and saying aloud, "To Phillip, a budding actor with whom I hope to work one day. Cheers, Oscar Asche."

"Thank you, sir. This was an honor. Good luck to you, sir."

"And to both you lads," Asche responded.

Their return train ride to Bristol was uneventful. They merely basked in fond memories of the previous fortnight.

Chapter 15
The Rehearsal Becomes a Play

Bristol, 1917

In January, Miss Joyce had a short meeting with her drama students. "I'm not going to be able to begin teaching classes for several weeks," she announced. "I've been cast in a Pinero play that's opening here in Bristol." Little did Ashley and Phillip know her small part would turn into a major learning experience for them.

"A part in a play, Miss Joyce? Pray tell, what is it? With whom?" asked Judith. Other students enthusiastically expressed their interest and good wishes for their adored teacher's good fortune.

"I'm to perform the role of Mrs. Orreyed in *The Second Mrs. Tanqueray*," Miss Joyce announced. The best news of all, however, is that Mrs. Pat Campbell, the original lead, is going to be the star."

"Mrs. Pat!" "The Mrs. Campbell - the famous actress?" "She's a legend," were among the students' reactions.

"She's England's greatest performer," Ashley said.

"Yes, Mrs. Pat Campbell. I'm very thrilled," responded their teacher. "And, the original Mr. Tanqueray, the equally prominent, Mr. George Alexander, is the producer. Phillip, because of your outstanding work in my school, I've asked Mr. Alexander if you could be my guest at rehearsals. I've told him about you, and, that despite your youth, you're going to be a talent to reckon with."

"Oh, Phillip, I'm so pleased for you," Judith expressed both the delight and the guarded envy of her classmates.

"Thank you, Miss Collins," responded Phillip, as he whispered to Ashley, whose amicable jealousy was written plainly on his face, "I'll try to get you a chance to go with me, Ash. Really I will."

"Phillip, the first rehearsal is tomorrow at seven at the Old Vic." Handing him a large envelope, she explained, "The script is in here. I'll expect you to have read it before the rehearsal. I'm leaving your name with the stage door-keeper." Knowing whom he'd choose, she added, "And you can bring one friend. Remember, only one. All right?" Phillip nodded his assent.

Addressing the group, Miss Joyce said, "Now class, As this is our last meeting for a while, and to celebrate my good fortune, I've purchased tickets in the stalls for opening night two weeks from Friday for all of you,"

Charles Robinson led his friends with verve, two hands waving in the fashion of an orchestra director, and they joined him with, "Hip, hip, hooray. Hip, hip, hooray." Miss Joyce blushed and happily shook every student's hand as they gaily and in animated conversation left the Green Room. Phillip and Ashley remained.

Phillip said humbly. "Thank you, Miss Joyce, for all you've done. I've really come around to this idea of an actor's life."

"You have genuine natural talent, Phillip. It must be shared. I'm going to help you in every way. And, Ashley, "You're learning. You just keep it up," she said assuredly. "Will you be coming to rehearsals with Philip?"

"Yes, he will," Phillip answered for his friend. "He'll tell his parents he has to make up work in the commercial school." The boys chuckled at this private joke. Miss Joyce extinguished the lights, and they all donned their hats and rainwear, collected their umbrellas, and departed into the rainy night.

Phillip laid The Second Mrs. Tanqueray script on top of his large Dickens's Tale of Two Cities, and, during two department store recesses, was able to read the entire Arthur Pinero work. During his lunch period, he had arranged a meeting with Ashley to exchange the script for the latter's digestion. Ashley put scrapes of an hour together during the afternoon at the office so that, he too, could finish the manuscript. They met for fish and chips at Duffy's near the Old Vic at half past five to discuss the play.

The boys learned from one of the actors that *The Second Mrs. Tanqueray* had originally opened in London at the St. James's Theatre on 27 May 1893. It ran for 225 consecutive performances and was unanimously accepted by the newspaper drama critics as "an unequivocal triumph." Mrs. Patrick Campbell, as Paula Tanqueray, was hailed as "the belle of the British theatrical ball" and "a magnificent actress." Pinero was praised as having perfected the "well-made play" and "written on a scale with Shaw."

Together, in preparation for the initial Bristol rehearsal, the boys took turns describing the complicated Pinero plot. Phillip went first. "The play opens with Aubrey Tanqueray, in his rooms at the Albany, explaining to his two friends,

Frank Misquith, a widower, and Gordon Jayne, that he intends to marry a second wife."

Ashley continued, "Tanqueray's wife and her husband had no real heart relationship. She was a cold person, one, who, Tanqueray's other male friend said, 'only showed warmth when she was dying of fever."

Phillip interrupted, "She was an elevated type of woman and of respectable virtue, but was too self-centered and unloving for her husband. Even so, they had a daughter, Ellean, who was brought up as a Catholic and put away in an Irish convent to become a nun."

"Right-o," said Ashley. "Lacking proper female companionship, Tanqueray sought a totally different type of woman than his departed wife, what I'd call a 'fallen woman,'" he suggested in adult fashion. Phillip nodded his agreement. "She had a doubtful past and was known under several names, Paula Ray and Mrs. Jarman...What was the other name, Phillip?"

"Mrs. Dartry," he responded, adding, "The second Mrs. Tanqueray was very beautiful, frail, and certainly not an iceberg like the first one."

"She reminded me of Angela. Remember Phillip, that governess I told you about?"

"Yes," answered Phillip with noticeable envy. Then sounding like Miss Joyce describing a play to the class, he said, "We first meet Paula in her future husband's quarters late that night. She feels bored and lonesome and questions Tanqueray whether he's done the right thing by marrying her."

"She's even written about all her earlier transgressions and sealed the note in an envelope," Ashley added.

"Tanqueray wants the past to stay there and puts the envelope in the burning fireplace without even reading it," Phillip inserted. "He wants everything to turn out happily and desires to begin a new happy marriage in his country seat at Highercoombe, near Willowmere, Surrey. He believes he can help Paula rise to his own social strata and dreams of contented bliss."

"Oh, such a happy ending," teases Ashley. "But it is not to be. He receives a letter from his daughter, Ellean. She's worried about his loneliness, so she's coming home."

"The next act finds the still disturbed couple at the country manor. Grandeur withstanding, the newly-married Mrs. Tanqueray is still sorry for herself and extremely bored with country life," Phillip said, adding, "Which is no life at all!"

"They're not even visited by the first Mrs. Tanqueray's closest friend, their neighbor," Ashley points his finger at Phillip.

"Mrs. Cortelyon," Phillip answers correctly. "With whom Cayley Drummle, Mr. Tanqueray's mate, is staying. Now what about the relationship between number two and the daughter?"

"It's a shambles that hasn't even had a chance to start. Their temperaments, their interests, their backgrounds..."

"And their morals," interrupts Phillip.

"Are all different," Ashley finishes. "To resolve her boredom, Mrs. Tanqueray invites her old companion, Mrs. Mabel Orreyed to visit."

Phillip interrupted. "Skillfully played by the splendid actress, the renowned Miss Joyce Russell. And her drunkard husband, Sir George Orreyed, a low-life among the aristocracy if there ever was one, also is to visit for an undetermined period of time." Changing the topic to reality, "Do you want another cup of tea, Ashley?"

"No thanks. Let's finish the play."

"All right. In the midst of the alienation found in the Tanqueray household, Drummle brings Mrs. Cortelyon to apologize for her neglect, but Mrs. Tanqueray is cool to her appeal for friendship, already jealous of the ardor that seems to flow between the neighbor and her stepdaughter. Mrs. Cortelyon invites Ellean to accompany her to Paris. Though her father tends not to acquiesce, Drummle counsels him. What's that superb line? Look it up, Ashley?" Phillip requests.

Reading from the script, "Even a saint should get the hem of her skirt a little dusty," Ashley smirked.

"While Ellean is abroad with Mrs. Cortelyon, she meets and falls in love with a certain Captain Hugh Ardale, a young officer who has gained conspicuous honors for bravery in the India theatre."

"And is very handsome," adds Ashley.

"Where does it say that?" questioned Phillip.

"I just supposed it. Shouldn't I?" asked Ashley.

"Meanwhile, because Mrs. Tanqueray has jealously intercepted, but not read, Ellean's letters, the home front is unaware of their contents." Phillip continues. "And so the wanderers return from foreign lands, Mrs. Cortelyon anxious to explain that she is not to blame for the daughter falling in love, and Ellean looking forward just as anxiously to introducing her father to her future husband."

"And we mustn't forget number two, Phillip! Remember, she's also jealous of the relationship between Mrs. Cortelyon and Ellean."

"Right-o," said Phillip. "But, the plot thickens. It seems that Captain Ardale, who has accompanied the ladies, and Paula have met before," he suggested with the expression of a police detective pleading his case. "As a matter of fact, there was a time in London when they lived together."

"Oh, the shame of it." Ashley mimed the reaction of a prudish lady.

"And now the plot unravels. Mrs. Tanqueray confesses to her husband. Hugh departs. Ellean realizes the truth. The father won't let her marry a tarnished man. He doesn't know what to do about his wife."

"And what of the Orreyeds?" asked Ashley.

"They're still upstairs. What difference do they make?"

"None. I just wondered if you read the whole play," teased Ashley. "Then what happens?"

"You know, she kills herself. Mrs. Tanqueray commits suicide. What a splendid ending!"

"Why do you think so?" asked Ashley.

"I'm not sure. I just think it's splendid!" was Phillip's response. "Come on. It's almost time for the rehearsal."

With permission granted by the stage doorkeeper, the two boys found their way into the fully lit auditorium, sitting far to the right side where they would not interfere with the proceedings. A few men and women were scattered among the seats. On stage, Miss Joyce stood with several actors and actresses. An extremely tall, handsome gentleman had their attention.

"That's George Alexander!" Phillip exclaimed. "He was the original Mr. Tanqueray. It said so in the newspaper. I recognized him from a newspaper picture. Where's Mrs. Pat Campbell?" he asked.

"Who else could she be?" responded Ashley, his eyes riveted to a slender, stunningly attractive dark-haired woman standing next to Miss Joyce. "She's absolutely keen! But, she's really pretty old, isn't she?"

Alexander turned to the fragmented audience. "You've all been invited here as guests of the actors. During rehearsals," he instructed, "I'd appreciate your being as silent and cooperative as possible. We've only nine days to prepare for our opening here in Bristol, and only two of us are familiar with the play. Just pretend you're not here. Thank you," he said as turned back to his cast.

"Remember my friends, the first Mrs. Tanqueray was a

cold and impassive saint; the second is a reckless, emotional, irresponsible sinner," the actor-manager instructed. "Can happiness be found on such terms? Can a man with one nature find satisfaction with an infatuation in an eccentric contrast of a woman? This is the essence of the play," he continued. "If such a thing were possible, life would have no moral laws. A person's character would be a scramble rather than one with definite and ineradicable tendencies."

"We are what we have made ourselves," Mrs. Campbell contributed. "Aubrey Tanqueray can no more win contentment than I, as the second Mrs. Tanqueray, can wipe out my sordid past. Mr. Pinero has shown me, as I am, a woman who has made it impossible, both for herself and the people with whom she lives, to win peace. Each of you must carry out your part as faithfully as the meaning of the lines you're reading. You must stay in character. The contrasts are very significant."

"Mrs. Campbell, give the speech about your future." Alexander asked.

Pausing to gather the words from within her vast theatrical memory, the famous actress closed her eyes, placed one hand over them, and, as she raised the other dramatically, with a voice that rebounded from the rear walls of the theatre, began the famous Pinero reflection, "And when the young ones gradually take the place of the old there will still remain the sacred tradition that the dreadful person who lives at the top of the hill is never, under any circumstances, to be called upon!"

Crossing from the center of the stage amidst the group towards her right, she continued, "And so we shall go on here, year in and year out, until the sap is run out of our lives, and we're stale and dry and withered from sheer solitary respectability." Glancing at the group, "Upon my word, I wonder that we didn't see that we should have been far happier if we'd gone in for the devil-may-care sort of life in town!" Fixing her eyes directly on her leading man, she looked longingly at him. "After all, I have a set, and you might have joined it. It's true, I did want, dearly, dearly, to be a married woman, but where's the pride in being a married woman among married women who are... married!"

Phillip grabbed Ashley's hands as the younger boy started to clap. "Don't. You mustn't."

"Wasn't she wonderful?" Ashley said, glowing with admiration, pointed to the stage. "Look they're applauding!"

And sure enough, the assembled cast was clapping their hands enthusiastically, adding appropriate compliments: "Bravo." "Splendid." "What a reading!"

"Thank you, Mrs. Campbell," the director commented. "You'll also notice Pinero's skill at reading people when he uses Aubrey to point out the 'out-of-the-way' comments that Paula makes so spontaneously. Listening to the one person he wants to be happy and contented, he hears curiously warped, and very selfish, dreadful utterances. It would be hard still to find any English piece so strong and powerful," he said. "But there is no figure, not a one of you, who is totally sympathetic. Paula, the heroine, uses words that make us shudder. Aubrey, our dutiful hero, has motives in his second marriage that are not very lucid. He's chivalrous because he's foolish. He's noble, even though he lacks common sense. What about your role, Miss Pennytree, what's your reading of Ellean?"

The young, mid-twenties, handsome actress, feeling tested, replied. "I'm not really of this world. I'm too different, too religious, too aloof."

"Too much the prude," interrupted Alexander. "You're right! And what of your character, Mr. Cavindish?"

Cavindish, playing the role of Cayley Drummle, took his time to answer, "I'm a good-natured chap, worldly, a bit like the Greek chorus. I bring messages, and I provide a bit of contrast to the other characters."

"There's another reality, Cavindish. Cayley Drummle might be considered as a male Mrs. Tanqueray. Yet, you see, his infidelities are taken lightly. He's not the tarnished soul of his opposite!"

"Umm. I never thought of him that way. You're right of course, Mr. Alexander. That's something to ponder," said Cavindish.

"If we paint all of our characters the same color, we'll have a bland portrait. If we treat each of them differently, it won't be black upon black, but blue on red, yellow on green, different roots for different human emotions. I approach Aubrey Tanqueray as a chivalrous aristocrat desiring to raise Paula Ray to his own level while still attempting to maintain the innocence of his daughter. He's not an easy character to portray or to comprehend. His motives are not really clearly defined. Nor are they decisive. His attitudes throughout the play are rather monotonous - chivalrous affection, unending patience, a quiet protector exercising neither temper nor strain. These are qualities he must exhibit. At the end, despite his world falling apart before him, he is resolute to still face the future. Are you all with me?" Alexander asked earnestly.

The actors nodded politely.

"Even the small part of Captain Ardale is essential to the plot," Alexander continued. "He could not be a person who the author refers to through his character's words. He must physically face Paula to enable the audience to actually feel the tension present and believe that the past relationship took place. Otherwise, it would be hearsay. With both actors encountering one another, it is believable."

Phillip whispered to Ashley, "He sounds like our school master, Dr. Norwood, interpreting Dickens, doesn't he?"

"True," Ashley whispered back, "but he's much more interesting."

"It was Pinero's intent," continued George Alexander, "to have his dominant character, Mrs. Tanqueray, stand out in contrast to the rest. She has to be a miserable woman whose nature has been poisoned by a wayward life. Every gesture, every action and tone of voice has to be a harsh and grating discord in this new existence that she must find impossible to endure. Mrs. Campbell must almost act against each of you rather than with you, do you understand?" he asked.

"And Miss Russell, how would you define your role?" asked the famed actor.

Pleased to at last be recognized, Miss Joyce responded eagerly, "I'm still what Paula was. I'm not trying to change. I don't need to. I've got a money ticket to the future in Sir George, and I'm not letting go, not for anything."

"That's the spirit, Miss Russell! You're another important contrast to the heroine. You're still happy wallowing in the mire that she wants to leave."

Before George Alexander left the theatre that night, Miss Joyce introduced her two pupils to him, suggesting that he might have to cast Phillip in a future production.

"I'll make note of that, young man," he said to Phillip. Ashley watched in awe.

For the next several evenings, the boys faithfully watched the unfolding of rehearsal after rehearsal of the famous play. During the first several days, the group of thirteen actors wandered about the undecorated stage in street dress, scripts in hand, with the stage manager reading the lines of Aubrey and Paula Tanqueray, all under the alert command of George Alexander. As he directed them in position, voice inflection, or movement across the stage, the actors made notations in their scripts. During each of the first four days, the actors carefully followed this procedure through each of the four acts three times, two during the day between ten a.m. and four p.m., and once in the evening starting promptly at seven p.m., with each actor reading his lines from the script. Phillip and Ashley, because of school and work, attended only the evening rehearsals.

The next four evenings, the cast, all having firmly memorized their respective lines and each other's, moved about the stage and worked together more naturally. Mrs. Campbell and George Alexander acted out their parts with the rest. Rather than interrupt them during their speeches, Alexander would stop the rehearsal and make his verbal comments between the "French scenes," which meant dividing the acts, as they had learned at the Russell Drama School, every time a new character entered the stage.

"This," Miss Joyce had told the boys, "changes the dynamics of the scene. Whenever one or more people come onto the stage, the relationships between the characters change. Each French scene is like a rung on the ladder leading to the final destination."

On the Wednesday night at the end of the rehearsal, Alexander stood on the forestage addressing his cast who were seated in the pit in front of him. Ashley and Phillip and a few others were inconspicuously scattered throughout the auditorium. "Tomorrow we will run through the play three times, twice during the day, the final time in the evening. In the evening, I want you in your costumes. Miss Meredith, the costume mistress, has worked with each of you on your outfits. You should be prepared. We'll also work with props like the drinking scene in Act 1 and the letters and envelopes. There will be no interventions during these rehearsals. We'll make straight runs through the play. I'll take notations and share them with you after each performance." Turning to his stage manager, Alfred, in the prompter's corner, he asked, "Fred, anything to say?"

The stage manager nodded his no.

"At this point," Alexander commented, "I must compliment you. You're all pulling together quite well. Are there any questions or comments?" He acknowledged the famous leading lady who had remained somewhat detached from her fellow players. "Mrs. Campbell!"

Rising from among the pit seats, the vivacious woman scanned the actors who had turned towards her. "George, I do believe that this cast is superior to the one we started with in London. I really believe it!" She sat down glowing in the appreciative smiles of the cast members and warmly took Miss Joyce's outstretched hand.

"Isn't that keen?" Phillip whispered to Ashley. "I think she's accepted them!"

"On Friday, you must rest the entire day for the opening performance," George Alexander told his cast. "We have a sell-out crowd. Leave your costumes with Miss Meredith tomorrow night. She must press them. Is there anything else?"

Silence was his answer.

"Good night and God bless," he said, meaning it.

Friday night, the company's opening to a full house was flawless. When the curtains rose for the first act, the sight of the famed George Alexander brought first a few appreciative whistles, added with light applause, which crescendoed into a thunderous collective clapping. Then the entire audience rose as one to pay its ardent respect. The male actors, all professionals, adlibbed their activities, pretending to continue a tête-à-tête over cigars and drink as if the din only prevented them from being heard. Once the audience had settled back into their seats, the dialogue onstage began the introduction to the characters and the moralistic Pinero plot.

Misquith opened the play with, "Aubrey, it is a pleasant yet dreadful fact to contemplate, but it's nearly fifteen years since I first dined with you. You lodged in Piccadilly in those days, over a hat-shop. Jayne, I met you at that dinner, and Cayley Drummle."

When the distinguished, still beautiful Mrs. Pat Campbell entered the set of the bachelor's quarter to embrace Alexander, the audience repeated itself in their collective overt welcome. The duo engaged in animated discussion before the appreciative noise subdued, until Alexander could exclaim, "Paula! Paula!" and Mrs. Campbell could answer with a soft adoring, "Dearest."

Ashley and Phillip had memorized every word in the play by now. They sat in the rear of the theatre, entranced by the theatrical spectacle unweaving before them. Soon, they were both immersed in the imaginary world of drama, mesmerized by becoming totally lost in the action that familiarly transpired. Each gesture, word, or movement carried their intense interest. They were also captivated by the realistic performance of their teacher, Miss Joyce.

"She's splendid, isn't she?" said Ashley to his friend, whose eyes seemed glued to his beloved mentor, despite her suggestive costume and overdone make-up.

Phillip finally managed, "They're all splendid."

And the Bristol drama critics agreed. So did the several London paper theatre reviewers. The next day's theatrical columns stated: "Mrs. Patrick Campbell gave a remarkable performance as Mrs. Paula Tanqueray, but it was the play and not the player that accounted for the extraordinary first night success." "Bold, trenchant, and heroic in treatment, subtle in thought, vigorous in portraiture, and happy and incisive in dialogue, *The Second Mrs. Tanqueray* is a dramatic masterpiece." "This revival is better than the original!" "London, take notice. It's coming back again!" "*The Second Mrs. Tanqueray* is very strong, very grim, and very true; and it deals with abiding and fundamental elements of human nature." And further down in several of the columns were such comments as "Miss Joyce Russell was a perfect casting as Mrs. Campbell's chum. She was everything she should have been, and more." "A rising young actress, Joyce Russell, almost stole the play from a most professional cast. Her performance was one of the finest ever seen on a Bristol stage. She is a talent that Alexander and Campbell reckoned with and both of them are the better because of it."

"Good for her!" exclaimed Ashley as he finished reading from the *Bristol Evening News*. "Maybe she'll have to close the school."

"I hope not," responded Phillip adoringly. "She's been my inspiration."

Chapter 16
The Birmingham Repertory Company

Birmingham, 1917

John Drinkwater, Birmingham's major playwright and director, was true to his word. After Richard Bates had written a letter on their behalf, Drinkwater mailed a promise to Phillip and Ashley that they were invited to visit the Birmingham Repertory Theatre. On Tuesday evening, February 1917, as arranged, the boys arrived from Bristol at the Birmingham Train Station. After a five-minute walk down Station Street, they entered the theatre through the backstage door, warmly welcomed by the stage doorkeeper, Arnold Towers. His name was painted on the wall by his glass cage with the round opening. He graced them with a happy smile, saying, "Mr. Drinkwater wanted you to see the rep company in action. Put down your bags in my office and come with me to the front of the house."

Setting their suitcases along the wall in the tiny cubicle,

Phillip and Ashley followed the middle-aged gentleman around the corner where well-dressed people were milling about, lined up for their tickets at the box office, hastily inhaling from a cigarette, debarking from taxis, or serving as models for all pre-theatre goers everywhere preparing for a night of make believe. The boys accepted the two tickets handed to them by Mr. Towers, gave them to a uniformed boy at the theatre entrance who was only a tad older than they, and walked up the carpeted stairs to the balcony. The walls were lined with black-and-white photographs of actors in scenes of previous plays and an occasional poster announcing a new play to be performed by the Birmingham Company.

The lady seated in front of them was wearing a dress appearing to be made from bird feathers; she was gossiping loudly with her male companion, a gray-haired gentleman in a tuxedo. She said loudly, "This triple bill, as a whole, was well received at the first two performances on Saturday and Monday. However, the newspaper critic mentioned that some might be offended by religious implications. I wonder what that means."

Her male friend responded, "When I purchased our tickets, I learned that almost the whole of the seats in the balcony were booked in advance for tonight, nearly half of them to one person for a party. Wonder why those six or eight police officers are lurking in the lobby."

The woman looked around the balcony audience nervously, smiling meekly at the two boys behind her. "There don't appear to be any hostile-looking people here tonight," she remarked.

Just then, the lights in the auditorium dimmed. The first play was about to begin. "Thrilling isn't it, Phillip?" Ashley admitted to his friend, as the volume of murmuring voices lowered.

Members of the balcony appeared somewhat restless before the first play, *The Workhouse Ward*, but apparently enjoyed it. Written by Lady Gregory of Dublin's Abbey Theatre, it had been quite successful as a quaint, realistic comedy of lower life. It received its usual reaction of laughter and applause. As the curtain went up on the next one-acter, *Everybody's Husband*, there was bit of hissing and booing, but it subsided quickly, and no one knew why it happened. But when *The Tinker's Wedding* began, pandemonium let loose. The row was dreadful. All around the boys, boos, hisses, shouts, and singing prevented a single word of the play from being heard. Items were thrown from the balcony onto the stage, one of which was a large latchkey. As the main curtain started to close, during a slight lull in the noise, actress Marie O'Neill picked it up, put it in her pocket and shouted out to the audience, "One of you won't get in tonight!"

Once the main curtain was dropped, the house lights turned on again. Slowly, the noise lessened. The curtain was again drawn open, and the actors began the scene. Unfortunately, after they had exchanged a few lines, the result was the same - pandemonium. Drinkwater appeared on the stage from the left wings. In his quiet, charming manner, he very quickly calmed the vocal storm and obtained a hearing from several gentlemen standing in the front rows of the balcony. Drinkwater said in a friendly tone, "I have no idea why you're making this disturbance. Will someone explain it to me? Will you choose a spokesman?"

Several balcony members each began speaking at once, drowning out one another.

When these subsided, one of the leaders of the uprising in the front row shouted out, "Our main objection to the play, gov'ner, is representn' the Catholic priesthood in an untrue and unfavourable light!" He went on to say he regretted that he and his friends had inconvenienced the Rep Theatre, but they considered it their duty to protest.

Drinkwater responded. "But I don't understand why you're objecting to something you've neither seen nor heard." The debate went on for several minutes but ended when Drinkwater informed the audience that the performance would continue. The protestors proclaimed that if it did, no one should hear it. This discussion had been quaintly courteous on both sides, rather like the ceremonious preliminaries to a fisticuffs match.

The play commenced; so did the deafening din. By the time the final curtain fell, the boisterousness had become a riot. The actors could not hear one another's lines, and all kinds of objects were still being thrown onto the stage. The very small body of police couldn't have been more polite, softly speaking to the protestors, pointing at the loudest and placing their fingers on their lips to encourage silence, but they were only standing by to insure that no serious violence occurred.

Fortunately, no one was hurt, but when Phillip and Ashley went onstage to thank Mr. Drinkwater, amongst the debris, they inventoried a metal cigarette case, two clasp-knives, three apples, two oranges, a large quantity of plaster that had been knocked off the walls, and other articles that had been thrown at the actors.

Phillip noticed that only a few members of the audience had left the theatre during the melee, with most remaining until the end; everyone seemed to enjoy the entire evening's unexpected excitement. The police had recommended to John Drinkwater that the comedy close that night. Drinkwater argued that this would have been unjust to the play and might be construed as an admission that the theatre had made a mistake.

The box office staff was informed that, in the future,

no more than four balcony seats could be sold to any one person for the rest of the week. The next evening, one of the actresses, Marie O'Neill, with a heavy dark shawl covering her face, and, in a loud, rough, Cockney voice, asked for fifty tickets. One of the girls phoned the business manager for advice, whispering that a low London peasant was making trouble. Marie had already disappeared.

The three-act set ran for a full week after Phillip and Ashley had returned to Bristol. No further disturbances occurred, but the incident itself and the following newspaper coverage served as invaluable advertisements for the plays, resulting in full houses for each subsequent performance of the *Tinker's Wedding* when it was on a billing.

John Drinkwater had asked Phillip and Ashley if they would like to join the Company as apprentices. Both were quite excited but admitted they had to gain parental permission.

Returning to Bristol, Ashley, sadly, attended his mother's anticipated funeral, and it was several months before he gained his father's blessing to join the Birmingham Repertory Company. Happily, he informed his employers that he was joining a theatrical company and left their service with a sizable bonus.

Ashley started correspondence with both the Townsends, who had emigrated to Canada, and Richard Bates, who was touring the United States with a Benson company.

Phillip's parents were both quite enthusiastic about his new opportunity. "It will help mature you, give you new insights on life. Then, you can return for me to groom you to eventually take over our store," his father suggested. Phillip doubted that outcome.

On the train bound from Bristol to Birmingham, Ashley and Phillip realized this was the opportunity they had hoped for over the last two years. They were finally members of a theatre company. They shared what they knew about the productions planned by the Birmingham Company for the coming season.

"There're several Russian translations," noted Phillip, looking up from the play list. "I've only heard of Chekhov's *The Proposal*."

"I've no idea except what the name implies," responded Phillip. "Here's a Tolstoy play. I thought he wrote novels. Remember? We read his book, *War and Peace*, in our literature course at BGS."

"And it was difficult reading. I wonder what his play'll be like." Ashley mused.

"Oh, good. Along with all that heavy-sounding drama, here's a comedy by Eden Philpot. It's called *The Farmer's Wife*. And here. This is an opera. I despise opera. Nothing interesting ever happens. Fat people in fancy costumes just stand around and sing to one another."

"It's really the music that people want to hear with operas," Ashley contributed.

"You're out of your flipping mind, Ashley," retorted Phillip. "They want to listen to the singers. That's what opera's all about. Except that this one is translated from Japanese. It's called *The Sumida River*."

"A-so, da Sim-a-da Lee-var," repeated Ashley, trying to sound as Japanese as he could.

"You don't even look the part, much less sound like it. Do you think the producer will want the actors to speak English with a Japanese accent or the Queen's English?" Phillip asked.

"The Queen's. If you couldn't understand my excellent pronunciation of English with a Japanese accent, how could a Birmingham audience?" Ashley pondered.

Just then, a distinguished, middle-aged lady entered their compartment.

"Do you mind if I sit in this compartment?" She asked. "It's far less crowded than the one I left." Her green velvet dress and silvery fur coat suggested wealth. Her wide brimmed hat with thick feathers extending from the sides added dignity. She nodded and smiled at them as she sat in the empty seat that faced the boys. For a long time, she read a newspaper, while Ashley and Phillip left to explore the train from front to back.

After they returned, the lady commented, "Oh dear, it's exceedingly hot. Do you mind if I open the window?"

"Oh, no! Allow me?" exclaimed Phillip, as he unlatched and slid up the window sash. "How's that?"

"The cool air is most refreshing," the lady acknowledged. "Thank you, young man. Let me introduce myself. I'm Miss Anne Fredericka Horniman of Manchester."

"My pleasure, Madame. My name is Phillip Outerbanks," Phillip replied. "This is my friend, Rupert Runbout," he added, pointing to a suddenly frowning Ashley.

"Miss Horniman, are you related to the tea company?" Ashley inquired.

"Why, yes, young man. It was founded by my father."

"It's very good tea," Phillip said.

"And what is your destination?" Miss Horniman asked.

"We're headed for Liverpool on a naval assignment," Phillip answered rapidly. "It's hush-hush. We can't talk about it." Ashley's eyes bore holes through Phillip's head.

"Aren't you two a bit young to be on military duty?"

"That's part of the hush-hush," Phillip responded. "It was the same way in India."

"India! India! What are you talking about?" questioned Ashley.

"Oh, it's all right, old chap. We've finished that assignment," Phillip said with a laugh. "It's no longer secret information."

"Pray tell. What were you doing in India?" Miss Horniman asked with peaked interest.

"You're not supposed to tell anyone. Remember?" said Ashley, catching on to Phillip's fibbing.

"Why not? Miss Horniman seems to be quite a lady. She should probably know why we were sent by the prime minister on our secret mission," Phillip insisted.

"Oh, yes. I'm intrigued."

Moving across the compartment to sit beside Miss Horniman, Phillip put a finger to his lips. "You mustn't tell this to anyone, Miss Horniman. Promise?"

She nodded.

"Rupert and I were trained in a British combat command near Bombay. Our orders were to infiltrate an Indian division as water carriers and find out why there were so many deserters. As boys, in disguise with heavy dark make-up and long white Indian garments with hoods, we wouldn't be suspected," Phillip stated convincingly.

Ashley, warming to the invented story, added, "We spoke English with the same stilted accent the Indians use. They, the Indian soldiers, accepted us without question.

We spent a fortnight with a roving patrol that inspected small villages looking for deserters."

On and on the boys carried their fictitious story. Miss Horniman appeared to consider every word carefully, asking questions as their narrative continued. "So, how did you eventually bring the Indian ringleader to justice, the one who was selling the deserters their liberty?" she asked.

"One night, it was very late and very dark on the patrol. He was the sergeant in charge and called for a flask of water. When I approached him, he reached for the flask I was holding and took a quick swallow. I said, 'That's poisoned. You're going to die. Do you want the antidote?"

"He clasped his hands around his neck like he was being

hung by a rope," added Ashley. "He looked like he was turning blue. 'Yes. Yes. Why have you done this to me? Yes, the antidote!' he shouted."

"I said, 'Sign this confession.' He did. I drank from the flask, and we put him in handcuffs and led him away to the station's commander."

"How brave you both were," complimented Miss Horniman. "What a fascinating story. Thank you for this delightful entertainment. Now I must prepare for my arrival in Manchester. Ta-ta, gentlemen." Miss Horniman left the compartment and headed down the narrow train corridor.

The minute she was out of vocal range, the boys collapsed in glee. "You rascal," declared Ashley happily. "Why do you make up such wild stories?"

"Wasn't it ripping?" said Phillip, a broad devilish grin on his face. "I had Miss Horniman reeled in on my hook."

When Miss Horniman returned from her primping expedition, the boys were ready to debark at the Birmingham station.

After their farewells, Miss Horniman mused aloud, "I thought those two charming young chaps were going to Liverpool."

As they were entering the station lobby, the boys heard their names shouted out. "Phillip, Ashley, over here."

"Oh, it's the good Mr. Towers, come to pick us up," acknowledged Phillip.

They greeted one another warmly and walked full abreast down Station Street.

As they entered through the open backstage doorway, Towers said, "Boys, Gov'ner Drinkwater has asked me to spend your first morning giv'n you a little history 'bout the Birmingham Rep. We don't start rehearsals 'til next Monday. This afternoon, you'll be off to search for digs. Until you find sompn', you both can stay in my flat. My boy's off for Army so the missus and I have a spare room for a fortnight or so. I've asked one o' our regular cast members, Miss Cecily Byrne, to join us. She knows the history of the Pilgrim Players more than I do."

"The Pilgrim Players? Who are they?" Phillip asked.

"That's where it all began," responded Towers. After locking the door and leaving a note to knock loudly, the middle-aged man led the boys to the property room where a sofa and two settees awaited them. A handsome young woman was already sitting on one of the settees, dressed comfortably in men's dark trousers and a rumpled white-collared shirt.

"Hallo," she said, rising and shaking the boys' hands. "I'm Cecily Byrne, one of the Company's actresses."

Phillip and Ashley introduced themselves and briefly shared their limited history in the theatrical business with Cecily and Towers.

"Well, actually, that's somewhat like we started, as amateurs," Cecily began. Barry Jackson and John Drinkwater, before he became my husband, formed the Pilgrim Players in 1907. It was strictly a novice theatre group, not a religious organization like many people thought because it played in St. Jude's Mission Hall. It opened with a morality play, *The Interlude of Youth*. The main characters were 'Charity,' 'Youth,' 'Riot,' and 'Humility,' two of them played by Barry and John."

"They wanted to bring new plays to the public, plays that weren't performed on tour by London-based companies, as well as old classics that local theatre groups were keen on," Towers contributed.

"Barry worked on the stage decoration and costumes. John acted and helped with the stage production," Cecily said. "After the first two plays were relatively well received and the newspaper critics approved, we attempted an ambitious rendering of Shakespeare's *The Two Gentlemen of Verona*. It was then that I had the pleasure of joining the company."

"And finding a husband," said Towers chuckling.

Acknowledging him with a nod, Cecily continued. "We used curtains on the sides, and Barry drew beautiful designs depicting outdoor areas. This became the signature of scenery for all our Shakespearean plays, what John termed, 'the draped stage,' one with only curtains. We moved from the Hall to a much larger space, the Edgebaston Assembly Rooms, which could seat 400 patrons. It had footlights and arc lights and a baton to hang more drapes over the stage. That would be our home until 1914."

"The success of the first shows and the general chorus of praise by both newspapers and the public lifted the status of the Players among Birmingham's amateur societies," Towers confided.

"We moved to a schedule of weekly performances of plays from October of one year to May of the following one. John began writing plays. The first one we performed was *Fifenella*, a children's fairy frolic that we've continued to improve over the last twelve years," said Cecily. "We also staged plays by Yeats and Shaw, and, of course, Shakespeare."

"Did you just play in Birmingham or did you travel to other places?" Ashley asked.

"Oh, right. Thanks for the question," Cecily responded. "We first visited Stratford-upon-Avon in 1909 to show off our Shakespeare plays and have returned there almost every year for a small festival with other companies. We've also played before local audiences in King's Heath, Henley-in-Arden, and Worcester. We even went to London to perform W. B. Yeat's *The King's Threshold*. Yeats liked our version so much he invited us to Dublin for three performances in the Irish National Theatre Society's season. That was our comeuppance because both the London and Dublin critics had no sentimental interest in us and, despite a few merits, told of our faults quite clearly."

"By the end of the season in 1911, they had done thirty-five performances. Most o' the cast still worked full time in commercial and government positions, so they played close by Birmin'm and on holidays," Towers offered. "Over the months, they gived Saturday night revivals and also six new one-or two-act plays, two each directed by Mr. Jackson and Gov'ner Drinkwater."

"We were quite heavy on Shakespeare," Cecily continued," Barry began handing out disbursements of cash to the actors. We had a critical need for rehearsal space and a central office. The summer of 1911, eight of us toured twelve local villages on bicycles with Barry's car carrying our luggage and properties. We performed outdoors, presenting scenes from *Twelfth Night* and *As You Like It* and one-act plays. In the villages, playing in gardens, terraces, and castle ruins, we had small but very supportive audiences. By then, we had gained quite a positive reputation."

"But you were still amateurs," Ashley stated.

"No, actually, that was about the time we began regarding ourselves as semi-professional actors. We had begun printing 'The Birmingham Repertory Company' on programmes and announcements, and Barry continued paying small salaries."

Towers contributed, "Now they had a hall, dressn' rooms, rehearsal and storage rooms. They had started printing a journal 'bout theatre and had a comp'ny o' actors. What more could they need?"

"A theatre," Phillip responded.

"Ah, yes. A theatre," Cecily chimed in. "From October 1911 to April 1912, we gave forty-one performances in

Birmingham, plus several short tours. In the autumn, we produced a number of plays. The most popular were *The Return of the Prodigal*, the lovable *Fantasticks,* and *She Stoops to Conquer.*"

"I 'eard Gov'ner Drinkwater had a new play everyone liked, too," Towers interrupted. "Wasn't that when he went into his sick act onstage?"

"Oh, yes, quite right. Thank you again, John. You're speaking about the Gov'ner's, as you call him, one-act, *Copheua*. That was all in verse, and most people preferred to read it in the Player's Journal. No, it was when we were giving a private performance to a group of students when John pulled his illness stunt."

The boys were all ears.

"One of the actors hadn't memorized any of his lines. He had a principal role, and John was playing opposite him. The man, whom Barry dismissed immediately after the performance, came on stage, stumbled around for a few minutes, began gagging in blank verse in an incomprehensible language and finally beckoned to John, who was waiting in the wings for a proper cue, shouting, 'Come hither, brother. I must go hence.' He left the stage just as John walked on."

"What an awful situation!" Ashley exclaimed.

"It was," Cecily said. "John, realizing that the show could not be picked up again, staggered abruptly, put his hand to his head, and fell flat. Doctors were called, and the audience released with their refunded tickets, and John was carried to his home. Those who knew him well proclaimed it his greatest bit of acting. When he appeared that same evening in another play, the audience acknowledged him as a hero rising from his deathbed and gave him a great reception."

"Good for Mr. Drinkwater!" Phillip cried out, clapping his hands.

"In December, we gave our first performance of Galsworthy's *Silver Box*, which was to be one of our most successful plays, and for Christmas, *Puss in Boots*, a straight forward telling of the nursery story."

"We're doing *Silver Box* this season, aren't we?" Phillip asked.

"Right-o, lad," Towers agreed.

"We also received outstanding reviews on our production of Ibsen's *Enemy of the People*. It was the first time many of our Birmingham patrons had seen the realistic characters conceived by this Swedish playwright and the naturalistic set designs of Barry," Cecily said. "Frank Moore's performance of Dr. Stockmann was proclaimed as 'brilliant' by the local press."

"Didn't you also tour for the first time to Liverpool?" Towers asked.

"Yes, and we had fantastic reviews. Since there was already a repertory company there, it's probably what finally convinced Barry to break ground on his own theatre."

"I remember the announcement," Towers recalled. "It was on the tenth of June, 1912. A site had been secured on Station Street and building would begin immediately, but it didn't."

"By then," Cecily said, "the society, in five years, had presented 160 performances of twenty-eight different plays, seven of which were originals. We continued to offer plays in the Edgebaston Assembly Rooms while Barry's theatre was being built."

"Construction started in September. The first production in the new facility was *Twelfth Night*. It opened on fifteen February. That's when Mr. Jackson hired me as the stage doorkeeper," added Towers proudly. "I've kep' things 'n order ever since."

"So you have, John," Cecily acknowledged. "Barry was

the director, John, the general manager, and Bache Matthews was the first business manager. T. Foden Flint, who was to last only one season, was the stage manager. Besant Rice, giving up his position as a drama critic, became our first producer. Additionally, our stage and theatre crew consisted of a stage carpenter, two electricians, a scene painter, two dressmakers, doorkeepers, a fireman, and labourers and cleaners."

"How many actors?" Phillip asked.

"There were twelve of us," Cecily responded, "seven males and five females. We women had all been Pilgrims; all the men, except for two beginners, were hired from other companies. *Twelfth Night* was well received. Audiences liked the simple draped backgrounds and the lighting effects we used. For garden scenes, we drew the curtains away from the plaster and used light blue lights to create a horizon. For interiors, we used steps and pillars in front of the curtains, and placed a few items of furniture where it was needed. We started with full audiences, but they dropped off during the week."

Cecily continued, "The next play was Galsworthy's *The Pigeon*, the first modern play of the season. The characters were well acted, each with strengths and some noticeable weaknesses. Clever author he was, but the plot was too empty. They tried it twice again during the season. It never worked. Audiences just didn't care for it."

"Shaw's *Candida* came along with Miss Madge Mackintosh in the lead," said Cecily. "She was marvelous. Her performances demanded such fine reviews that the London producers took notice. She's now in a new production on the West Side. She was Birmingham's first loss to the London stage."

"*Everyman* and *The Importance of Being Ernest* both went well," Tower voiced. "Course, many o' the cast had performed them as Pilgrim Players. They knew the characters like old friends."

"I'm familiar with *Ernest*," Ashley announced. "It was performed by a professional company on a voyage I once took."

"That's nice," Cecily responded, and then continued the Birmingham theatre history lesson, "After well-attended performances of *The Silver Box* and *The Tragedy of Nan*, we moved into our April Shakespeare plays. On the whole, it was a most successful first season."

"In ninet'n weeks, thy'd done twenty-two plays. Fifteen full length," Towers indicated, reading from a sheet of paper he had just unfolded.

"Besant Rice, our talented and wise producer, was in charge of ten of them, and my John directed six. He was learning on the job. We closed for nine weeks with all of the actors and stage crew receiving full salaries from Barry. He reported that, although the season had lost money, it had been, and would continue to be, a worthwhile investment in the long run."

"What a valuable tale," Phillip responded. "It's quite enjoyable to know all this about the Rep Company. Don't you agree, Ashley?"

"I'm all ears for more."

"The thirteen-fourteenth season saw a few changes," Cecily offered. "Maud Gill joined us as an actress, and Frank Clewlow, who had been an actor, stage manager and producer of wide experience, became our own stage manager. Mr. Flint, who realized the task was a bit much for him, dropped back into the assistant stage manager position. Stuart Vinden signed on as an actor. Audiences especially enjoyed Bernard Shaw's *You Never Can Tell* and our revival of *The Tragedy of Nan*. We brought in a London Shakespearian actor, Allan Wilkie, to play the part of Falstaff and character roles in several of our other Elizabethan offerings. Do you recall when we first used the moving clouds, John?"

"Oh, quite well," Towers concurred. "The first night, I 'eard loud applause and cheern' a quarter a' hour fore the final curtain was to drop on the second one-act play, *Miles Dixon*. I run to the house doors to see what was happen'n. There, right on the rear plaster wall, clouds began to move slowly across the backstage. It was a magic lantern Mr. Jackson found that could throw light through openn's in a round tin. They looked just like the real thing."

"I've never seen that before. Have you, Phillip?" Ashley asked.

"Never."

"We tried another triple bill of one-acts that didn't go so well," said Cecily. "One was written by Strindberg, the Swedish dramatist. Our most prominent Birmingham play critic called it 'a wretched play by a wretched author.' People stayed away in droves. However, our Shakespeare plays in May were quite well received, and John's new play might have been the most successful of the entire season."

"Yes, Miss Bryne, you're correct," agreed Towers. "His work was full of strength and colour, the blank verse was musical and comfortable for the actors to speak, and the plot held the audience in the palms of the Gov'ner's 'ands. His words mesmerized 'em."

"And Barry's costumes and scenery may, by that time, have been the best he's ever conceived," added Cecily. "They were designed in an Assyrian manner, which added to the poetry. Before our summer vacation, we performed four more plays and finished late in June."

Again pulling a paper from his trouser pocket, Towers noted, "That season, the second, thirty-three plays had been presented in forty-two weeks. Nine were revivals. The rest were new to the cast and crew. Now, that's saying a lot for a creative repertory comp'ny, don't ya think?"

"I certainly agree," said Cecily. "Mr. Rice and John directed most of the plays. We had to use a new structure Barry built next door to the theatre to store our properties and the scenery we had made during our first two years. It also still holds the carpenter's workshop and scene-painting room. We'll take you there in a few moments," she added.

"It was then that the war started. Most o' us were out on summer holiday, but we came back to the theatre to find out about our jobs and what was ta become o' our rep company," Tower indicated. "We had several old Army and Navy Reserve gents, who left and never came back. Two o' our young male actors enlisted before the new season began. But the rest o' us agreed ta continue on, even with a depleted comp'ny."

"We started our third season in late August 1914," Cecily recalled, lying further back on the settee. "Five of our male actors and ASM had been replaced, and three of the ladies. At first, it was very difficult. Business dropped to almost nothing. But, instead of cutting down on expenses, Barry tried to add to the attractiveness of performances by adding a string quartet and piano. But that didn't work out well. To cut expenses, we trimmed out parts of plays where several actors were required and turned their roles into single ones. We reduced the number of properties and scenery and lighting effects on stage. We doubled up on parts for different plays, used the crew for walk-ons, and the director appeared as a character in every show he produced, whichever producer it was: John, Mr. Rice, Mr. Vinden, or Barry. Surprisingly, business went better than expected. People wanted to forget about the war raging close to us but not directly in Birmingham. To pick up the spirits of nearby villages, we took five plays from our repertoire to

Wolverhampton, Croydon, Brighton, and Leamington, and, along the way, rehearsed and performed our first production of Ibsen's *The Master Builder*."

"Durin' the five weeks the Company was away," I stage-door kept for two touring comp'nies," Towers proffered. "We had the Esme Percy Company for a month and A .E. Drinkwater's troupe with *Caste* for one week. We had turn-away audiences. When our own comp'ny returned, it opened with Wilde's *A Woman of No Importance.* It was so well received, it ran for two weeks instead o' the usual one."

"That's one of my favorites, too," said Ashley.

"We surprised our audiences by moving the first scene of *Tempest* onto the apron," Cecily said. " Do you know that word, apron?"

Both boys nodded affirmation.

"We played it in darkness with feeble glimmers from lanterns carried by some of our actors. It was so much fun," continued Cecily. "At the end of the scene, we exploded magnesium powder, and, during the flash, the curtain rose to reveal our replica of an island scene, which stood for the rest of the play. The stage looked as if it were covered with great jagged rocks rising from the mouth of a cave on the left side. Beyond the silhouettes of the scenery, only the colour of a brilliant blue was seen on the rear wall. Prospero, Miranda, Caliban, and Ariel were dressed in blue, green, and grey; the shipwrecked crew in scarlet and brown. It caused a sensation with our audiences. They loved it."

Again reading from his list, Towers related the following: "After a disappoint'n fall, there was marked improvement 'fore Christmas, good attendance durin' the winter and marked improvement in the spring. We were appealin' to Birming'm citizens who were new to theatre and yearned for any type of entertainment." Looking up at the boys, he said proudly, "We were train'n our own new audiences."

Taking up his paper again, he continued. "Dur'n this first year of the war season, we produced twenty-two plays, with Gov'ner Drinkwater and Mr. Rice responsible for most of them. It says here that four of the actors and fifteen of the working staff were in the Army. I know two o' em what died in France," he said, a sad look covering his face.

"All of our company spent Sundays working in a local munitions factory," Cecily added. "We were very fortunate that Maud Gill turned out to be a magnificent stage manager and was very popular with both cast and crew. She became a worthy captain of our repertory ship. I was even more heartened when I was cabled to take up an engagement in London to play the leading female role in *Othello*. I didn't want to leave my husband and the Company, but it was an opportunity I couldn't dismiss."

"But you're back now, aren't you?" asked Phillip.

"Yes, our production only lasted three weeks," she responded gaily. "Now, Arnold, let's take them next door before they go out and look for digs."

Chapter 17
The Theatre Apprentices

Birmingham, 1917-18

Ashley and Phillip had been well prepared for their first theater season as apprentices, which would begin in September 1917. Arnold Towers had faithfully sent Phillip weekly clippings from the Birmingham newspapers to keep him and Ashley aware of the Repertory Company activities during the year. Over a number of months from spring through September, they had followed the news faithfully. For their fourth season, the Company had performed seventeen different plays, of which six were one-acts. Sheridan's Restoration play, *The Rivals,* with good reviews and healthy audiences, opened the season, running a fortnight.

After that, the months sailed like a ship at sea. Turbulent waves and storms represented the difficult times and the controversial plays, and the calm, comforting seas occured when patrons and critics enjoyed the productions and praised the acting. Protesters picketed *King Lear's Wife*, a verse play by Gordon Bottomly. Critics called it a "tragedy that prostitutes art," "a beastly play," "almost shockingly crude," and "a drama of blood, lust, and death." It met with little appreciation. A new play by Conal O'Riordan, *His Majesty's Pleasure*, a satire, delightfully witty, well played, and charming to look at in its French boudoir setting, also did not arouse much encouragement. The Shakespearean offerings, as usual, were enthusiastically appreciated.

The highlight of the theatrical year was Drinkwater's direction of a translationi of a Japanese play, *The Faithful*, through which the translator was reported by a local drama critic "to have capably demonstrated his emphasis to portray the poetic beauty of a distant land." Another journalist wrote: "He simplified action by using standing tableaux of his stage pictures, with the impressive great passages ringing out through the stillness." Still another newspaper critic credited the Company's general director and founder, "Jackson had designed a dignified, yet simple, grey setting, which formed a somber background for his brilliantly colorful dresses."

For the Company itself, by the time the boys arrived, numerous new comings and goings of adored stage colleagues were reported. Rice had resigned after a falling out with Jackson, leaving Drinkwater to produce the majority of plays. Established actor Ribton Haines, and the promising John Dunn-Yarker, had enlisted in the military. Ion Swinley, Ivor Barnard, and Miss Mary Merrall were hired for London productions. Newcomers included Arthur Rose, recruited from the Liverpool Repertory Company, and Miss Mielle Maund, with a few others working from time to time as character roles, bit parts, and walk-abouts were required. It was also reported that Barry Jackson spent most of the year in London driving an ambulance. However, he continued to send designs and instructions, and he visited when he could. This was not the same as his being on the spot. The required Military Service Act had come into existence, and it had been a struggle to retain sufficient actors and staff.

By the end of spring, the boys were anticipating their promised appointment as full apprentices come September 1917. They returned to Bristol for the summer, Phillip to the Maggs' furniture store as a salesman, Ashley to the grocery business. His father insisted that he become a delivery boy, so Ashley attended driving school and obtained both an automobile and a lorry license. Both boys attended at least three plays a week by local Bristol amateur or professional groups, as well as the productions of touring companies. After each play, they would dissect the production at a local teashop in terms of acting, set design, lighting, direction, plot, and character development. Ashley faithfully kept rough notes on all of their discussions, saving them in a large metal container, along with the clippings they collected from the newspapers.

As promised, John Drinkwater cabled the boys with confirmations of their Birmingham Theatre apprenticeships.

This fifth Birmingham Repertory season started with a permanent professional group of thirteen who had been joined by several apprentices, including Ashley Thronson and Phillip Maggs, who began working both on and off stage. Mr. Towers had provided the boys lodging in a small room at his home where Mrs. Towers served them a delicious dinner each evening. They relished their apprenticeships and their occasional onstage appearances as walk-abouts. To reduce expenses, casts had to be supplemented with local amateurs, most of whom were entirely without onstage experience. The boys' offstage duties were to serve as needed, paint settings, construct and obtain properties, apply make-up, fill in as dressers, make and fetch tea as directed, and perform whatever other chores stage manager Maud Gill, assistant stage manager Dennis King, or the crew expected of them. If the entire Company was considered a theatrical family, the two boys were its servants. Miss Dorothy Taylor, just a few years older than the boys, who had experience as a pupil of the Company, joined as an ingénue.

The first production of the season was Oliver Goldsmith's *The Good-natured Man,* followed by a new Drinkwater play, *The God of Quiet*. The author of the next play, *The Inca of Perusalem,* was listed in the playbills as anonymous, but the author was a member of the Royal Society of Literature. It was an intellectual play, one that stimulated immediate and extensive thought, with meaty major roles and persuasive Socialistic speeches. The mystery of its unknown writer was a source of conversation, from the time the actors first read the script and began memorizing their parts to its last performance. Performers relished the richness of the play's content. As both critics and patrons raved favorably about the drama, all manner of suspicions arose. Most decided it couldn't have been the product of a novice playwright. The stage directions were so sophisticated, the name of George Bernard Shaw kept emerging as the unidentified author.

Next, *The Silver Box* was revived and favorably received. Three Russian repeats, including Chekhov's *The Proposal* were so popular over a fortnight in September that they were repeated in early December. *The Farmer's Wife* by Eden Philpot was produced for the first time to favorable audience attendance and newspaper reviews. Phillip wrote Richard Bates that Maud Gill had stepped out of her role as stage manager to play the challenging character of Thirza Tapper, wearing the same frumpy costume onstage that she donned for her backstage responsibilities in running the entire performance. "She was smashing," he recounted.

The Japanese opera, *The Sumida River*, was as mysterious for audiences to consider as the unknown name of *The Inca's* author. During Christmas, *Puss and Boots* was performed during the day and *The Critic* by night. Dennis King left for the military and was replaced by Richard Wayne. William Armstrong and Harold French took the posts of two other actors who had departed for compulsory service. *Candida, Thompson*, and *Nan* took the group through February. Two sets of triple bills were offered during the next two months, the first including *The Wounded*, a play written by a Belgian man of letters who had moved to Birmingham because of the war. The second set included Yeat's *The Hour Glass*, validating the influence of Dublin's Abbey Theatre.

By this time, it was apparent that Phillip and Dorothy Taylor were smitten with one another. Phillip always managed to find a seat next to her during play readings and rehearsals, and they often took tea together. If Ashley couldn't find him, he always knew he'd be visiting the downtown Birmingham flat where Dorothy and several actresses resided.

After a run of *The Merry Wives of Windsor*, there was again a triple bill of one-acts, which featured Drinkwater's next original effort, *X=O, A Night of the Trojan War*. Driving hard at the uselessness of war, the play had only male characters, so Gilbert Cannan, who had just joined the Company, hurriedly threw together a one-act satire in which there were five women and only one man. If anything, the Company was extremely adaptable to every condition. Audiences appreciated both plays.

To celebrate Shakespeare' birthday, *Twelfth Night* and *The Two Gentlemen of Verona* were restaged. Jackson, now in the Navy, submitted a new setting for the latter, consisting of platforms and staircases in front of black velvet drapes, which was carefully followed in other productions. As each scene changed, lights would illuminate only one area of the stage. Jackson called it "space staging."

The three one-act plays, staged in pandemonium the previous year because of *The Tinker's Wedding*, went swimmingly. Drinkwater reminded the press that, unless you're aware of the content of a production, you should weigh your protests carefully. The following weeks included *You Never Can Tell* and a rerun of *The Farmer's Wife*, *Partnership*, and *The Charity that Began at Home*. A triple bill consisting, of *X=O, The Cobbler's Shop,* and Gilbert Cannan's newest effort, *James and John*, carried the season to its last night, 23 June. Over this season, the Birmingham Company had added twenty-one plays, including eleven one-act plays, to its repertoire.

Throughout their first long theatrical adventure, Ashley had kept a journal, particularly to stay in close touch with Richard Bates, still on an American tour with the Bensonians. So did Phillip, who included in his letters to Richard his every acting moment on stage, his observations of various actors' techniques: the formalized, intoned, overemphasized performances of Shakespeare; the more realistic dramatics required by playing a peasant in a Russian one-act; and the differences in the delivery of lines for a comedy versus a tragedy. He also sent a weekly review of his own new role as a budding second assistant stage manager. Ashley, inserting his observations of their first real stage experiences and sending his letters along with Phillip's, recounted to Richard his set construction and backstage endeavors, continuing to store his considerable notes in the metal box.

War difficulties were acutely felt: rationing of food and petrol, blackouts, slowed train schedules, fear of bombing raids, and male actors and crew leaving for the service, among them. Drinkwater had appealed to several military tribunals that the theatre was unable to keep enough actors to continue the Company's work. With skilled workmen being taken away, it was hard to find adequate substitutes, and both Phillip and Ashley became indispensable members of the Company, though, at age sixteen, they were still not accepted as professionals.

During the season until June, onstage, the two boys played butlers, restaurant waiters, medieval townspeople, Roman soldiers in togas and golden helmets, frolicking children, wounded soldiers, and even heavily bearded old men in long, dark overcoats. Ashley had no spoken lines, just a few crowd murmurs. Phillip had three: "Your highness," "Aye, sir," and "As you wish."

It was in their construction, painting, and behind the scenes contributions that they flourished. Phillip became the stage manager's shadow, holding the script in the prompt corner, running endless errands, fetching refreshments, bringing garments from the wardrobe lady for actors making changes in the wings, and chalking the players' positions on the stage floor. During rehearsals, assisting Ashley as a provider of various special sounds, he became adept at winding the wind machine, dinging the telly bell, and barking realistically like a Great Dane. Ashley was the darling of the scenic designers, especially Barry Jackson, during the rare times he was present. Beginning as a colour mixer for two set painters, the young apprentice was soon assigned to sketching out the muslin curtains and scenic panels in perspective, while others filled in the colours. He also excelled as a prop maker and staircase builder. Jackson remarked to Maud Gill on one occasion, "This lad is a find in himself. He'll make a splendid backstage worker."

Every Monday morning, a week prior to a play being performed, the cast and crew would gather in chairs set upon the stage in a large circle for the first play reading. Whoever was producing the work would introduce each of the characters and which actors were performing which parts, describing their roles and relationships. He would review the plot and the previously agreed-upon settings and the layout of scenery by the set designer. He identified the placement of three-dimensional objects, furniture, and properties on the stage floor. After answering questions from both the cast and crew, the play-reading would begin, with the actors sitting in place and the stage manager reciting the written stage directions from the script.

Ashley and Phillip enjoyed these sessions immensely. Each new play offered an entirely different opportunity for everyone. Actors who had played leads in the previous play would relish a solidly written character part or comic character for the next one. This was one of the marvelous features of repertory theatre. Over one season, one could play many different roles, each requiring appropriate costumes and make-up. Every participant was usually quite excited about an entirely new theatrical creation, but, at the same time, invigorated and eager.

The boys soon realized how each participant in any given production interpreted a script differently. The general and business managers read plays with an eye for artistic merits and box office potential. Each actor concentrated on what could be done with the part allotted to him. The set designers were absorbed in how their scenery could represent realism, symbolism, or mysticism, how colours would complement the settings and costumes, and ensuring that the sets and properties would be ready by opening night. The director envisioned ever-changing stage pictures, not only how his actors would move on stage, but, more important, why. He insisted that there were always reasons for stage crosses, providing actor placement support for long speeches and appropriate places of stage entry from the wings or through onstage doors mounted in the scenery. The most difficult overall task, they agreed, was that of the stage manager, who had to read a play with, in this case, her mind on its scenic, lighting, and property requirements; special sound effects; and what articles were available, could be adapted, or must be built immediately.

Phillip proved himself capable during his first week with *Good Natured Man*. After that, his weeks were filled with requests from Miss Gill.

"Mark the actor's places in this scene with chalk." As the actors' delivered their lines, Phillip made outlines of the shoes on the stage floor with a white marker.

"We need a high-backed chair for the next act. Here's four shillings. Fetch one from Mr. Collin's furniture store and bring me the receipt." Phillip would leave the theatre, returning in fifteen minutes with a sturdy hardwood chair.

"For the wedding scene, we should have a white cake with four tiers and little figures of the bride and groom on the top. Have Ashley make one out of cardboard tonight so it's ready for tomorrow's rehearsal." Phillip relayed the message to Ashley who complied.

Occasionally, Phillip commented on his orders, learning as he went.

"Take the finished timesheets for this week to Mr. Matthew's office so he can prepare the cheques when the crow flies."

"What? What does a crow have to do with timesheets?" Phillip asks.

"You Dunderhead!" Miss Gill said with a smile. "The crow always flies on Saturday mornings. That's the name of the theatre's traditional payday." Phillip left for the business office.

"Phillip, write up a list of all the actors and actresses and bring it to me for dressing room assignments for the next three one-acts."

"Why can't they stay in the ones they already have?" Phillip asked.

"Mr. Drinkwater likes to mix the cast up occasionally, especially the actors who have several scenes together, don't you know," responded Miss Gill.

But, mostly, he just followed orders.

"Look in *His Majesty's Pleasure* prompter's script, act two, scene six. What's the line before the king's cross from upstage right to downstage left? We have to cue Charles to focus the spotlight with the blue gelatin after the cross." Phillip diligently turned the promptbook pages until he found the essential information.

On the third day of rehearsal for *The God of Quiet*, Miss Gill, calling him over, said, "Phillip, after the actors have left the stage, list all the properties we need for this scene and where they should be placed. Bring me the finished copy as soon as you can, so I can make the set-up assignments. Do the same thing the rest of the day so we can be prepared for tomorrow's rehearsal."

"Go through the *Silver Box* script and mark in red all of the curtain openings and closings and sound effects so we can discuss them later with the crew," Miss Gill requested.

In short order, Phillip learned that the life of a stage manager was nothing but technical details, high order organization, and problem-solving. To him, acting was much more attractive than coaching from the wings.

Ashley, on the other hand, was engaged in the more technical aspects of scenery building and repair, property maintenance, special effects, and lighting. During the week, he was busy painting. He learned how to stretch canvas on a wooden frame called a flat. Usually two meters wide and three meters high, flats were hinged together to form an interior, such as a drawing room, a dining room, an office or an inn. They could also represent exteriors such as a palace wall, the front of a small hut, or a Japanese temple. Two to five doors had to be constructed of canvas and frames and hinged into openings in the flats representing a large interior room. They were held erect on stage by tall triangular supports held upright by stage plugs, large screws with handles, which were attached to the stage floor. Ashley became adept at sketching the exterior of buildings or forests on canvas curtains called drops, which descended from the tall rafters of the stage house, hoisted up and down by ropes through ceiling pulleys from a loft, offstage left, called the flies.

One of Jackson's clever ideas had been to design his scenery shop with a long slot in the floor so that by attaching canvas to a paint frame, the scene painter could have a vertical surface which could be raised or lowed to ground level to enable him to sketch the necessary images and apply the appropriate colours. It also provided space for him to step back and view his work from the audience's perspective. Ashley learned to cut thin pieces of wood into two-dimensional profiles of bushes, trees, statues, and other objects, which, from an audience's viewpoint, strongly suggested the real thing. A scene in the woods was depicted by a drop painted with three to four trees surrounded by bushes, hedges, or bramble and one or two profiled silhouettes of small shrubs strategically placed in front of the drop. A village exterior would be represented by a rendering of an inn and one or two shops designated by signs identifying them as "Baker," "Greengrocer," or "Butcher." Configurations of a water well, a horse-hitching rail, or a tombstone would help to suggest locations.

"Ashley, come hither," Rolph, the Swedish born, fiftyish,

master scenic artist, would regularly begin his instructions. "Come hither, Cecil," he would call to another apprentice. Placing a sketch of the desired scenery that either he or Barry Jackson had prepared, he would painstakingly review every line and colour he wanted Ashley or his assistant scenic designer to reproduce in drops or smaller scenic pieces. Together, they discussed what previously used scenery, protected in the storage area, could be used in its present state or adapted for a different setting. For economy's sake, they knew it was always wiser to utilize what was on hand rather than constructing a new scenic item.

Depending on the length of a play's run, from two days to a week, or whether they were alternating plays nightly, settings could be erected only the night after a final performance or early the following morning to allow the cast one or two rehearsals in full costume before the opening night of the next play. Easiest for the scenic crew were the Shakespearian plays incorporating the so-called draped scene, featuring pillars and steps, so preferred by John Drinkwater.

Ashley also was schooled in the preparation of stage meals and beverages. If it was unnecessary for the actors to pretend they were actually consuming food, he would create a roasted pig or baked chicken out of paper. However, to duplicate real meals that had to be eaten, one never used the real thing. Cold tea, often with added colour, could serve as a substitute for whiskey, rum, cocoa, or coffee. Water was always used for white wine or gin. Bits of bananas could be covered with breadcrumbs to resemble meat, or ginger bread would suffice. Lettuce could be used when it was fresh, but often green paper worked just as well. Apples were also used to perform as themselves or were cut up to copy crumpets, chicken slices, or small sandwiches.

When authors added lit candles to a scene, it had to be

decided whether or not real candles would be incorporated or electrically-controlled candles. The former required candles, candlesticks, shade-holders, fireproofing the shades, and snuffers, if the candles were to be extinguished, as well as matches. Electric candles demanded a separate line to the switchboard, a private switch and attention to the cues when it would be lit or exhumed.

During the middle of the season, Cecily was onstage about to begin a love scene. Crossing from the offstage kitchen, she had carried in a plate containing a large bone, suggesting that she had just dined, and set it down on a table. William Armstrong, playing her fiancé, was pretending to hang a painting on the rear wall of the set. It was a difficult scene that followed a comic episode; the actors had to deliver lines meant to move the audience into a more suitable sentimental frame of mind. While Cecily was kneeling by a sofa straightening the pillows, her back was to the table. The audience began to collectively titter, then roared with delight. The actors' lines couldn't be heard. Then, Armstrong turned and whispered to Cecily, "They're not laughing at you. Turn around!" Instantly, she realized the audience's diversion. Two small cats were playing tug-of-war on the table. Cecily was perplexed but took the offending animals in her arms and tried to rescue the scene. The audience continued their amusement, especially with both cats trying to wrench their ways out of the actress' grasp. One finally escaped as the curtain rang down prematurely. The owner of the cats was Arnold Towers. But Ashley was blamed for the fiasco because he had bartered with the local butcher for a bone that still contained a healthy amount of meat.

As to properties, Miss Gill gathered her small crew together during the early cast readings of the next play to be performed to review the available inventory in the properties' room and determine what needed to be added.

In one instance she remarked, "When the meal is over, Jack, who has been drinking goodness knows where, strolls from the billiard room. Rolph note, we have a curtained opening, so we must paint a flat with a billiard-table and lights as a backing behind the entry door."

"Yes'm," Rolph agreed. Rolph and the apprentices always agreed.

Miss Gill continued, "He has to carry a cue stick, doesn't he? Ashley note this. He has to do this so the audience will know he's been playing billiards, so he can't be overly inebriated. The moment he arrives, Jack will ask for a whiskey. Note, Ashley, silver tray, glasses, siphon of soda and watered tea to be carried in by the butler. Then he wants to smoke. Ashley again, he'll require the silver box, ashtrays, match-stand, and supplies of matches."

"Shouldn't they already be on the table next to the settee?" Ashley might inquire.

"Naturally, he can't bring all those things onstage with a cue stick in one hand and a drink being handed to him," Miss Gill responded patiently.

Relative to another scene, Miss Gill followed along the same routine, "Eustace, left alone, will toy with a book, write a brief note, stamp it, look up the date in the calendar and seal the letter with wax and matches. She also will enclose a cheque, so we have to have a chequebook. Do you have all this down, Ashley?"

Phillip was the first to notice and relate to Ashley the fact that actors often came on stage holding on to something: tennis-racquets, croquet-mallets, cigarettes, bouquets of flowers, canes, or bumbershoots. He also learned early on that one of the hardest tasks of an actor was to pay close attention to whoever was reciting lines and to react to the words with intense listening expressions and reactions.

Mr. Drinkwater constantly reminded his actors to face

a speaker and play opposite or downstage of him to refer the audience's collective eyes in the same direction. Additionally, he and his cast members would discuss creative ways in which actors could avoid looking like immobile statues by smoking a cigarette or cigar, quietly sipping tea, or writing in a notebook in a non-distracting fashion. He always reminded them of the necessity of building stage pictures as a series of tableaus in a play and never the same.

The actors chidingly called these the "you" sessions. Pointing to each of his actors in turn, Drinkwater would command something like, "We must have you, you, and you standing, you sitting. You're over here. You're over there. When Jack enters from stage right, William, you cross to meet him with your hand out to welcome him."

Ashley had difficulties with the many technicalities of lighting. He was always afraid of receiving an electrical shock and worried when gas or lime were used because of a possible fire. He learned that a mild sunset was not as simple as it looked from an audience's standpoint and that a burst of fall snow took a great deal of manpower. A sunset involved slowly dimming lights but also realistic shadows reflecting the dimming, and believable colours cast upon the rear wall or scenic drop, as well as an adjustment of other lighting instruments and onstage lamps to insure the actors could be seen by the audience. For a snow scene, white paper had to be waterproofed, hung on lines to dry, and torn up in small pieces, often cutting and poisoning fingers. During the performance, the paper is taken up into the flies and gently shaken through a perforated cloth, falling onto the stage. If the paper is damp, it can fall in lumps and land like rocks. If it is swept up and used for additional performances, it can gather handfuls of tacks and screws that ruin the effect of snow falling.

Sound effects such as a popping champagne cork

required slapping a table with your hand, but that had to be done carefully and exactly on cue, requiring eye contact with the actors and in close proximity offstage. Miss Gill was known to have said, "When the audience is looking at Jack opening the champagne downstage right, and the 'pop' of the cork is downstage left, we have a problem."

Thunder and lightning were also challenges. Wind could be duplicated by rapidly turning a round sheet of metal in a container. Rain could be reproduced by a rain-box suspended from the fly gallery, being gently rocked or by throwing handfuls of rice at a sheet of glass. The Birmingham Repertory Company retained what was commonly called a magic box. It was used for most of the special effects required by a multitude of plays from Shaw to Shakespeare. After moving a pointer on an indicator, one simply turned a handle like an organ grinder to reproduce the sound of a railway train, rain, wind, waves, galloping horses, or a motor car.

Ashley always looked forward to his responsibilities as the sound effects boy. He would position himself and the magic box so he could follow all of the hand signals given by Miss Gill. "Start" was a quick raise of her right arm; "continue" was a turning motion by her right hand; and "cease" was a rapid drop of the same arm. On several occasions, she would be distracted by a question from an actor or an unfamiliar occurrence onstage such as the leading man falling over a footstool in the dark. One of several times when Ashley was reprimanded occurred when an incoming tide sounded more like horses' hooves. However, the abilities of cast and crew to immediately adjust themselves to overcome a mistake or to change their lines on the spot always amazed the two boys.

One night, after a successful performance of *The God of Quiet*, Phillip related to Ashley what he interpreted as "a brilliant adjustment made right in front of audience." He said, "Arthur Rose and Cecily Bayne had taken their places downstage right in a scene depicting a picnic in a park. Two profiles of shrubbery were behind them; a blanket had been laid on the stage floor upon which they both descended. Miss Gill directed the electrician to bring up the spotlights on them with a soft, 'Now,' and the lights came up on stage. But, instead of illuminating the downstage right area in which the actors were to deliver their opening lines, the downstage left was brightened instead. Instantaneously, Mr. Rose picked up the blanket, took Miss Bayne's arm, crossed the stage with her, and, looking out into the audience, said, 'The light's better over here, isn't it?' and they began playing their scene.

Water was always a troublesome element on the stage. Real water, even used moderately to depict showers dropping on the heads of actors entering onstage with their bumbershoots and raingear, had to be mopped carefully during blackouts and scene changes. Rolph had built a replica of a fountain, which was used in all the plays requiring one. It was a light curved structure on hidden wheels behind which a technician could siphon the water with a hand pump. After a fortnight, Ashley, because he was smaller than the other crewmembers, had the assignment of lying under and behind the apparatus, monitoring the water flow. His worst experience was during *Twelfth Night* when the actors were seated on a mossy bank made of grass matting. After a short time, water began seeping through the material finding the actors' fannies deep in slush. Somehow, the fountain had sprung a leak. That night the scene ended earlier than usual and commenced moments later on another part of the stage without the fountain and mossy bank.

The cloud machine, though a favorite with audiences, was a nemesis to Ashley. It required that he start up the machine before the curtain rose, because of the noise it made before it began whirring in a quieter tone, and to mask the front of the lantern until the cloud movement was required. Ashley, who had a dreadful fear of heights but was young and agile, was always the selectee to climb up a ladder and reach high in the air to manipulate the clumsy machine. He never looked forward to this assignment. One night, falling from his tenuous perch, he fortunately grabbed the sides of the ladder on his rapid descent, preventing what could have been a noisy landing requiring immediate medical attention.

At the end of the season in June, Phillip and Ashley were highly complimented by both the performers and their fellow crewmembers. Dorothy Taylor and Phillip had a sad parting, promising to write each other daily. Barry Jackson was very pleased with Ashley's work.

As for Phillip, John Drinkwater had noticed spurts of real talent in his stage portrayals of servants, soldiers, and other walk-about appearances. Taking Phillip aside for a private hour of conversation, Drinkwater laid out a training plan for Phillip to follow in the coming year. He concluded with, "I'll cable Basil Dean. He was the Liverpool Repertory Theatre's first producer. We've worked together several times. Let's see if we can arrange another year of apprenticeship for both you and Ashley. This time, we'll make an actor out of you, Phillip. Oh," he continued, "and George Bernard Shaw did write *The Inca of Persusalem*."

Chapter 18
The Liverpool Repertory Company

Liverpool, 1918

After another summer of Phillip working in the furniture store and Ashley making grocery deliveries, the boys used their contacts to arrange another apprenticeship, this time in Liverpool. Now the youngest members of the Liverpool Repertory Theatre, they arrived in the prominent seaport, picked up their bags, stepped down from their railcar, and walked towards the main section of the train station. They soon noticed an anxious gentleman, mustached and in his early twenties, standing on a wooden bench holding up two signs reading "Mr. Phillip Maggs" and "Mr. Ashley Thronson."

Approaching him, Ashley made the introductions, "I'm Ashley Thronson and this nice looking chap is Mr. Phillip Maggs, soon to be known as one of the finest actors in the Commonwealth."

"Pleased to make your acquaintance, gents," responded the pleasant young chap with a ruddy face, disposing of the signs in a dustbin, then shaking their hands with gusto. "I'm Rex Gerard, the first assistant stage manager. Thank the Heavenly Father you're here. I'm gratefully looking forward to your assistance. For the past three days, I've been the entire stage crew all by myself. We'll take a taxi to your digs so you can meet Mother Sawyer; then we'll pop off to the theatre to meet Rice, the stage manager."

"We're at your service," Phillip said.

After chatting briefly with Mother Sawyer, who was to be their landlady for the next nine months, the boys inspected their second story flat consisting of a small drawing room and a bedroom. The former had a fireplace, two heavy, high-backed chairs, and a large table. A mullioned window faced a waterfront street. The bedroom was small with a trundle bed. The outside loo was also pointed out. Satisfied with their lodging and still in their travelling attire, the boys set off with Gerard for their first look at the Liverpool Repertory Theatre.

Unlocking the front door of the theatre, Gerard motioned them in, "We're waiting until rehearsals begin before we start the stage doorkeeper," he said. "We're on a very slim budget for the session. Every pound counts. We'll be meeting Rice in his office backstage."

Both boys noted the attractiveness and warmth of the foyer, handsome with rich red-velvet-covered walls, ornate lamps, and dozens of framed photographs of past productions. As they passed through the darkened auditorium, they sighted the two protruding balconies, both essentially similar in size, the large main floor without a center aisle, and the rows of seats extending to both sides.

"This is a beautiful theatre," remarked Ashley in awe.

"Agreed," said Phillip, noting the half columns and ornate decor on the walls of the large hall.

They climbed the short set of stairs adjacent to the forestage and entered through the proscenium arch door to the stage. Gerard led them towards an open door on stage right into a small office. Once inside, they saw a very thin, white-haired man seated behind a small secretary's desk. Several wooden chairs completed the furnishings.

The man rose as he greeted them, "Welcome, gentlemen. Hearty welcome. I'm Rice Cassidy," he said warmly. "Sit down. Make yourselves comfortable. I want to give you an orientation to our repertory company. Help yourself to some tea. You've had a long journey and need to relax before your hard work begins."

The stage manager described the modest early movement of repertory theatre first in Dublin, followed by Manchester and Glasgow. He told them about how a small group of influential members of Liverpool's commerce and university sectors had begun discussions on the feasibility of such an enterprise beginning in 1910. The most important and fashionable theatre for touring companies was the Royal Court, where such notables as Henry Irving, Ellen Terry, Forbes Robertson, and other actor-managers had trod the boards. Other theatres, including the Shakespeare, Kelly's Theatre, and smaller houses, the Queen's, the Rotunda, and the Star in Williamson Square, all offered touring dramas, operas, melodramas, and variety shows. There were also several amateur groups producing plays, but the possibility of a local, resident, professional group staging classical, modern, foreign, and new plays was appealing to community leaders. Known as the Playgoers' Club, the group had enthusiastically supported a touring company's two Ibsen productions.

"Weren't they *A Doll's House* and *The Master Builder*?" asked Gerard.

"Yes, Rex." Cassidy responded. "The plays alternated during a week's run in September 1910. They received great acclaim. Further fanning their initial fire of zeal, the Club invited prominent lecturers from the repertory movement to speak at a special gathering. The main invitee was spokesman Granville Barker who declared that Liverpool had a moral and social obligation to sponsor a year-round municipal theatre. He also suggested that such a venture might cost between 600 and 700 pounds per week. He was supported by Nigel Playfair, a London theatre manager, who emphasized the splendid health of theatre in London and the need for provincial theatre to help in the development of actors, plays, and audiences. Annie Horniman spoke of her work with the repertory company at Manchester's Gaiety, intoning that the wealth of Liverpool should certainly support a theatrical competitor. However, talk rather than action appeared to be all the meeting produced."

"But, eventually, there had to be action, or we wouldn't be here, would we?" offered Ashley.

"Annie Horniman! Ashley and I met her on a train last year," Phillip recalled. "We tried to convince her we were government spies."

"I really don't think she believed us," added Ashley.

"She's a deceptively bright female," Cassidy declared. "She'd be hard to fool."

"Not by a good actor," Phillip injected.

"Quite so," Cassidy replied. He continued, "Sensing the possibility of expanding his own theatrical base, Alfred Wareing, Director of the Glasgow Repertory Theatre, who had also lectured to the Playgoers' Club in October, began making plans to bring his company to Liverpool for a trial season in February or March of 1911. The plays he chose were *The Voysey Inheritance, The Fountain, The Tragedy of Nan*, and *The Cassilis Engagement*, all of which had had successful London runs. He contracted with Liverpool Theatre proprietor, W. W. Kelly, to lease his theatre for six weeks. The leaders of the Playgoers' Club agreed to this plan as a possible beginning of a permanent theatre, pledging to raise a guarantee fund of 500 pounds for productions. I'm doing all the talking. Tell the boys what happened next, Rex."

Gerard informed them that, unfortunately, Wareing, who had to spend a good deal of time in nightly travel between Liverpool and Glasgow, was having problems in his own theatre. With the burden of an additional trial season, he suffered a nervous breakdown. He wired Kelly he would be unable to fulfill their agreement.

In the meantime, there were three actor friends in London searching for an opportunity to become their own theatre producers. One was Miss Darraugh, an experienced actress from the Manchester Repertory Company, who had been looking for suitable leading roles; the second was Basil Dean, a twenty-two-year-old fellow-Manchester actor, desiring the chance to direct productions; and Charles Kenyon, Miss Darraugh's actor friend, who was willing to put up some money for her career. They had learned of Wareing's situation and approached the Playgoers' Club for support of their own scheme for a six-week experimental theatre trial.

"We know of Basil Dean," said Phillip. "He's famous for playing Jack Barthwick in *The Silver Box* in Manchester, isn't he? He also played the part in London."

"Quite so," Cassidy responded, appreciating the recognition of one of the theatre company's founders. "With this new alternative before them," he continued, "Club members excitedly pledged their backing. Kenyon invested 500 pounds and Kelly agreed to a fifty-fifty split with the threesome of anticipated profits. Miss Darraugh and Dean both agreed to additional small salaries, and Dean immediately headed for London to collect a company."

Cassidy said that Dean had hastily recruited a talented and experienced group of players, all older than he, and returned to Liverpool to begin rehearsals of John Galsworthy's *Strife* as the opening play. Despite an untried producer and members of the Playgoers' Club all offering strong but conflicting advice, the beginning days went well.

Cassidy told them that Galsworthy, himself, had helped with rehearsals, and the city's two major newspapers, *the Post* and *The Courier* strongly encouraged the venture. "*Strife* played to full houses for a fortnight," he said. "Critics were unanimous in praising its superior staging, fine acting, and thought-provoking content." *Strife* had been followed by a series of one-act plays in which the actors proved their talented virtuosity. "The *Cassilis Engagement* demonstrated the considerable skills of Estelle Winwood in comedy. The concluding play, Masefield's *Tragedy of Nan*, provided a balanced enjoyable ensemble effort. The trial season was an unqualified triumphant success. One thousand six hundred pounds profit had been realized to divide amongst the investors. Who said that repertory couldn't pay for itself?"

"I was touring with a variety show in Scotland when I heard about the success of the experimental venture," said Gerard. "It sounded quite exciting for a first tryout."

"Before the trial season was over," Cassidy continued, "Basil Dean convinced the leaders of the Playgoers' Club that he should be retained as producer; he prepared a prospectus for potential investors in a new Liverpool theatrical company. The concept was a comfortable, attractive theatre, with affordable prices, in which an experienced resident company would alternate a variety of plays over a nine-month season. A board of directors would operate the theatre, and there would be an initial issue of 20,000 shares at one pound each. By May, when the prospectus was distributed, the Star Theatre in Williamson Square had been selected as the new company's home."

"And it still is," Phillip said with admiration.

Cassidy explained that, in their enthusiasm and eagerness, board members had not anticipated the costs in the Star's having to be altered, re-fitted, and redecorated. "A foyer had to be built," he said. "The stage was extended, the dressing rooms expanded, a paint room added. Two properties adjacent to the theatre also had to be purchased to provide more space.

"While all of this was going on, Basil Dean took a fortnight abroad to study innovative lighting techniques and stage settings in Berlin. They had been created by Max Reinhardt, a famous German theatre technician and entrepreneur.

"After the first rush of financial commitment, shareholder applications slowed disappointingly, and many contributors failed to fulfill their original promises. By June, only twelve thousand pounds had been subscribed by 900 shareholders," Cassidy concluded.

"Undeterred and hopeful that the forthcoming season of plays would overcome the financial barriers," pouring the three young men another cup of tea, Gerard said, with a pause for theatrical emphasis, "The Liverpool Repertory Company gave its first performance of *The Admirable Crichton* on thirty October 1911 in Manchester."

"Manchester, why Manchester?" asked Ashley.

Cassidy responded, "Dean wanted the new company to have exposure before an audience accustomed to a repertory company. He wanted their reaction and encouraged his actors to very carefully hone their parts and practice ensemble acting. Besides, workmen were still readying the Star at home. Manchester received the play warmly rather than enthusiastically, so Dean made several changes in his actors' stage movements and line delivery, which helped it immensely."

Cassidy told the three young men that the initial opening in Liverpool was one of the city's finest cultural events. "The theatre was magnificent. It still smelled of plaster and paint. The seats were comfortable, and a staircase had been added between the dress circle and the stalls. There was a new foyer, and the columns and walls had been decorated with colourful formal festoons and palm trees in low relief. Fresh flowers were everywhere. Playgoers included not only the finely dressed elite of Liverpool but prominent visitors from London, Manchester, Bristol, and Birmingham, including playwrights and theatre owners. *The Admirable Crichton* was a trustworthy choice, never having been seen in Manchester or Liverpool. The acting and directing were superb, awarded with multiple curtain calls and congratulatory speeches. The second night was almost as gratifying as the first. Reviews were laudatory."

"Ashley and I have done *Crichton*," Phillip inserted. Ashley nodded.

"*Justice*, also by Galsworthy," Cassidy continued, acknowledging them with a wave, "was the next offering, and it was well received, although not so highly praised nor attended as the initial production. Next came the afternoon Christmas plays for children with evening performances of Sheridan's Restoration play, *The Critic*. During the new year, 1912, a comedy, Sutro's *The Perplexed Husband*, was running at the same time in London. It dealt with the pressing dilemma of women's rights and was just the vehicle to display the extreme talents of Estelle Winwood and Dorothy Massingham. Other plays followed. I have the list here."

Reading aloud, Cassidy continued, "They produced *The*

Tyranny of Tears, The Return of the Prodigal, and *You Never Can Tell. The Pillars of Society* was the greatest financial success, and, after a series of revivals of previously presented plays, the first season closed with Charles McEvoy's *The Situation at Newbury,* accompanied by speeches, criticism, applause, and bouquets. Dean had also been successful in introducing new lighting equipment and different methods of staging, from plain draperies to realistic and elaborate interior and exterior stage settings. Although the board of directors rarely agreed on anything, they collectively informed Basil Dean and his company of actors, and designer George Harris and his backstage staff that they could count their first as a fruitful season. All were asked to return for the following season. With a well-earned summer vacation, the theatre was rested, actors returned to their respective homes, and Dean and Harris left for Vienna and Berlin to study the latest in Continental stagecraft."

Cassidy's reflections also included the second season, which began on 9 September 1912. Improvements included giving Dean some relief in producing by assigning ten of the twenty-nine planned productions to actor Laurence Hanray and exchanging several plays for one-week stays between the Manchester and Liverpool Repertory companies.

Opening with successful performances of *The Importance of Being Earnest,* followed by *A Doll's House,* and *The Mollusk,* a production by the Manchester Repertory Company of *Devil's Disciple* brought additional deserved theatrical prestige to Liverpool. Through the rest of the season, several plays fared well, while others were disappointing in terms of attendance and response. The delightful and bright multi-coloured settings and costumes of the Christmas production of *Fifinella* brought six weeks of successful matinee performances. Dean's thoughtful productions of a new play by Lascelles Abercromie, *The*

Adder, in blank verse, and his ambitious staging of *Hannele* were ambitious adventures. The latter was Dean's greatest triumph, expensive, challenging, and difficult. It was also taken to Manchester where it created a great stir as well.

"Yet, even with these artistic successes, the financial picture was bleak. With the strain of responsibility for the company's economics and constant bickering with members of the Company's board, Basil Dean resigned."

"Where did he go?" Phillip asked.

"London, where else?" Gerard resounded.

Cassidy went on. "During its first two years of existence, the Liverpool Repertory Company's hard work, enthusiasm, excitement, and opportunity were the bywords. Basil Dean, though not a financial wizard, was still considered an artistic genius; the actors were praised as being of London quality; the scenery and lighting deemed superior; and the theatre a palace of pride. Plays by Shaw, Ibsen, Galsworthy, Barker, Sheridan, and their likes had been presented. Several originals had been introduced."

The stage manager recalled that the same pattern of producing had been continued after Dean's departure. New stagings were given every week. Mondays were reserved for final dress rehearsals and opening nights. After the first performance and before going to their digs, actors were presented with scripts to memorize for the next week's play with rehearsals beginning the following day, Tuesday. Rehearsals lasted from ten-thirty a.m. to four p.m., with a half hour for lunch. With mandatory arrival at the theatre by seven p.m., a curtain at eight, and performances lasting until eleven p.m., actors and crew had little time to themselves, even with Sundays as days of supposed rest. Thus was the life of repertory theatre.

"Well, we're certainly prepared," inserted Phillip. "We were thrown into the fire in Birmingham."

"And emerged unscathed," interrupted Ashley with a dramatic sweep of his hands.

"You were highly recommended. We have great expectations of both of you," Cassidy affirmed.

"And I certainly need the help. I came here to act, not to run errands," complained Gerard.

Cassidy continued his history of the Liverpool Company. He told his three listeners that, with considerable debt and facing new expenses, the theatre began the fall of the 1913-14 season in retrenchment: a smaller cast and crew, no more expensive productions, solely tried-and-true play choices geared to the skills of the actors, and minimal salaries. "The first six productions through Christmas were not well received. The financial future spelled disaster," he admitted. Arguments and criticism of the Liverpool Repertory Company filled the local newspapers and pubs. The directors eventually agreed that they could only continue to support the theatre through May, pledging a new collective investment of 2,000 pounds to cover existing expenses. Laurence Hanray, given the new title of stage director, was to have full control behind the scenes; ticket prices would be reduced, and a coupon system was installed for shareholders.

"I understand Hanray changed a number of former conventions," Gerard encouraged.

"True," was the response. "After a surprisingly long and unexpectedly profitable run of thirty-two performances of *Twelfth Night*, he established a new strategy for Liverpool's repertory. In January, the real experiment began with Ronald Jean's *Two and Two*, performed on Monday, Tuesday, and Friday nights; *Twelfth Night* on Wednesday evenings and Saturday afternoons; and, on Thursday and Saturday nights, *The Importance of Being Earnest*."

"So, only three plays a week. That's better for the actors," Ashley observed.

"Quite right," Cassidy responded. "The new system had the advantage of flexibility. Successful plays could continue to be alternated. A failure could be quickly abandoned, and new plays could be introduced for either short or long runs. During the spring, some of the standard plays were replaced by *The Liars, Caste, The Tragedy of Nan,* and a production of *The Gay Lord Quex*. The new system rescued the sinking ship."

Cassidy indicated that, by the end of the season in May, the debts of the previous year had been paid off, and all current expenses had been met. "Optimism resurged," he added, "and there was hope for the autumn season. Madge McIntosh, a fine actress and producer for the Glasgow Repertory Theatre, had been hired as the new managing director. She was presented with two lists on her arrival, a list of plays selected by the board of directors for the coming session and a list of actors under contract. Then came the war."

"The bloody war," Gerard reiterated.

"The war changed everything in theatre, everywhere, as you know," Cassidy stated. "The directors informed Madge McIntosh that the theatre was to be closed, all contracts were to be cancelled, and she would receive one half salary for her efforts to date. In an empty theatre, whilst inventorying scenery and properties to be sold, she chatted with the Company's most popular actress, Estelle Winwood. Estelle insisted that the theatre should not be shut down. Now planning her own unexpected departure, she proposed her own scheme for a Commonwealth Company. The innovative scheme called for a collective organization: each member of the cast would donate one pound, the crew and house staff contributing half of that amount, with all becoming members and receiving one half of their normal wages. Of weekly gross receipts, twenty-five percent would be paid to the Repertory Theatre Ltd. for standing charges; seventy-five percent would go to running charges and wages. If there were a positive or plus balance at the end of the season, any existing standing charges would be paid before distributing the rest of the funds for cast and staff wages."

"Jolly good idea," added Ashley.

"Miss McIntosh was positively overwhelmed with the scope of the new plans. She immediately arranged for a meeting of local Company members and wired and telephoned others. Agreement on behalf of the cast and staff was unanimous. Presented to the directors, this willingness of the cast and staff to take over the running of the theatre at half their normal salaries was an offer they couldn't refuse. As they say in theatre, the show must go on. And it did."

"Both Birmingham and Manchester have sole ownerships, don't they, Mr. Cassidy?" Ashley asked.

"Yes, both are supported by members of wealthy families. Since theatre is always a risk," Cassidy responded, "healthy financial backing is essential." He continued his narrative on the repertory company. "For the next two years, Madge McIntosh and Estelle Winwood teamed together to insure the success of the Commonwealth. There were enormous difficulties: finding directors for the plays, trouble with the trade union about low wages, men leaving for the service, finding replacements - a never-ending turmoil. Throughout the first year, the positives clearly outweighed the negatives. Outstanding actors, performing for half salaries, excelled in their onstage roles, bringing new, paying, entertainment-starved playgoers to the theatre. The Liverpool community rallied around their fearless Commonwealth. Emphasizing comedies, an occasional Shaw play, previously performed successful revivals, and a few original plays, the enthusiasm and consistently sterling performances of the actors continued to attract large audiences. Unexpectedly, the first season of the Commonwealth saw all of the cast's and house and stage staff's full amounts of regular wages received, the standing costs covered, and a profit of ninety-five pounds on the year."

"That's not much profit," Phillip said.

Cassidy nodded his agreement and continued with the company's history. "The next year of the Commonwealth was much the same as the first. *Helen with the High Hand* and *The Call,* a controversial new play by a Welsh woman, which detailed the romantic life of a revivalist preacher, followed two trivial comedies. Repeating previously successful productions, the Company also added such new shows as *Alice-Sit-By-The-Fire, The Second Mrs. Tanqueray, The Pigeon,* and *The Silver Box.*"

"Additionally," Cassidy reported, "they created two satirical musical reviews about various plays, periods, and personalities in the evolution of the Liverpool Repertory Company. With respected theatrical performers stepping out of their ordinarily dramatic characters, making good fun of one another, mimicking one another and members of the Company's board and past producers and directors familiar to audience members, along with costumes of clowns and animals, dancing and singing of comical parodies, the result was overwhelming. The critics were so favorable, it was decided to take the review for short runs to London. Unfortunately, the humor was too local for the sophisticated tastes of the West End audiences."

"But, aren't the provinces expected to produce entertainment that suits the provinces, rather than London?" Phillip asked.

"London considers itself the theatrical capital of the world," Gerard suggested.

Cassidy credited John Galsworthy, dedicated to the continuance of the Liverpool Company, for provided them with his new play, *A Bit o' Love.* It was so well received as an event, it was taken in its entirety to London where it had a distinguished reception. The company also performed a number of summer productions in Portsmouth. The Commonwealth's second year's profits amounted to 685 pounds.

"Unfortunately, the Commonwealth came to an end," the theatrician said sadly. "Problems had increased: finding male members for the cast and crew, actors and crew members leaving for better positions or military service, choosing plays appropriate to the abilities of the performers, rationing of food and products, and shortages of set building materials created miserable conditions. The hopelessness of a second year of war and air raids kept people at home. The early zeal and enthusiasm had diminished, and the directors wanted to regain full control of the Company. Nevertheless, the theatre would have surely closed had it not been for the Commonwealth."

"In 1916," Cassidy continued, "Muriel Pratt, who had been leading an experimental theatre in Bristol, and her husband, Bridges Adams, who had to hobble around on two canes, became co-producers."

"We've seen Bridges' work," Phillip spoke up. "He's a smashing director, I think. His staging of Sybil Thorndyke and Lewis Casson in *Julius Caesar* was the best Shakespeare I've ever seen."

"Right-o," added Ashley.

"He is clearly one of the best," Cassidy remarked. "This new company, still including mostly previous Liverpool Rep performers, opened in September with the parody, *Iris Intervenes.* The 'real repertory' scheme was continued with light comedies and memorable productions of *She Stoops to Conquer, Prunella,* and *Quality Street.* In November, a gripping translation of Emile Zola's *Therese Raquin* was staged. Its only previous production in England had been by Grein in his independent theatre at the end of the previous century. In that rendition, the unforgettable performances of Muriel Pratt and Margaret Yarde were exceptional. Another review, *Nothing New*, was developed. It failed locally because of the lack of local colour but, surprisingly, it succeeded in London with another company. It was a witty and lighthearted skit about the backstage antics of a repertory company."

"Soon after Christmas, 'real repertory' was abandoned," Cassidy said, "and it was possible to have runs from three to as many as eight weeks, depending on the popularity of the play and the polishing that longer runs provide. *What Every Woman Knows, The School for Scandal*, and *Everyman* went well, adding more variety to the repertory system. Unfortunately, although they were very popular both with the Company and our audiences, both Adams and Pratt had to resign because of his declining health. The loss for this past season was 1,440 pounds. And that, gentlemen, brings you up to the present. The producers are very concerned that we turn a profit."

"How can we do that?" Ashley asked.

"Max Jerome, who has been our business manager, has been elevated to managing producer. He plans to implement his fiscal policies carefully by keeping strict economies in management, retaining low salaries, using actors as directors, employing a smaller theatrical company with actors playing more than one role in most plays, and reducing production expenses. Times are very difficult, as you know. The condition of the country is serious. We also have an influenza epidemic, and there is a great shortage of men and of any products and materials."

The following morning, Phillip and Ashley attended their first rehearsal with the Liverpool Repertory Company.

Nine males, including Rice Cassidy as stage manager, and an equal number of women were engaged as the cast. They were not sure they were looking forward to meeting Max Jerome.

Chapter 19
More Liverpool

Liverpool, 1918-1919

Neither Ashley nor Phillip was impressed with Max Jerome in a theatrical sense. He seemed to them a "by the books" type of businessman, whose vocabulary was filled with commercial words like "accounts," "billings," "ticket sales," "auditorium occupants," "credits," "assets," "debits," and "bookings."

"He sounds more like Britain's Minister of Finance discussing war debts than a managing director," Ashley noted. "I'd call him a very negative person."

"He must know something about the theatre. I did appreciate the fact he considered me more of an actor than a stage crew member," Phillip responded. "At least he went over all the plays and told me what parts he expected me to play."

"Do you really think he read them, the plays I mean?" Ashley asked. "As he turned the pages of a script, it was more like he was adding up how many lines each character spoke, and he gave the shorter male and juvenile roles to you. It would cost him less. Notice how he also assigned you to make all the background sounds like front door bells and telephones ringing, wind, rain, and storms."

"That's because he's given you all the on stage calls and dressing and scene changes to accomplish," Phillip said. "Anyway, he said that all his specific recommendations would have to be reviewed by the new producer, George Bellamy. After all, he's a businessman, not a play director."

The next morning at precisely ten a.m., Max Jerome addressed the assembled company of eighteen sitting in a half-circle facing him, all dressed in clothing suited for leisure. Seated to Jerome's right was a thin, pale-faced man with a drooping mustache, wearing a dark dress suit. "Ladies and gentlemen," Jerome announced proudly, "I have the distinct honor of introducing Mr. George Bellamy to you." There was a modest round of applause.

Jerome continued, "Mr. Bellamy is a distinguished actor who has appeared in eight London productions, toured South Africa, and played various characters in several repertory theatre companies. He will now direct our plays this season. I will, of course, as general manager, oversee all productions, especially the financial aspects, and assist Mr. Bellamy in the selection of actors for each of the parts."

Company members had been hired by Jerome but were still surprised his producer wasn't in charge of who played what. "As I mentioned to each of you previously, we'll strain your acting skills to the utmost, since we must, because of our limited budget, have to double up, and, in some cases, triple up the parts. We must call upon your versatility to its fullest extent. Mr. Bellamy, will you please continue?" Jerome remained standing.

Bellamy rose from his chair, bowed courteously to his audience, and, in a strong, articulate Elizabethan tone, began speaking. "Because of the peculiar financial circumstances upon which this season rests, we must abandon the normal procedure of principle actors and actresses sharing the better parts with the rest of the ensemble. For each play, we will have to have our more experienced actors perform the major roles. As stage director, I have also agreed to serve in an actor-manager type of capacity. Are there any objections?"

There was a titter of murmuring.

"Mr. Bellamy, I had presumed I would be asked to play the role of Sir John Timbley in the first production," Terence O'Brien stated rather sternly. "Is that still the case?"

"No, Mr. O'Brien. I intend to take that part. I played Timbley in the Queen's Theatre in London three years ago," Bellamy answered. "Mr. Jerome and I have identified you for the second male lead."

"Remember, Mr. O'Brien," Jerome added, "There were no parts specified in your contract. We agreed only on a weekly stipend and that you would appear in every play."

"But, gentlemen, I came to Liverpool on the premise that I would be the featured leading man in this company," O'Brien insisted, looking to his colleagues for support. "I have too much stage experience to be limited to secondary roles."

Several of the acting company members nodded, and talking softly among themselves, generally supported O'Brien.

"I'd also expected to play opposite Terry in this first production," Dorothy Dewhurst suggested. "Actually, we've already begun rehearsing on our own. He's perfect for the part and…"

Interrupting, "I'm the general manager of this company!" insisted Jerome. "Let me make that perfectly clear! I make the final decisions! Do you all understand?" His finger swept in a pointed arc at the assemblage. "Do you all understand," he said more calmly. "Now continue, Mr. Bellamy."

Bellamy read the names of the cast members and their roles. Phillip was to play the part of the leading man's butler and would appear in most of the scenes of *The Country Mouse*. He was delighted with this opportunity, but both the boys noticed that many of the cast members appeared unhappy with their assignments. "Now, let's go through a first reading of the play," Bellamy requested. Stage manager J. Rice Cassidy passed out parts, calling them "sides," to the cast. Jerome, with loud, heavy-sounding footsteps, had left.

The initial reading of the new play lasted until lunchtime. After a one-half-hour rest period, the cast reassembled on the stage. Bellamy went through each of the scenes, positioning his players and indicating when and where he wanted them to enter and leave the stage, and what movements and actions should take place during each scene. The actors made notes in their side scripts.

Rehearsals continued through the next five days. They were to open on a Monday night, so the final dress rehearsal was held on that afternoon. It was obvious to everyone that Bellamy thought well of himself as an actor, though others thought he was more of an orator. He overemphasized his movements around the stage settings, delivering his lines louder than anyone else, gesturing broadly with almost every sentence.

For each of the three acts of *The Country Mouse*, there was a set change: an interior drawing room, a courtyard, and an interior gallery. Ashley, though disappointed that his name would not appear as a cast member, was content with making the "on set" calls, placing and removing properties, and helping cast members with their costumes and make-up. Bellamy, who insisted on perfecting his make-up and costume to make him appear younger, delayed the start of each final rehearsal act. "No, that eyebrow needs more blackening," "Comb the wig in the back so it lays flatter," "Pull the corset tighter, Ashley."

Every audience seat was occupied when the curtain rose on the Liverpool Repertory Company's initial play of the 1918 season. During the first act, Bellamy's acting was believable; the audience seemed interested and relaxed. However, after the interval, the next act moved slowly. There were always delays prior to Bellamy's entrances. The audience grew restless; their impersonal chatter became louder, distracting the actors. Throughout the final act, several misspoke their lines, a stage worker forgot to place a telephone on a table, and, when the actress went to answer the ringing sounding offstage, she had to leave the stage and deliver her lines from offstage where she was presumed to have found the missing telephone. Another actor corpsed, forgetting his lines and what play he was performing in. The audience heard the prompter attempting to place him back on the right track. Before the act had ended, many audience members had departed.

On Tuesday afternoon, the Liverpool newspapers unanimously suggested that its readership select other evening diversions than attending *The Country Mouse.* One paper read, "Mr. George Bellamy, in the principle role, was not only suspect as a proper leading man, he was far too ancient for the part and seemed to dash around the stage like a lost courtier searching for Hamlet."

The *Porcupine* drama critic wrote, "In his small role as a butler, Phillip Maggs shows promise." Another critic reported, "When they had Mr. Terence O'Brien, why was Mr. Bellamy playing the principle character?"

Rehearsals for the next production, *His Excellency the Governor*, began the same day. For the following several nights, the audiences for *The Country Mouse* were so paltry, the Friday and Saturday evening performances were cancelled. The cast was despondent. Many had begun talking behind

Bellamy's back, making fun of him both on and off the stage when he wasn't looking, imitating him from the wings, and purposely giving him incorrect cues before his lines. In their scenes together, O'Brien would often repeat Bellamy's last line before he delivered his own. One actor overheard Jerome speaking with Bellamy on the theatre telephone backstage. Jerome said sarcastically, "I'm watching you from the rear of the house. Wish you were here."

"You know, Ashley?" Phillip remarked offstage to his friend during the final evening of the show's performance, "I'm going to teach Mr. Bellamy a lesson."

"How will you do that?" Ashley asked.

"You'll see," Phillip answered.

As Ashley peered through a false window from the wings on stage left, Phillip, in his butler's costume was carrying a tuxedo for his master, Sir John Timbley, across the stage and exiting stage right. Bellamy delivered a final line to his two cohorts before following Phillip offstage to change into the tuxedo. The onstage pair continued speaking for a minute or so. However, after they had spoken all their lines, Bellamy had not re-appeared for his final scene. Reginald Gatty made up a few sentences for Frank Milray's response. They continued to adlib on stage, talking about horse races. The few members of the small audience didn't appear to notice anything unusual.

Bellamy, re-entering and crossing to a chair behind the two actors, said, in his exaggerated stage voice, "Is the horseman preparing to take us to the ball?" He seated himself comfortably.

"Your butler has just gone to the stable to fetch him," Milray responded.

Gatty spoke his line, "I understand the prime minister will be attending the celebration. You certainly look like he'll make a special presentation to you, Sir Timbley."

Bellamy started to rise but something seemed to hold him back. He tried again to no avail. Gatty, in a soft stage whisper to Milray, said, "My Gawd, he's glued to his seat."

Sure enough, as Bellamy again tried to lift himself from the chair, it would not budge from his rear quarters. A voice from the audience clamored, "He's stuck to the chair! Look, he's stuck to the chair!" Audience members roared in glee.

Bellamy, in a state of horror, screamed, "Curtain! Bring down the bloody curtain!"

His request was granted.

The next day, Friday, daytime rehearsals continued for *His Excellency the Governor*. Bellamy and Jerome had met early that morning in Jerome's office to discuss both the dismissal of whomever had played the deliberate trick on Bellamy and what could be done about the loss in revenue with the first production of the season. Bellamy, who was to play the leading role in this production as well, insisted that the matter of the chair be considered as one of the many instances when actors normally played jokes on a closing night and be forgotten.

Jerome was livid, unwilling to dismiss his wrath. "We must catch the culprit! Who do you reckon it was? Do you think O'Brien wanted revenge on you?" he asked.

"No, O'Brien's too sophisticated for an act like that," Bellamy, answered. "I think it may have been one of the stagehands, someone who carried the chair onto the stage. It could be one of our apprentices, Phillip or Ashley. Do we have any cash to post a small reward for someone naming the person?"

"Of course not!" responded Jerome angrily, "That's what you and I have to address. If we have another fiasco like this first one, I'm going to have to sack you. Perhaps, I should direct the next play."

"Never!" Bellamy said loudly. "You take care of the

business side of things. I'll take care of what goes on onstage," he insisted. "I have a rehearsal to conduct." He slammed the door as he left Jerome's office.

Rehearsals appeared to go well for *His Excellency the Governor*. The leading role was much more in keeping with Bellamy's physical stature, theatrical stage presence, and booming voice. In not blaming anyone for the glued chair incident, he gave the impression that he might be, after all, a good sport. Jerome was not seen very often for he was out and about Liverpool tacking up posters, visiting newspaper rector's offices, attempting to effect enthusiasm for the Company's next venture.

During one rehearsal, Phillip, with his back turned, had missed sitting upon a chair someone had improperly removed and had fallen to the stage floor. As he rose, unharmed, Ashley immediately said, "I always knew you'd make an impression on the stage." Those rehearsing laughed uproariously.

Opening night saw a packed house. *His Excellency the Governor* had had a long run in London; Jerome expected a favorable response. Everything went well, better than expected, until the last scene. The actor who had become a corpse sneezed.

The audience couldn't stop laughing. The curtain was brought down and raised again with an ensuing scene, but the audience had lost control. They laughed and commented aloud on everything, the costumes, and the manner in which lines were delivered. Chaos reigned.

The next day, the corpse, George Cowans, was fired. His wife, Dorothy, who was playing small parts, departed with her husband. Both their roles were hastily recast with members of the present company, and the play was performed through its final Saturday date without further mishap.

However, the die was cast. Jerome was able to locate another husband and wife acting team from London who agreed to come to Liverpool. His loud parting with Bellamy was overheard by Phillip. who reported his version of the tense meeting with the cast.

Mr. Bellamy said, 'Thank gawd, I don't have to act for you anymore."

Mr. Jerome responded, 'I didn't know that you had, old chap.'"

After wiring Miss Annie Horniman in Manchester for help, Jerome gathered the cast around him, announcing that the new stage producer, Percy Forster, would be arriving on the morrow. In preparation, Jerome led a read-though with the cast of the next dramatic choice of the repertory season, *Lady Huntworth's Experiment*, a play about a woman's search for a wealthy suitor. Phillip was to appear as Lady Huntworth's son. The playwright, R. C. Carton, would be attending rehearsals.

The following morning, Jerome introduced Forster. He was tall, blondish, very handsome, and he had a rich baritone voice. The Company welcomed him warmly as did Terry O'Brien. He had worked with Forster before in Hull. Forster believed O'Brien's acting ability and fine reputation would serve well for the rest of the company's season. Many of the plays to be offered were revivals in which O'Brien had played major roles both in Hull and elsewhere.

Dorothy Dewhurst was a natural to play Lady Huntworth, who was presented by playwright Carton as a wealthy, "do-as-she-cared" widow with a roguish son. Comedy was her forte, and she basked in the character she was performing. In the play, Lady Huntworth selects three possible suitors, all representing the highest-level businessmen in Brighton. As the play evolves and she, aggressive as a male, pursues each one independently, it comes clear that two of the wealthy gentlemen had acquired their riches through illegal means, and one had done so through hard work and ethical practices. The audience's challenge was to figure out which was the righteous one to become Lady Huntworth's next husband. Phillip's part as the son was to serve as a foil. He was to play various tricks on the suitors to test their reactions on behalf of his mother. Who were the good sports? Who was not?

Everyone enjoyed the rehearsals. It was a delightful play to perform, and they learned to carry out small bits of business when laughter from an audience would be expected. Forster, who portrayed one of the untrustworthy gentlemen, also had a special flair for comedy, always making a deadpan stare at the audience when he delivered a humorous line. Frank Simmons, a London character actor, played his unsavory role as a heavy-handed villain, almost a melodramatic type. O'Brien played a delightful character and carried out his part as a charming, debonair business tycoon who had risen from the bottom of the pile as a former valet.

Spirits of the Company were high on opening night. Playwright Carton had made constructive suggestions to Forster during the rehearsals and appeared very pleased with the development of the production. The play moved along swiftly. One could actually feel the audience's enjoyment as smiles, chuckles, and occasional light applause followed the lines the actors delivered. In one scene, however, Lady Huntworth was sleeping on a four-poster bed. Only her head and shoulders were seen above a comforter, a pearl necklace loosely strung around her neck. A hand appeared in the window adjacent to the bed. It slowly unclasped the necklace and quickly pulled it out of sight. Lady Huntworth awoke drowsily, her hand moving to her unclad neck. She screamed. She screamed again. She threw the comforter aside and rose from the bed in a pink nightgown, running from side to side, still screaming at the top of her lungs. No one came to her rescue. She screamed some more. The set depicting the bedroom started shaking.

Suddenly, a loud whisper from backstage could be heard throughout the theatre. "The door's stuck. I can't get in."

Lady Huntworth ran to the door, turned the knob and said aloud, "The bloody door's locked. I don't have a key." She started screaming again. Muffled noises continued from offstage. The scenery shook violently as someone tried to open the door adjacent to the bed from the wings.

The actress stopped screaming. She walked downstage, faced the audience, and said, "This is ridiculous. I'm sorry. We have to bring the curtain down because the rest of the cast is supposed to come in now and rescue me. But they're locked outside."

The curtain fell. The audience thought this was hilarious, especially with the apparent openings between the scenery and the wings on either side of the stage next to the proscenium arch.

This was the last scene before the second interval, so, when a somewhat subdued audience reassembled in their seats, the last act went on as if nothing had been amiss. O'Brien had won Lady Huntworth's hand; Simmons had been caught by the bobbies; and Phillip, as Lady Huntworth's son, had forced the character Forster was playing to confess his issuance of false securities. Despite the stuck stage door, the Liverpool papers were kind to the opening performance, praising the players' performances, even noting that Phillip's acting was a pleasant surprise.

The following afternoon, after reading the reviews aloud to the cast, Forster evaluated the first performance with those assembled. "Those terrible situations are bound to happen in repertory theatre. I can remember our locking the leading man onstage in a coffin, and we lost the key. We had to carry him offstage and saw the case open. We had two more acts to go. I've seen door handles come off in actresses' hands. Dogs wander onstage. Actors get drunk and forget to put on their make-up. Wigs and mustaches fall off. My own worst moment was when I was playing *Hamlet* in a small village in Somerset. I was way down on the apron, reciting 'the soliloquy,' yes, 'To be or not to be?' A woman appeared on the aisle, completely naked. I was mesmerized and so was the audience. But, I continued talking. I'm not even sure I was reciting the proper lines. She kept coming down the aisle, towards the stage, walking slowly, as if she were in a trance. The audience was stunned, but murmurs could be heard. She almost reached the footlights, but she ran in front of the first row to a large window, opened it, and, as she was astride the frame, two men in what looked like blue pajamas ran down the aisle and climbed out behind her. The audience burst into applause. *Hamlet* continued. After the performance, we learned the woman had escaped from the local insane asylum."

"I was playing in Bristol," said O'Brien, "portraying a policeman. "I had moved close to the footlights. I felt a tug on my trousers. I tried to pretend nothing had happened but the tugger wouldn't let go. I looked down. A woman said to me, 'We think you were so good last week.'" The cast roared as one.

"If you think that was bad, I can do you one more. I was playing a small role in London and I had several costume changes," Dorothy Dewhurst reminisced aloud. "The play was about a 'Jack-the-Ripper' character who was murdering women right and left. In my last scene, he was supposed to stab me in the back as I walked down a dark alley. As I fell, one of my breasts popped out. Since I was dead, I couldn't do anything about it. The story's followed me all of my theatrical life." Several members of the cast voiced their sympathy.

Other bad-luck experiences were shared, especially opening night ones. An actress trying to knit onstage for the first time heard an audience member cry out, "She can't knit. She may be a queen, but she hasn't a clue how to knit."

That reminded another actor of having to smoke onstage for the first time and someone yelled from the audience, "Anyone can see you can't smoke."

Others spoke about fluffed lines, missed entrances, and suits of armor being stuck.

"I was playing in *Ghost Train*," Reginald Gatty, a character actor, contributed. "An actor playing the villain, who'd evidently been drinking during the interval, fell asleep under a table onstage. The stage manager turned out the stage lights so we could awaken him. The actor who revived the villain asked if he had his prop, a gun. 'No, I forgot was the response.' The lights came on again. We had to retrieve the gun from offstage, and pass it behind our backs from one to another until it finally reached him."

Forster, laughing, said, "Now, let's get back to business. I want to hand out your sides. We open with *Smith, the Builder of Bridges*, next Monday. Let's do a read-through. Those of you unfamiliar with the play, start learning your lines, and we'll have a walk-through tomorrow.

Throughout the week, the performances of *Lady Huntworth's Experiment* went swimmingly. There were sold-out houses every night. Surprisingly, Max Jerome was seen actually smiling for once.

On 11 November, the entire Company happily participated in an onstage gathering prior to a Tuesday rehearsal. They learned that the Great War had ended.

Germany was defeated at last. Everyone's mood changed to the better.

Smith, featuring Frank Simmons as the successful engineer, was also highly praised at its opening, and filled houses continued. *Sowing the Winds*, again with Dorothy Dewhurst and Terry O'Neil in starring roles, was also well received. Everyone now looked forward to preparing *The Rivals*, a popular Renaissance play by Sheridan.

First produced at Covent Garden in 1775, the play is one of stereotypes. Actors, with little depth in their characters, can perform perfectly to audience's expectations. It was a perfect vehicle for the Liverpool Company, which appeared to have come together like a well-oiled machine. They interacted well on stage, complimented one another offstage, and benefited from one another's unique talents.

Phillip having made positive impressions in all of his small roles to date, was already recognized by his fellow actors as a rising young talent. He memorized his parts rapidly, changed his voice and mannerisms to fit each of his roles, was a believable onstage listener, and made a favorable stage impression.

Drawing him into the rear row of the theatre one Thursday afternoon, Terry O'Brien, recognizing Phillip's talent, began tutoring him about the acting education one could gain through repertory theatre. "Phillip," he said, "You're a comer. And, in a place like Liverpool, a repertory company of actors can become like family to the theatregoers. They have little to do at night. They sit in the same seats. The same actors play different roles. Audiences like seeing them pop up in a variety of interesting characters. Some people have special favorites. When I was in the Manchester Rep, we had grande dames who automatically received applause as they walked on stage. Everyone knew them. They'd been there forever, week after week. It made the actors feel loved, to receive presents like flowers or candies. Sometimes, it spoiled them."

"I think introducing audiences to good theatre is tremendously exciting," Phillip said. "*The Rivals* is a good example of a comedy that survived for over 200 years. People still enjoy it."

"You're quite right, Phillip. But let's talk a bit about acting. You've already gained some new skills by working with experienced professionals: voice variation, gesturing for emphasis, moving confidently onstage, using business that doesn't distract from other actors' deliveries. I've watched you closely. You're a natural actor. It just comes to you easily and comfortably. It's confidence. Many actors see a production in London, and, when performing the same production in repertory, they imitate the interpretation of the part by the original actor. That's not acting. That's mimicry; that's miming. Some actors play themselves in every performance, not the character they're supposed to recreate. That's not acting either."

"I've noticed that in the past," Phillip responded, "Even in different frocks with different lines to deliver, they're still the same."

"Acting has changed in the last decade or so, Phillip. The actor-managers were larger than life. They could be heard in the rear rows, but their characters weren't really believable. They were acting formally. Acting has become more naturalized. Roles, for the most part, have moved from royalty and upper class situations to replicating common people in 'real life' situations. I believe all acting demands imagination and emotion, not technique. Play the person. Create your own vocal power. Treat your audiences with respect. They'll let you know whether or not you're getting through to them. Good actors, and you have the makings of one, use instinct. They do what they feel is right. They try not to act but be absolutely real. Using the intimacy and immediacy of the stage medium requires a more believable style of acting than in the past."

"But in rep, we have to play all kinds of parts. I was an eighty-year-old man in *Smith*."

"True," O'Brien agreed. "That's what's wonderful about repertory theatre. It helps you develop a range of characterizations. It's how you learn to interpret your characters through performance and actual experience. However, more and more, especially in London, directors look for 'types,' actors who possess the looks, walks, mannerisms, clothes, hair, speech and accent to make themselves become the character. Unfortunately, in rep many people are given roles for which they're totally unsuited. They're just not believable."

"What about having to play the same role in the same play in the same theatre over and over for a year?"

"That kind of a role is what supports some good actors, but it doesn't give them new opportunities to stretch themselves. When I was a young actor, I wanted all kinds of acting opportunities. I played the rear end of a cow once. When I was nineteen, I played a 100-year-old man whose son was actually an eighty-six-year-old actor. That same year, I needed to increase my weight for a role. I wore three jackets and an overcoat. I loved it."

Ashley smiled at the mental image.

"I learned that playing a wide range of parts helps you discover different sides of your own nature. It's beautiful when you discover what's really required with each new character you play. You can test out your comedic skills, expand your natural sense of timing. Rep taught me what I was really good at and what I was very bad at. It taught me about hard self-discipline and low financial rewards.

It also gave me the tremendous gift of making mistakes, watching seasoned actors ply their wares, picking up stray bits of advice like 'When you do that, you face the audience.' 'Speak up, or they won't hear you.' They gave me the rhythm of a line. They taught me that even if you were playing a small part, you treated it as if it were a leading part."

Just then, there was a voice off stage.

"Uh-oh, the stage manager's calling for you, Phillip. You'd better go..."

Chapter 20
The Unforeseen

Liverpool, 1919

The Rivals proved to be the Liverpool Repertory Theatre's most successful production. It was so popular the run was extended another month. Word-of-mouth proved to be the most effective publicity. Jerome wasn't even in Liverpool. He had traveled to London to review current plays that the Liverpool Company might produce towards the end of the season.

The Rivals was bawdy, it was bold, and it provided challenges to all the Company's actors, which they met. It gave them a collective sense of ensemble acting, everyone contributing equally.

The play is set in Bath in the eighteenth-century. With its waters believed to have healing qualities, Bath was an ideal setting for the play's characters. The plot revolves around Lydia Languish, an attractive lady obsessed with the romantic ideals of love she reads about in the popular novels of the time, and Captain Jack Absolute, who pretends to be a poor soldier called Ensign Beverly. In reality, Absolute is a rich gentleman. A marriage is arranged, but, when Lydia learns of Absolute's real identity, she refuses to marry him, clinging to her romantic notions of eloping with a poor soldier. Captain Faulkland, a close friend of Absolute, has fallen in love with her. Another friend, Bob Acres, a somewhat buffoonish country gentleman and a coward, plans to win her hand by defeating the fictional Ensign in a duel, and Sir Lucius O'Trigger wants her money and a duel, as well. Each of the characters conforms completely to the audience's expectations. The lack of depth of character allows for a complex plot and broad comedic interpretations.

Lydia is carried away with her romantic ideas of love. Jack Absolute is courageous, recognizing both money and marriage are important. He is also manipulative. In the end, when Absolute's identity is revealed to everyone at the site of the duel, Lydia admits she loves the real him, and everyone is resolved to live happily ever after.

Throughout the rehearsals, Phillip as Bob Acres was brilliant. Despite his youth, he was more than convincing. His practice performances invigorated the rest of the cast. Sometimes he overplayed his role, other times, he held back. Often, during rehearsals, because of his humorously timed lines, the actors broke into laughter, despite themselves. Phillip had created a ridiculously funny man.

The entire cast had looked forward to opening night. By the end of the first act, they knew they had a hit on their hands. Many members of the audience were familiar with the Sheridan play. They had seen it in school or on tour. However, they had never experienced an entire cast so perfectly suited to the roles they were playing. As the first act commenced, a number of spectators began laughing at Phillip before he even uttered a word. The way he strolled about the stage, the manner in which he rolled his eyes, screwed up his facial expressions, pointed and waved, and flung his arms around, made Bob Acres an impossible, but believable, characterization. In the dueling scene, he was a whirling dervish, swinging his sword insanely and wildly at everything and everybody onstage. Laughter rang throughout the theatre. When he bowed at the end of the fifth act, the entire audience rose as one, applauding enthusiastically. All of the actors onstage joined in the impressive outburst.

As the main curtain lowered, Forster and other members of the cast warmly embraced Phillip. An ecstatic Ashley ran onto the stage, yelling, "Phillip, you've done it! You've captivated the entire audience. You were just magnificent," hugging him.

Phillip, very humble with all this attention, acknowledged the praise with nods and thank you's. "Excuse me," he uttered softly and went up the stairs to his dressing room.

After picking up the properties left on stage and helping several of the actors with their costumes, Ashley entered Phillip's dressing room, which he shared with several male actors. Noting his absence, Ashley asked, "Where's Phillip? Why isn't he here?"

"He changed his clothes and left without a word, just left," Reginald Gatty said. "Look in the pub next door. Maybe he needed a pint after all that energy he used up."

Ashley ran down the stairs and into the adjacent pub. He looked everywhere, but Phillip was nowhere to be seen. He chased down several more blocks, peeking into pubs and restaurants. With growing concern, he returned to the flat they shared at Mother Sawyer's. Phillip wasn't there either.

Ashley located his script for his role as a young schoolboy in next week's production of *Rutherford and Son* and began studying it, worried about Phillip. Within minutes, he had fallen asleep.

When he awoke in the morning, Phillip was still not in

the flat. Ashley arrived at the theatre. He asked everyone he encountered if they had seen Phillip. No one had.

Forster, very concerned himself, said to the Company members who had assembled, "I know we're all concerned about our newest star. We all are, but we have to do a first reading of *Rutherford*. Would you all bring chairs to the center of stage and sit around me? Cassidy, could you send someone to the local hospital? Phillip might have met with a mishap."

"Yes, sir," was the reply.

The reading went on for three hours. No word of Phillip's whereabouts was forthcoming. A sad pallor descended on the cast. "What's happened to Phillip?" "Where could he be?" "Has an accident befallen him?"

Before the luncheon break, Forster approached Ashley. "Ashley, I'm going to have you fill in for Phillip for tonight's performance."

"I can't, sir. I can't play that role the way he has. He's magnificent."

"As they commonly say in this business, Ashley, the show must go on. You've got to do the best you can. We'll all appreciate that, and so would Phillip, wherever he is."

"All right, sir. I'll try," Ashley replied. "I'll go to Phillip's dressing room and start to memorize the part."

"That's a good lad."

Before the review of actors' movements in *Rutherford* began, Cassidy reported that Phillip had not been seen at the hospital.

"Let's go about our stage business, everyone," Forster directed. "I'm sure he'll turn up." He asked the Company members to take up their sides and mark them as they moved around the stage, being told when and where they'd enter and depart.

At three p.m., a uniformed man entered from the stage door. He approached Cassidy who pointed to Forster.

"Sir," he said as he walked towards Forster, "I'm Higgins, sir. I work at the train station. Sir, there's been a terrible accident. We just found a bloke, sir. We've rushed him to the hospital. It was a boy, sir. He had a worker's card in his wallet. It said Liverpool Repertory Theatre. His name was..."

"I know his name. It's Phillip Maggs, isn't it?"

"That's right, sir."

"Did you say, 'was?"

"I donno, sir. He was all bloody. He wasn't moving. We had to wrap him in a blanket to get him to the hospital."

"What happened?" Rex Girard asked the station man.

"He fell under a moving train," was the response.

As one, the actors groaned. "How terrible." "What a tragedy." "Will he live?"

"I'm going to the hospital," Forster announced. "Cassidy, you take over the rehearsal. Come on everyone, we can't all rush off. We have a play to rehearse. He started to leave the theatre.

Ashley, suddenly appearing at the stage door, said, "I'm going with you."

Once at the hospital, they were told to wait in a private room. "Mr. Forster, I'm going to telephone Phillip's father at his department store in Bristol," Ashley said.

"I think we should wait," Forster answered. "We don't really know what to tell Mr. Maggs, do we?"

"I guess you're right. I'll wait before telegraphing our acting teacher, Miss Joyce, too," Ashley responded.

Ashley studied the Bob Acres part but had trouble concentrating. He'd read a passage, and immediately forget what he'd just read.

Forster paced the room. There was nothing he could do but wait.

Two hours passed. "I'm going back to the theatre. You stay here, Ashley," Forster commanded.

As he was leaving, a tall, grey-bearded man in a white smock entered the room. "Are you the two here about Phillip Maggs?" he asked.

"Yes," Forster and Ashley said in unison.

"I'm Doctor Wolfe. Mr. Maggs is seriously injured. Are you members of his family?"

"No, sir, we're with the Liverpool Repertory Theatre. Phillip is one of our actors," Forster said.

"Can you contact his parents? Mr. Maggs is close to death."

"Oh, my God!" said Forster.

Tears rose in Ashley's eyes. "Death? Phillip is dying?"

"Ashley, run back to the theatre and telephone Phillip's parents. Tell the cast to keep rehearsing. Go back to your flat and learn your lines. I'll see you tonight at the theatre."

"I'm going to telephone Miss Joyce," Ashley responded. "She'll want to know about Phillip, too." He let himself out the door as the doctor continued talking with Forster, explaining in medical detail Phillip's actual condition. If he survived the night, an operation was imminent.

Back at the theatre, Ashley was able to make telephone contact with Mr. Maggs and with Miss Joyce. Both were devastated, promising to take the next train to Liverpool.

Ashley arrived onstage at six-thirty p.m. Forster was waiting for him. "I can't go on," Ashley said. "I can't learn the lines. I just can't remember them. I can't get Phillip off my mind."

"All right, son," Forster said gently. "I understand. We'll have Cassidy read Phillip's part from the script and make all his movements onstage. You go back to the hospital and wait," he ordered. "Maybe you'll get a chance to see Phillip."

At eight p.m., Forster stood on the apron with the main curtain closed behind him. He addressed the audience.

"One of our fine young actors has had a tragic accident. He's currently in the Liverpool Hospital. His condition is undetermined, but it's serious. We have no understudy. So, for tonight's performance, our stage manager, Mr. J. Rice Cassidy, will read the role previously played by Phillip Maggs. If any of you would like your admission refunded, we'd be happy to do so, or you can use your tickets for another play during our season." No one in the audience rose. "All right, then, let's make the most of this performance," and Forster slipped backstage through the main curtain slit. The complete cast was already assembled.

"I know this is difficult for all of you," Forster said. "We have no idea what Phillip's condition represents. We have to perform a comic play when our feelings are quite the opposite. Are you up to it?"

Terry O'Brien was the first to speak. "We're all concerned about Phillip. Certainly we are. But, remember all, we're actors. We've got an audience out there. They're here to be entertained. That's what we're paid for."

"We just have to put our feelings aside and be the professionals we're supposed to be," added Dorothy Dewhurst.

Several others joined in with positive comments that troupers must be troupers and acting helped face reality. The show went on. Cassidy did an admirable job even though he was script bound. The cast often repeated lines he read, turning them into more witty statements, and this spirit prevailed over the footlights to the audience. The ship had made it through the strained emotional storm.

Immediately after the final curtain fell, Forster, after praising Cassidy and the cast, left for the hospital. He found Ashley asleep in a chair. Sitting next to him, Cassidy, also, was soon quietly snoring.

Early the next morning, Mr. and Mrs. Maggs appeared,

shortly followed by Miss Joyce. Dr. Wolfe was informed by a staff member and met with the Maggs, Miss Joyce, Forster, and Ashley. "Phillip had a turn for the better early this morning. He recovered consciousness and even had a bite to eat. We shall perform the operation post haste."

"The operation," questioned Mr. Maggs. "What operation?

They all listened intently as the doctor responded, "Phillip's right leg was crushed by a railcar wheel. It's going to have to be removed," he admitted bluntly.

"His leg? His whole leg!" Mrs. Maggs cried out. "But he's only a boy. My boy! This can't have happened."

"I know how you all feel. This is terrible news, the doctor said. "But Phillip's life is still in danger. He's lost a great deal of blood. The leg can't be saved. It has to go."

"I can't believe it. What will happen to his career?" Miss Joyce asked no one in particular. "He had such promise as an actor."

"How can he act with no leg?" Ashley asked.

Forster and Ashley were silent in their remorse as both women broke down in tears. Mr. Maggs was in complete shock. He repeated over and over again. "I can't believe this. I can't believe this."

Three hours passed. Nurses brought food and tea into the waiting room. Phillip's parents and friends spent much of the time in prayer. Mrs. Maggs shared several of her fondest remembrances about Phillip's childhood at Miss Joyce's request. She wanted the mother's mind off the operation taking place close by. All of a sudden, the door burst open and Mr. Thronson appeared.

"I'm so sorry this happened. Phillip's father alerted me. I wanted to be with you, Rupie," he said. "I know your friend's been seriously injured. How is he?"

Ashley quickly rose, and taking his father's arm firmly

in his hand, he said, "Come outside, Father. I'll tell you all about it."

Just as Ashley finished relating what had happened to his father, Dr. Wolfe appeared in the hallway and entered the waiting area. Ashley and his father followed him.

"I'm pleased to announce that Phillip's operation was successful. His condition is still serious, but we are much more hopeful than before. We'll know more this evening. Why don't all of you get some rest and return about six to meet with me? I'll bring you up to date then," he added.

The Maggs, Mr. Thronson, Senior, and Miss Joyce all checked into the Liverpool Hotel. Miss Joyce told Forster, whom she had known from a previous theatrical tour, that an understudy was assuming her role in Manchester. She wanted to be near Phillip. She wanted to help him recover. After she had unpacked her luggage, she joined the Liverpool Company at their afternoon rehearsal as Forster's guest. Still apprehensive because of Phillip's undeclared condition, she was overwhelmed by the affection and respect cast members expressed about her former pupil. Ashley resumed his stage duties, arranging to meet his father for dinner at four p.m.

During their meeting, Mr. Thronson tried to persuade his son to return to Bristol and take a position at Shirley's Grocery. "Acting's an unworthy profession, Rupie," his father declared. "Look what happened to Phillip. If he'd stayed in Bristol, working in his father's store, this wouldn't have happened."

"Father, acting has nothing to do with Phillip's accident. It just happened. It could have happened anywhere to anyone, any time," he responded. "Right now, Phillip's the most important person in my life. I'm not going to leave him. He needs me. I'm his best friend."

"I respect you for that, son. I'm going to stay to see if there's anything I can do to help."

"Thank you, Father. I appreciate that."

They both hurried to the hospital. Miss Joyce, Forster, and the Maggs had all been informed that Dr. Wolfe wanted to meet everyone at six p.m. When they had gathered, he said, with a smile, "Phillip is awake and alert. He wants to see all of you together."

The group reassembled in Phillip's large hospital room. Two nurses were attending him when they arrived with Dr. Wolfe. Phillip wore a white hospital gown. He had bandages on one side of his face and covering his right arm. One leg was outstretched. The other, a stump, was heavily wound in white tape.

"How's our young patient," Dr. Wolfe greeted him warmly.

Phillip, despite being weak and covered with medical dressings, said in a meek but confident voice, looking at each in turn, "Hello everyone, Mother, Father, Miss Joyce, Mr. Thronson, Ashley, Mr. Forster. Thank you for being here. I'm going to be all right. I promise."

"Oh, my darling boy," Mrs. Maggs said. "I'm so happy you're alive."

"You're a brave lad, my son," added Mr. Maggs.

The others gave their wishes for a rapid recovery.

"Now, ladies and gentlemen, may I have your attention," Dr. Wolfe requested. "After Phillip leaves the hospital, there will be a period of several months of rehabilitation. He must regain his health and must learn to move about in a wheelchair. I've spoken with one of my colleagues in Bristol, and we both feel that's the best place for Phillip to recuperate, to gain back his strength and mobility. He'll have his family around him and sufficient medical support. I assume that is all right with everyone?" he asked.

"That's fine with me," Mr. Maggs answered. "His mother can remain with him in Liverpool until he's ready to return to Bristol. He'll also have Ashley and Mr. Forster to visit with him here."

"And the entire Liverpool Repertory Theatre Company," Forster said.

"And everyone who's seen Phillip act in Liverpool," added Ashley.

"I'm staying as long as I can too, Phillip," Miss Joyce promised. "I want to see you recover as soon as possible."

"Bully," Dr. Wolfe said, "Phillip, it appears that your immediate future is pretty well decided. I've other patients to see. I'll return later. Let's all leave now. Phillip needs his rest."

Departing, everyone thanked the doctor for his splendid efforts in rescuing Phillip from the brink of death and insuring his recovery.

"We'll be beholden to you for the rest of our lives," Mrs. Maggs confessed. "I'm sure Mr. Maggs will be making a contribution to your splendid hospital, Doctor." Maggs nodded his assent.

Forster had invited the Maggs, Miss Joyce, and Mr. Thronson to that evening's performance. Mr. Cassidy again filled in with the script, and the audience accepted this unique way of acting out a comedy with one member of the cast running around the stage with a script and reading his lines aloud. Cassidy hammed it up, making the most of his silly situation. "After all, I'm an actor, too," he proudly claimed.

Miss Joyce, after several visits with Phillip, returned to her company in Manchester. Thronson Senior, after admitting that Ashley, in his words, "Rupie," had been quite convincing as a mail delivery man in the play, left for Bristol.

Forster and Ashley continued their respective positions with the Liverpool Company, with Ashley visiting Phillip on a daily basis. During one of their hospital visits, Ashley asked Phillip, "What were you doing at the Liverpool train station after that wonderful opening night. You were just outstanding!"

"I was so excited, I didn't know what to do, where to go. I couldn't face the cast. I was really too embarrassed with all the adoration they were displaying. I didn't think I deserved it. I wanted to get away and celebrate quietly. I wanted to savor what the night had really meant. I wanted to think about every move I made and every line I delivered. I decided to take the train down to Manchester and surprise Miss Joyce. It was only a short train ride away. I could come back the next day. I knew Miss Joyce would understand how I felt. After all, she was the one who first encouraged me, besides you, I mean."

"I was worried about you, mate," Ashley admitted.

"I was standing in front of a large crowd of people on a narrow platform when the train approached. As it was pulling into the station, I think someone pushed onto the platform. I lost my balance and was plunged down under the train. I don't remember anything after that," he said sadly.

"How terrible," Ashley remarked. "An awful accident just because someone was late getting to the train. He destroyed your life as an actor, Phillip. He really did."

"Well, there's nothing I can do about it now, is there?" Phillip said despondently.

It took two more weeks before Phillip could be moved from the hospital to a rehabilitation home for medical purposes. His mother was given a room in the same building. She spent much of her time reading to Phillip and helping him with his correspondence with Richard Bates, Miss Joyce, and other friends.

Members of the Liverpool cast also made visits to

Phillip's room. His health had swiftly returned, and he had mastered his wheelchair quickly. Even Max Jerome paid Phillip a short visit to relay his concern.

Two months after his accident, Phillip announced to Ashley, "I'm returning to Bristol, tomorrow."

"I'll go with you, Phillip. You'll need me to push the wheelchair."

"No, I won't Ash. I've got arms. I can roll myself around quite well now. Besides, I'm thinking about finding a false right leg."

"A false leg? How on earth could you do that?

"As you're aware, Ash, many soldiers lost limbs during the war. There are military hospitals now that have developed new kinds of aids for crippled people. I've been reading about them in both newspapers and magazines. I've even been looking at medical journal articles about artificial arms and legs. I don't want to spend the rest of my life in a wheelchair. You can bet on that."

Ashley saw Phillip and his mother off at the Liverpool railway station in March. Phillip had encouraged Ashley to remain with the Company and complete his apprenticeship.

Ashley had been gaining confidence in his scenic design skills as well as his acting. The sad news was an irony that, ever since Phillip had had his accident, the Liverpool Repertory Company had been losing money. It was just not filling theatre seats.

After the unlikely success of *The Rivals*, the next three productions, *Rutherford and Son, David Ballard*, and *The Manxman*, all revivals of previous plays produced in the Liverpool Theatre, failed to attract audiences. *The Manxman*, an adventure in melodrama, wasn't successful because it did not suit the main actors.

Due to their familiarity with the plays and the fact that the costumes and scenery were already in local storage and didn't have to be created, cast members, instead of having to attend rehearsals, pursued other diversions. They frequented Liverpool's many clothing and general stores. As a major seaport, the city provided an ample amount and variety of goods, including teas and perfumes from faraway places like China and Japan. The men had also located a local school ground where they practiced cricket, even occasionally challenging local teams in the late afternoon. Before his accident, Phillip, several times, had reversed his social position with the male members of the Company. In cricket, he was one of the leading men with the others playing the lesser roles. Allen Johnson left in May to join the British Army in Germany, helping to maintain the Armistice. Lane Bayliff, a London actor, filled in for him between May and end of season in July.

The next production was a new play, *The K. C.* by Dionne Titheradge, who had been a member of Basil Dean's company. Opening night began well but met with a small crowd, the result of the influenza epidemic that had kept many at home. But the actors were lethargic and under rehearsed. So uncertain was the company in words and moves on the early nights of the run, it was impossible to judge the play fairly. Newspaper reviews were scathing from the acting to the set design to the script itself. For the second time in the season, only five performances rather than the seven scheduled were conducted.

The following play, Ronald Jean's *Give and Take*, a melodrama, didn't suit any of the principle actors and actresses, who brought no believability to their roles. It had been a poor choice. Audiences continued to be sparse.

Percy Forster and Max Jerome were distraught. They couldn't agree on a positive path to pursue in their choice of plays. They had no time to review new productions in other locations or to read scripts. They had relied on the tried and true – the old standards. Each of them attempted to counsel and encourage their actors. Morale had never been lower since Phillip's accident. The set designer was disappointed as an artist; Jerome found the bills piling higher than the receipts. When he reported the financial problems of the company to Liverpool Repertory's Board of Directors, he was told bluntly, "Do something about it!"

The Dewhursts and Rex Girard turned in their resignations and left the company. Terry O'Brien and Reginald Gatty were terminated, salaries being the principal issue. Telegrams sent to London agents for replacements went unanswered. Rehearsals now began at nine a.m. and went to six p.m., with some continuing after the evening performance until the wee hours of the morning. Actors were often rehearsing in their dressing rooms during performances of the current production. Ashley worked harder than ever.

With an almost complete change of company, staff, and management, surprisingly, the next two productions, *A Midsummer Night's Dream* and *Cupid and the Styx* were well performed and had relatively good audiences. However, the theatrical season was still well in the red.

The Liverpool Repertory Theatre directors vowed that another losing season would not be tolerated. Max Jerome agreed. He left for a business position in London. Although five of the season's productions had been performed for the first time in Liverpool, three of them for the first time on any stage, the board decided that new productions would not be included in succeeding years. They agreed to bring in experienced actors, highly regarded plays, and a proven stage director for the coming season.

In July, Ashley returned to Bristol, uncertain as to his next step.

Chapter 21
The A.L.S. Travelling Theatre

On-the-Road, 1919-1920

Back in Bristol, Phillip to recuperating and helping out at his father's furniture store, Ashley to delivering grocery items in the grocery company's lorry, the next several months were also spent in Ashley's continuing search for acting jobs. He subscribed to several theatre magazines and followed up on every advertisement possibility by phone, mail or telegraph. One day, he had a telephone call from Rex Gerard whom he had known when working with the Liverpool Repertory Company.

The previous year, Gerard had joined the Travelling Theatre, founded by Eleanor Elder, who had resided in India during the last two years of the war. He was to be her stage manager and a principal actor. Elder had returned to England "anxious to take up work in the theatre again, filled with the desire to help in the developments in drama and education."

She had a solid theatrical background, having initially watched several rehearsals of director Granville Barker, later appearing in one of his companies. She had joined a touring Shakespearian company, first as a young pupil and walk-about, and, a few years later, as a full member of the company. She was a member of Margaret Morris' dancing troupe in Galsworthy's *Little Dream*, at Annie Horniman's Gaiety Theatre-based Manchester Repertory Company. The producer was Iden Payne, who had apprenticed at the Abbey Theatre. She had even appeared on stage in London with Laurence Irving. To Gerard, she had impressive and versatile credentials.

Mustering her persuasive talents, she had assembled the performing wing of the Arts League of Service, popularly known as the A.L.S., a broad national representation of all the arts, "taking arts to the people, if you will." This vast endeavor included transporting portfolios of original drawings and paintings to be sent to all parts of England and a block of studios erected in Chelsea for painters and sculptures. This movement was to provide a government-sponsored rebirth of national culture after four years of fruitless war and a long intermission for the furthering of the visual and performing arts. An important linchpin was known as the A.L.S. Travelling Theatre. Elder's mission was "to take into the country a dramatic company that would, in their productions, touch the imagination of the people and lead them to a better understanding of the arts."

With the unbalanced lure of small salaries and considerable travel, Elder gathered a small company from among her many stage friends, along with a few amateurs, who combined experience, spirit, and humor with a desire to perform in variety performances of song, dance, and drama. However, she desperately needed a competent lorry driver for the fit-up. One of the questions asked of everyone involved was "Do you drive an automobile?" No one felt confident enough.

Rehearsals were held in Elder's large flat. Her neighbors were James Barrie, and, within window view, Bernard Shaw, who lent Elder useful advice and bits from his plays on a sliding scale rather than fixed-amount royalties. The first production was to consist of dances by sisters Muriel and Hermione Baddeley, musical soloists, and three one-act plays: Lady Gregory's *Workhouse Ward*, Gertrude Jennings' *The Rest Cure*, and Harold Brighouse's *The Price of Coal* – a mixture of variety and plays. The costumes were to be striking in colour and design, with folk songs performed in smocks and peasant dresses. During rehearsals, every gesture and movement was timed exactly to the music. W. G. Fay, who had started a theatrical group in Ireland that eventually became the nucleus of the Abbey Theatre, was Elder's producer. He encouraged his players at every step, laughing at their apprehensions. Because of the sparse funds, volunteers made their costumes, scenery was at a minimum, and arrangements were made to take the roving players in as guests in homes along the way. By the end of the first week of rehearsals, no one felt strong enough as a driver of a small lorry to transport scenery, costumes, and properties on narrow curved roads to unfamiliar destinations.

Gerard urged Ashley to come to London at once, to the League offices on Robert Street, Adelphi, to apply for a position as an actor/driver for the touring company. "I'll put in a favorable recommendation for you, Ash," he promised.

Dashing to the Clinton flat, throwing clothing and toiletries into a rucksack, and catching the first train to London, Ashley arrived at the League's offices and was promptly sent to Elder's flat where the entire cast was rehearsing curtain calls. Arriving at his destination door, he heard voices singing inside. No one answered his knock. Ashley opened the unlocked door quietly. As it widened, he saw the performers holding hands and raising them to the ceiling. Applauding, Eleanor shouted loudly, "Cast dismissed."

Glancing in Ashley's direction, she announced, "I do hope this is our new driver. The office said you'd be coming. Is this the one, Rex?" she shouted over the din of actors congratulating one another after the practice finale.

Gerard called out, "Yes, Eleanor, this is Ashley Thronson."

"Welcome to our company, Ashley," Elder said as she approached him. "Want to see our lorry?"

"I've brought my credentials, and I'm prepared for an audition," Ashley said, anxiously, his rucksack in hand.

"No need, Ashley. Rex had ripping things to say about you. The job's yours, if you want it," Elder said gaily.

"Oh, I do. I do." Ashley responded enthusiastically.

"Let's see if you can drive the vehicle. Then, we'll have to find you a room."

The first tour, beginning in January, was to be for a fortnight in several Sussex villages. The local Labour Party had made all the arrangements and rented the halls. Under Ash's supervision, into the motor wagonette went the curtains, which would serve as a false proscenium and hide the wings; pieces of a wooden structure to hang them on; folding chairs and tables; and all the rest of the stage paraphernalia. If they couldn't share auto rides with those who owned vehicles, the cast and luggage would have to be transported by rail and picked up at the train station by Ashley. It was still an enormous challenge to him and his aides to pile one item after another into whatever room was available in the lorry. Several times, he stacked a bag confidently in a space, only to have it fall to the floor before he had picked up another item. Once his precious cargo was loaded, he and Gerard made their way to the first performance stop in the small village of Lindfield.

The "take in" went well for a first time. The fit-up had never been assembled in a hall before, and Miss Elder had to show Ashley and his actor-helpers where the scenery and properties were to be placed. Ashley accidentally put his foot through a piece of muslin on a flat-framed surface. Gerard hung a curtain upside down, and another actor had broken the leg of a small table. Aside from those minor incidents, the mistakes were readily repaired where necessary. While Miss Elder was perched on a ladder tying curtains to battens, she directed all the necessary tasks, and the costumes were unpacked and the properties laid out. The Travelling Theatre was ready for its first live performance, the weather perfect, and spirits were high.

There were no serious hitches on opening night. The small hall was packed, and cast friends had come down from London to provide a send-off. When the needle stuck in the phonograph, Hermoine Baddeley improvised onstage in pantomime until Miss Elder corrected the problem. The audience wasn't even aware that a phrase of Grieg's *"Anita's"* had been repeated ten times and her clever solo ended in a roar of appreciative laughter. The Baddeleys were, without a doubt, the successes of the evening, even if a few in the audience whispered their embarrassment over bare feet being shown in one number. At the end of the performance, an agitated teacher even lodged her personal protest with Eleanor Elder. "Stockings and petticoats worn with the costumes would make the dances decent and much more beautiful."

One of the cast members noted in her journal and quoted her words to Ashley:

> "Lindfield is incredibly picturesque. Pond with swans, terraced and balustraded Georgian houses, and a wisteria-covered hall. A pressman appeared and we had a lot of photographs taken in costume, making up in the open air (though why, I couldn't discover!) and so on. At the hall there was an excessively allegorical proscenium, designed by a Royal Academician, we were told, and it certainly looked it…Quite an excellent house, and the show went very smoothly and was apparently a huge success."

The second stop was Burgess Hill, although the cast remained with families where they had lodged in Lindfield. The company was to play in a filthy, musty, mildewed, rotting Victorian hall. After a major cleaning of the stage area and the setting up of sets and props, the performance went swimmingly. The audience especially enjoyed *The Workhouse Ward*, which Elder thought they might not understand.

By twenty-nine January, they were in Handcross, where the set-up was delayed. They had arrived at the church, where they were to play, in the middle of a Mothers' Meeting taking place. The piano was badly out of tune, and the rear-door to the hall locked. Fortunately, the vicar's wife was a skilled pianist and technician, and a rear door key was located so the scenery and properties could be unloaded. The meeting, strangely, ended with women marching out of the hall arguing, pointing accusatory fingers at one another. The company's one night performance, however, went well.

A few villages later, they came to Groombridge, where, once more, a key was missing, this time to the hall itself. It was in the possession of a particularly bloodthirsty butcher, who appeared with gore on his hands and apron, much to the chagrin of Miss Elder, a vegetarian.

The entire cast stayed in an old rambling house in Withyham, the town in which they played the next night. It was opposite a lovely lake, with a well-kept flower garden surrounding it.

Ashley, now eighteen, was in theatrical heaven. His status as a driver provided him an elevated presence as an important, actually irreplaceable, member of a touring theatrical company. He had the same duties as in Birmingham, including serving as callboy and dresser. Additionally, he was in charge of delivering, unloading, and loading scenery, property, and costumes, and returning to villages where they had played the previous night to pick up cast members or transport them after performances to their lodgings. He hadn't yet appeared on stage but was reassured that this would occur before long. He quickly came to know the young Baddeley girls, Enid Guest, Michael Hogan, Felix Irwin, John Powell, and other members of the touring group. Ashley developed an especially strong bond with Rex Gerard, who was sharing the mysteries of stage management on the road with him. But, most important of all, he had re-united with Rosie St. John, whom he had met on the *Lusitania* and with whom he had continued to communicate by mail. She was most attractive and had a perky personality and a curious mind.

Ashley had served "wing" duty as a second prompter at the sides of the stage where an actor might possibly forget his lines; he had dutifully moved scenery and props behind a closed curtain or when the stage lights were turned off. As in Birmingham, he had also assisted the men with their makeup and costume changes. Occasionally, he assisted the female cast members, as well. He found that Rosie St. John was blessed with a lovely singing voice and skilled as a solo dancer. She began giving lessons in both to a willing Ashley.

In Handcross and Groombridge, Michael Hogan, Rex Gerard, and Felix Irwin had put the finishing touches on a one-act play about the Boer War, which was to be launched in Withyham. The story began with four soldiers playing a game of whist and concluded with a humorous, exaggerated argument about who had made the greatest heroic contribution in terms of self and "Jolly Ole England." The short play had been announced in forthcoming event posters and in the Withyham weekly newspaper as an original farcical takeoff on the short-lived fortunes of war – a timely and needed topic at this moment in history. After the performance in Groombridge, John Powell, a former rugger and pugnacious talker, had walked through a fierce downpour to a local pub to share his numerous views of the world war with his newly acquired local friends.

When Ashley, who had transported cast members in shuttles back to their quarters in Withyham, finally located Powell in the middle of a sentence at the pub to drive him to his lodgings, it was past closing time. "Do-n't fret, La-addie," John slurred through the maze of smoke and the blaring of rowdy conversations going on about him. "I'll find me way 'ome. Go on now."

All the "but's" Ashley uttered did no good. Powell had turned his attention to his worshipping, badly inebriated audience. Tired to the bone, Ashley left the Groomfield pub, walking through pounding rain to the lorry, drove the eight kilometers to Withyham, and returned to his soft, warm cot in the Withyham guesthouse.

How Powell had mysteriously found his way to the doorstep in front of the old lakefront house where he was staying, no one could testify. Miss Elder discovered him lying on the wet ground at nine in the morning, a bottle of Whitbread still in his hand, in a seeming nightmare, talking wildly to himself, coughing, turning about constantly.

Summoning aid, she and others hauled the heavy body up the stairs, stripped him, and lay him, mumbling words only he could comprehend, on the bed he shared with Michael Hagan.

Calling Ashley to the sitting room, Miss Elder announced, "Ashley, you may have to take John's part in the skit tonight." Noting his look of protest, she added, "Don't worry. He'll probably bounce back in good health. Anyway, there are only one or two lines. You'd be fine."

"But Miss Elder, I've always been backstage. I've only been onstage as a walk-about," Ashley pleaded. "I'd like to be an actor, but I don't think I can do it."

"Ashley, you entered the theatre to become an actor, didn't you? Now, here's your chance. Here's a copy of the script. Study it. Just in case we lose John, I'll call the others for a rehearsal here in the sitting room in an hour." She left the room. Ashley opened the script and began reading it to himself.

The rehearsal went swimmingly. Ashley, with several bits of advice from Miss Elder and Charles, was a convincing young Boer War British soldier, even with his noticeable Bristolian accent. It even provided variety in the sound of the dialogue. The others complimented him on learning his four lines so rapidly. They conducted three run-throughs and then joined the others for lunch in the old inn's dining room.

Powell awoke in mid-afternoon. To Miss Elder, he still appeared drunk, and he couldn't be heard above a whisper. Knocking on the door to the men's quarters, Miss Elder announced, "Ashley. John is in a terrible state. You'll have to go on tonight."

"All right, Miss Elder," Ashley's heavily pitched stage voice rang through the door. "I expect a raise in wages."

Laughing, Miss Elder responded, "So do we all, Ashley. Start transporting the cast at five-ish."

At the theatre, after he had checked in the performers, and Rosie had given her best wishes, Ashley and his actor friends tried to adjust a soldier's costume made for a man of immensely large proportion into one for a medium-sized one.

"Let's lay this folded blanket along your front, Ash? It'll fill a lot of this empty space," Rex said as he stuffed an afghan into the tunic. "Your arms and legs are too thin," he insisted. "Let's take off your trousers and shirt and wrap bandages around your limbs. That'll fatten up your appendages."

"Ash, try these wads of cotton on both insides of your mouth," Felix insisted. You need to fatten your face."

Ashley, already quite uncomfortable with the bulging padding under his uniform, carefully inserted the two cotton mounds inside both sides of his face.

"Say something! "Let's hear how you sound?" Felix asked.

"H-h-m – m try-ing to ta-a-lk," Ashley mumbled, stuffing the wads further back in his mouth. "I'm trying to talk," he repeated. "Hear me?"

"Splendid," Felix offered. You look a thousand stones heavier. Those fat, rosy cheeks add a lot to your appearance. Now, try on the hat."

The non-commissioned officer's cap was also too large, so Rex hastily took out a pair of scissors, reduced the hat's radius, threaded a needle, and sewed the cut pieces together. Placing the cap on his head, Ashley stood before the mirror, admiring his new, massive appearance. Turning and walking a few paces, he deemed himself ready to go onstage as a more sizeable replica of himself. "I'm going to call 'halves' to go onstage in my new outfit and see if people recognize me," he promised.

As he made his rounds of the dressing rooms, everyone acknowledged his familiar voice; each one also had something to contribute about his appearance: "Hello, fatso. Where's the war?" "Ashley, you've got to watch the ale." "When did this hippopotamus join our company?" "John Powell, I thought you were still in bed," and "You could have fooled me."

The curtain rose to an appreciative audience in the small Withyham theatre. Built for a local amateur group, it seated approximately eighty people, with a tiny stage platform and a false proscenium arch made of scenery. The most distinguishing characteristic, however, was that the audience seats were on a decidedly flat surface, but the stage was sharply-angled, raked to insure every seated occupant an unobstructed view of the performing area.

"I've never seen such a rake in me life," said Rex, when he had first entered the theatre. Observing the angle of the stage, which was higher in the rear than the forestage, he said, "It's going to be hard to keep your balance moving downstage. We'll have to tape down the chairs and tables so they don't slide down into the audience."

The first two dancing numbers went well, as did the *The Rest Cure*. After the interval, Rosie St. John sang a folk song. The four males entered through the side curtains from stage left for their first performance of *Foppism or Heroism*.

"Break a leg, Ashley," Rex said. The other two followed suit.

"I've heard that often, Rex. What does it mean?" Ashley whispered to his friend.

"It's an old superstition," Gilbert answered quietly, as Rosie pranced around onstage earning laughter for her ditty. "It means good luck, but it's bad luck to say good luck. It's like 'bend your leg when you're making a bow.' It's a wish for success."

The setting for the sketch was a table in front of a dark rear curtain with three dark curtain legs hiding the wings on either side of the stage. The main curtain was red, and two panels were gathered upwards to the sides by pulleys opposite one another at the top of the false proscenium arch. It was literally a "the aris was drawn" operation in the Greek Classical sense.

The curtain closed on the applause for Rosie, and the actors brought four chairs and a table onstage. Behind the closed curtain, all in British military attire, they seated themselves in sturdy hardback chairs around a card table pretending they were engaged in a game of whist. Ashley had the second line in the scene, "When will we march to the front?"

The two red curtains lifted together on either side. Rex, in his deep stage baritone, boomed across the small table, "The enemy looks to have been very busy today, mates." Ashley looked up from the cards he had drawn. He was seated directly in front of the audience. He stared at the collective assemblage; naturally, they stared back at the four card players onstage.

In a louder voice, Rex repeated, "The enemy looks to have been very busy today, mates." Felix nudged Ashley's leg under the tale. Ashley was mesmerized. He didn't move a muscle. His eyes were fixed on the audience.

Elder whispered loudly from the prompter's corner, "When will we march to the front?" Ashley sat like a marbled stone statue. His fellow actors ruffled through the playing cards they held in their hands, each undecided what to do next.

Elder whispered the line again. No response.

Suddenly, a voice called out from the front row, loudly, "My God. He's peed his pants!" Agreement and laughter rippled through the crowd.

Sure enough, a large trickle of liquid was slowly moving down the inclined stage heading, towards the front row.

Quickly, Elder grabbed the cane Desmond Green was leaning on for his next scene and burst out on to the stage. Placing the hooked portion around Ashley's motionless neck, she pulled him upright. The curtain closed to a chaotic uproar of glee. Members of the first row moved to the aisles.

Backstage, Ashley, resembling a swimmer emerging from the water after a long exercise, admitted sadly, "I corpsed. I corpsed."

"Yes, Ashley," said Miss Elder, directing the Baddeley girls towards the stage for their next number. "It appears you've never faced an audience before. It's going to be a long while before I put you on stage again, young man."

During the next several months, Ashley continued only his driving, set-up, and backstage endeavors for the group. He did, however, continue developing song and dance numbers with Rosie at every opportunity. At the end of tour in June, he bade farewell to all the troupers, and, despondently, returned to Bristol to assist with deliveries from his father's store.

Chapter 22
Stratford-upon-Avon

Stratford, 1920

The September train ride from Bristol to Stratford-upon-Avon was not long. Ashley was excited as he entered the railway station. He looked about anxiously for Richard Bates who had insisted that Ashley meet him here. History was in the making and, thanks to Sir Frank Benson, they would be a part of it.

This was Ashley's first trip to Stratford, birthplace of the Bard, William Shakespeare. He looked forward to touring the city about which he had heard so much: the Avon River winding its way around the city, colourful punting boats, the ancient thatched-roofed buildings, the perfect place for a conference on British theatre.

As he stepped out of the entrance to the railroad station, he heard his name called. He spotted Richard at the kerb seated on the rider's bench of an open, large-wheeled wooden cart with a grey horse strapped to its steerage.

"Rupie! Over here!" Richard shouted, cupping his lips with his hands.

As Ashley approached the cart, Richard, lending him a hand, said, "Step up, now. Here's your seat. I've chartered this beautiful carriage for the afternoon until the drama conference starts. I want to show you Shakespeare's country." Ashley flung up his travelling-case and followed it over the side of the cart, shaking Richard's hand as he seated himself.

"Richard, remember? I'm Ashley. Right-o?"

"Sorry. I forgot your stage name," Richard paused with a wide grin.

"This rig is smashing," Ashley said with admiration, "but isn't it dear?

"No problem, mate. This is only one of several carriages owned by my actor friend, Rex Harrison. He makes more money from the visitors to Stratford than he can on the stage. Ash, Stratford-upon-Avon is a simply gorgeous little town," Richard announced with a sweeping wave of his arm. "It's amazing to think that it was new in 1196, added to the English medieval grid system. This is why the streets are so straight and why it's so easy to find your way around. Even though some of the first-level shops are modern, always look up from time to time. You'll find wavy roofs with terracotta dragons on them, odd little windows, and lots of black-and-white buildings. The Victorians painted them this way because they thought it looked neater. Who knows, you may see the living spirit of a very young Shakespeare unwillingly 'creeping off to school like a snail.'"

They started up Henley Street near the statue of a smiling Jester, a lasting reference to the many comics, fops, and fools who livened up Shakespeare's plays. As they moved down the street, Richard pointed out the family home, where William Shakespeare was born in an upper room in

1564. On the right side of the Tudor style half-timbered farmhouse was the workroom and shop where Richard indicated Shakespeare's father, John Shakespeare, had made and sold gloves.

"They came from the skin of sheep, which had been slaughtered and butchered. These animals were one of the main sources of income for the early Stratford community. Meat, wool, and leather goods from the animals and the tanning activity supported many families. That's Sheep Street over to your left," Richard indicated.

"Ash, see that white arched building?" he continued. "That used to be the old Market Hall. People could just walk in and out under the arches that go all the way around the building. The women sold their butter and cheese there. It was called the 'gossips' market.' Directly across the street is the site of the market cross and the whipping post. Any bargain or sale carried out under the cross would be honest and binding. See, beyond the roundabout? There's Bridge Street, going down towards the river and its fifteenth-century bridge."

As they crossed onto High Street, Ashley noticed an especially attractive shop with a sign over it, The Trading Post. "What's this place, Richard?" he asked.

"There's a little bit of everything in there. It has a long history. It was once a gaol with a cage for prisoners on the outside," Richard mused. "Later, it was the home of Shakespeare's youngest daughter Judith. She was married to Thomas Quiney who, rumour has it, was a womanizing wine merchant who drank more than he sold."

On the left side of the road was a large, black-and-white building with a sign outside, "Marlowe's Restaurant." Directly opposite was a beautiful, wood-carved house, which Richard said had been the home of John Harvard, the founder of America's famous Harvard University. Further down High Street was the Town Hall with the words "God Save the King" painted on the building.

"Do you know where the name 'Stratford' came from, Ash?" Richard asked.

"I haven't the faintest idea," was the response.

"In Roman times, this was a crossing point, a ford over the Avon. 'Strat' meant street and you know what 'ford' means. That's why there're so many Stratfords and Stretfords throughout England. You always had to get across the rivers. At first, they built wooden bridges. Later, stone ones. This bridge is called the Clapton Bridge. Oh, here's the Shakespeare Hotel," Richard announced, "where all the rooms and suites are named after Shakespeare's plays. You wouldn't want to spend a romantic holiday in a room called 'Much Ado About Nothing' would you? Over there's the Nash House. It's now the town museum. Thomas Nash married the girl-next-door, Shakespeare's granddaughter. See that green plaque? It tells about this being the site of the house where Shakespeare died on his fifty-second birthday in 1616."

The boys passed the Guild Chapel, Richard pointing out the boys' grammar school which Shakespeare was alleged to have attended, King Edward VI School. As they rode into Old Town, there were a series of red brick houses, all looking alike. One was Hall's Croft, formerly the home of Shakespeare's daughter Susannah and her husband, Doctor John Hall. Richard said Hall grew his own herbs and plants in the garden behind the house, using them for his medicines. Next, they paused at the Holy Trinity Church where the graves of Shakespeare and his family lay.

"This is really impressive," Ashley remarked, finding the solitude refreshing.

A mile out of town, they entered the hamlet of Shottery, home of Shakespeare's wife, Ann Hathaway, and her family.

It was a small, thatched-roofed cottage with the exterior cross beams surrounded by lovely flowers, with a bubbling brook running beside the path next to the house. The boys dropped off the cart, tied the horse to a tree, and walked a short distance from the cottage where a large pond had been formed by the brook. Surrounded by reeds and overhung by willows, it had a calming atmosphere.

"Just think, Richard, Shakespeare himself might have written one of his famous plays right at this spot," Ashley suggested.

"I doubt it, mate," Richard answered. "I reckon he wrote most of his plays in a London pub when he was with his repertory company. He only had time to write at night because they performed during the day. A pub was the only place where he had candlelight."

"You're probably right about that, Richard. I never thought about it before," said Ashley.

Resuming their ride on the cart, they returned to Stratford's downtown area. Richard pointed out the Dirty Duck pub, in Shakespeare's time known as the Black Swan. They again descended from the riding cart and walked along a footpath where a sign indicated that John Shakespeare had had a house there. It was close to the Shakespeare Memorial Theatre where the important conference they would both be attending was to take place.

"Come on. We'll have an ale in the White Swan Hotel to celebrate our tour," Richard declared.

The minute they entered the hotel, they couldn't help but notice that seated around one of the tables in the crowded bar were several famous theatricians: Barry Jackson, Frank Benson, John Martin Harvey, and playwrights John Drinkwater and G. B. Shaw, all deep in concentrated conversation. Jackson and Drinkwater rose in greeting the boys.

Benson looked up, recognizing Ashley. "Good, very good, Ashley Thronson. You made it. I'm happy to see you, young man. We need some members of the coming generation to help us decide what kind of theatre they're going to have in the future. And who is your friend, Ashley? Wait, I remember. It's Richard Bates. You toured America with one of my productions, didn't you, Richard?"

"Right you are, sir. And a grand tour it was."

Benson identified the renowned men around him. "We were just talking about Annie Horniman," Benson said. "Care to sit down with us and listen? Gentlemen, Ashley and Richard are here in Stratford to be my note-takers. "Ashley was an excellent prompter for one of our Company voyages to America. Richard is a Bensonian."

The boys hastily retrieved two chairs and joined the circle of colleagues. Each was handed a mug from a buxom serving girl who poured from a pitcher of ale.

"Well, I think we should name the new Stratford repertory theatre in honor of Annie," G. B. Shaw suggested. "She started repertory in Dublin and then in Manchester. She's the mother of rep," he added.

John Harvey held up his hand and asked to speak. He said, "Miss Horniman, even with her first Irish company, followed the group idea of a continuously changing programme and group responsibility with regard to acting. An actor would play a minor character in one play and a star part in another."

"You're correct, John," John Drinkwater interrupted. "In the fourth year of the Manchester Rep's existence, 1911, the company went to America to spread the good word about repertory theatre. They were enthusiastically received and asked to return. The next year, she took a company of eighteen actors and her business manager to Canada with eleven plays and fifty tons of scenery and properties. Of the plays brought from England for their first performance in America, they produced George's *Candida* and *Man and Superman*, *The Silver Box, Nan*, and Shakespeare's *She Stoops to Conquer* - all plays in the Company's repertoire."

Benson spoke up. "After returning to Manchester, Annie and her Gaiety Theatre rode the crest of the wave of theatrical triumph. It was very successful. She also played a six-week season in London at the Coronet Theatre, the first provincial repertory company ever to perform there. Again, she sent two companies for three months each to Canada and America playing to sell-out audiences."

Barry Jackson broke in. "By that time, Anne had two full theatrical companies, one in Manchester and one performing repertory for nine weeks at the Royal Court Theatre in London. But then the war came with what our Birmingham Company called 'all those cheery plays.'"

The boys listened in awe, Ashley recalling his own personal knowledge of the famous lady on a train ride some time ago.

Shaw noted that, primarily because of the war, Horniman's company of actors disbanded in the summer of 1917. The theatre was leased to other companies, eventually being turned into a cinema. "However, she's spent the rest of her life enjoying herself, travelling, dispensing advice." Changing his focus, he stood, declaring, "Gentlemen, the war's over! British theatre must have a new beginning! Stratford's the place to start! We all share the failure of theatre. We all should bear the blame. But we must start somewhere. I vote that it's with the new Horniman Theatre."

"But, George," broke in Jackson, "Stratford's the home of Shakespeare. It's the birthplace of our traditional theatre. I think it should remain as such. We need to establish a national theatre in London, not just a place for repertory actors to perform,"

Shaw seated himself, reaching for his mug of beer.

"Let's look at the facts." Drinkwater said. "Of the theatres Annie has nurtured, Glasgow was the first to lose its repertory theatre. Bristol's theatre had only a short life. Amateurs now run Sheffield's rep. Birmingham still has a repertory company, primarily due to Barry Jackson himself, and his family's chain of Maypole Dairies. And the Abbey Theatre's still going. That's about it."

"Are we talking about a resident national repertory company, or a national theatre that would feature the best actors and the best playwrights in the nation?" asked Benson. "You know I've been producing a Shakespeare summer season here for years."

"That's the real question," Shaw said. That's why we're having this conference. We have the greatest theatre minds in the country to help us figure it out. We can't decide in this pub what the future of the stage is going to be. It has to be part of the larger forum."

"I agree," Jackson offered. "However, I like the idea of a national repertory company named for Annie Horniman. Besides, she still has a large endowment from her family's tea business. We can't just depend on the government to build us a new theatre, can we?"

"Does anyone know how Annie got started in Manchester?" Benson asked.

"I do," Barry Jackson responded. "Remember, our Birmingham Company was the fourth British repertory theatre historically. Annie had done well with tours of the Abbey Company in Ireland. She saw the early potential of rep, the ability to bring theatre to the people, to make their leisure time worthwhile. When she started in Manchester, there were already eight commercial theatres in the city, offering every form of entertainment – music hall, variety, spectacle, Shakespeare, serious drama, ballet, opera, and circus. It was a circuit of suburban theaters. The people were interested in the arts and music. Culture was less tedious than punting in their canals. Manchester also had the first public library, you'll recall. The people were ready for her kind of theatre. She and Iden Payne, her British director from the Abbey Theatre, got the confidence of the press. She wanted to be in control. She knew how a theatre company was to be run."

"I remember that time well," John Drinkwater commented. "I was an actor with Barry's company before I became a playwright. I know the way she handled actors. With Horniman, actors would have secure contracts, but they were also open to dismissal for good reason. She insisted on discipline, from the manager down to the prompter. She demanded that her repertory theater would offer the best plays of all ages, while emphasizing new and original drama. With plays performed by a stock company of first-rate actors, seats would sell at top popular prices and productions would be efficient."

"But, best of all, Iden Payne was totally free for his artistic direction," Jackson commented. "Annie read every original play sent to her besides reviewing successful productions from London. She'd make her own recommendations to Iden, most of which he followed. She also replaced the old seats in the Gaiety Theatre and put an entire new face on the interior. She insisted on an orchestra. Her company identified with her new ideas and developed a new style of acting. It was more realistic. Their scenery moved from a bare stage to an overflowing extravaganza. George even gave her his new play, *Candida*, which became Sybil Thorndike's first great triumph. That went very well, didn't it, George?"

Shaw nodded.

"She 'discovered' Lewis Casson when he joined her touring company," Jackson continued. "As you all know, he married Sybil during their first run together. Horniman's company was even a success here in Stratford during several short tours. Before that, John Drinkwater and I attended several of her early productions in Manchester. Her new theatre had an all-white interior with plaster filigree work. The proscenium was framed in veined marble. It actually looked more like an art gallery than a theatre. The red upholstered, tip-up seats and cushioned seats in the gallery gave the theatre warmth and comfort. The top of the proscenium arch even had a replica of an ancient ship. Do you remember that, John?"

Nodding his agreement, John Drinkwater reminisced. "The Gaiety went from success to success. Galsworthy's *Strife* ran for three weeks. Ben Jonson's *Every Man in His Humour* and *Wanted Freedom* were played in 1910. Shakespeare's *Much Ado About Nothing* had full houses every night. By then, Annie had a full-time stage manager and a permanent scenic designer. Scenery, stage properties, and costumes were constructed right on the premises. Her staff included stage carpenters, electricians, callboys, and programme sellers. I believe she revolutionized travelling theatre." Jackson waved entry to Shaw who held up his hand to speak.

"Gentlemen, with eighty actors vying for roles, she had enough of them to divide into two companies. This enabled half of them to rehearse or to tour while the other half played at home in Manchester. This was an ideal arrangement for the actors. It gave them a chance to experience both touring and resident theatre and to try out a great variety of roles, from leading parts to walk-ons. Rehearsals ran from ten-thirty to four with a lunch recess at Miss Horniman's expense. Strangely, there were no jealousies, rather friendly competition and a stimulating challenge in a happy atmosphere. The actors had forty-week contacts, which expired each year but could be taken up for another year. Annie didn't want them to be legally bound to her. The wages ranged between three and twelve pounds per week, the same average as in London, except for the stars. There was no star system at the Gaiety. Good working conditions helped keep talented players."

"Having been one," Drinkwater said, "I know new playwrights became aware of her courage and pioneering spirit in presenting their works. The first three weeks of her company's performances in London gave the sophisticated audiences a good idea of the high standards of this provincial company. Annie Horniman became a London celebrity, a woman rising in a man's world."

Shaw re-entered the conversation. "Although she was attractive and a meticulous dresser, Annie never married. There were always rumors about her relationships with Yeats, her leading men, even me. As early as her Abbey theatre experience, Annie was forthright in spreading her theatre magic. She arranged for tour dates in England at Oxford and Cambridge. She even had a few bookings in London. Mostly, they toured the larger cities here in England and played to full houses everywhere. When she left the Abbey Theatre, which she had funded, after a nasty set of disputes, Annie broadened her scope greatly. She visited theatres, opera houses, museums, and art galleries all over - London, Paris, Prague, Bayreuth, and Dresden. She met the theatre managers and producers. The Abbey Theatre became a company of one production per month without Annie's continuing endowment. They even stopped sending touring leads to towns and villages with local supporting cast members."

Benson waved for attention. "I think it was in September of 1907 when she first tried out Manchester for size, with a short season of plays at the Midland Theatre. 'Brilliant' was the word used by the major local theatre critic to describe the opening night. George had given her his play, *Widowers' Houses*, which was most successful, and she also produced *David Ballard*, a realistic drama about lower middle-class life by newcomer Charles McEvoy. Her following four-week programme continued successfully. Additionally, she had discovered Charles Bibby, who was described by Iden Payne as the finest character actor he had ever known." Benson went on to say that Iden felt Bibby was unique in his capacity for grasping a character in a flash. He said, 'Without effort and, apparently, with instinct free from thought, he would instantly create a finished picture of whom he had to represent.' Having roused great interest and confidence in the future of Manchester theatre, Annie bought the rundown Gaiety Theatre on Peter Street, almost opposite the prestigious Theatre Royal, where Sir Henry Irving and Ellen Terry had built their reputations over many years. After, that, she made reporatory theatre history."

"Well, this has been a stimulating conversation, gentlemen," Benson said. "I'd previously thought that the conference would just be about forming a national theatre for the entire country and deciding on building Stratford-upon-Avon as our Shakespeare Center. You've provided me with considerable food for thought. Thanks, boys," he said to Ashley and Richard, "for listening in. You were certainly quiet."

"This was a fabulous learning experience for me," Ashley admitted. "What do you think, Richard?"

"I can't wait until tomorrow," the young aspiring actor responded as the group dispersed.

Chapter 23

The British National Theatre Conference

Stratford, 1920

The magic day had arrived. The royalty of British theatre had assembled for the first time to discuss the future of the profession in which each was involved. The seventy-five-fold included prominent actor-managers, both professional and amateur actors and actresses, theatre managers, scenic designers, theatre critics, directors, playwrights, and six young temporary scribes, such as Ashley and Richard, who would record the proceedings. Academic notables represented the various colleges and universities providing classes in dramatic history, Shakespeare, and other theatre disciplines, or contemplating to do so. Additionally, the leaders of several amateur theatre groups thoughout the U.K. had been invited.

The morning began rather chaotically. Once in the auditorium, everyone was engaged in handshaking, calling out to former colleagues, waving over the din to friends in distant seats, slapping a few backs, nodding almost continuously. Only a few sat silently awaiting the proceedings to begin. Ashley and Richard were as boisterous as everyone else, noting familiar faces in the crowd, dashing up to greet several former chums, talking excitedly about the occasion. Both had pens on the ready with large pads for codifying the theatrical history that would be taking place.

Eventually, with the din at its heighth, Sir Frank Benson rose, with great dignity, from the first row where all the speakers were positioned, strode vigorously to the rostrum, and lifted his arms to signal a command for silence. Like a knob control being slowly dialed on a radio, the vocal din subsided.

Benson began. "My theatrical friends - all of you." He flourished a sweeping broad gesture. "It's the twelfth of February 1920. We're here at Stratford-upon-Avon, the birthplace of England's greatest playwright, William Shakespeare. The occasion is the first British Theatre Conference ever held." There was a friendly murmur of proud acknowledgement. "We have assembled members of the British Drama League and the Workers' Education Association, as well as university professors - the leading theatre people in the British Empire. We have been called to discuss the formation of a national theatre that will not only serve both professional and amateur theatre but also be linked with the faculties of British colleges and universities.

"Shortly, we will divide ourselves into discussion groups, each headed by a respected professional, to consider the following four significant issues, all of which are listed in your programmes: One, to promote and assist in collective and individual efforts in the development of acting, drama, and theater as forces in the life of this nation. Two, to recommend governmental policy changes addressing the cultural needs of its people. Three, to encourage the development of theatre that is related to the lives of our people. Four, to take theatre, which is currently isolated and remote, into every town and village of our nation.

"Upon discussing these four key issues, we must also recommend to our government the structural form which we believe a future national theatre must assume for the good of our country, a national theatre performing Shakespeare and his medieval contemporaries, a national theatre featuring more modern fare including the classics of George Bernard Shaw and other playwrights in our midst, or a national theatre combining the best of England's dramatic output as well as America's and translations of the best of European works."

Richard whispered to Ashley, "I'd prefer the latter – the best of the best." Ashley nodded his affirmation.

Benson, adopting a professorial tone, continued, "As all of you recall, British theatre actually began with foreign material, with the Roman fireside dramatics of our early invaders. Later, it extended from the religious wagon stages of Mystery, Miracle, and Morality plays." When he commented that *Everyman*, written by the famous author, Anonymous, was still quite popular, he drew scattered laughter from the crowded auditorium. "In fact," he continued, "it was our own William Poel who rediscovered *Everyman* 400 years after its initial performances." Benson highlighted the Elizabethan period, crediting Shakespeare and his contemporaries, the jolly plays of the Restoration, and the great days of the actor-managers, performers who both acted and directed as well as toured their productions throughout Great Britain.

"I'd like to acknowledge the distinguished presence of several of these fine gentlemen actor-managers. I'm also looking forward to their collective recommendations as to a British national theatre. Gentlemen, will each of you please stand as I call your names." The famous theater notables, in turn, rose, nodded to the appreciative crowd, and bowed as if after a stage performance to a grateful audience: Ben Greet, John Harvey, Nigel Playfair, Seymour Hicks, Matheson Lang, and Johnston Forbes-Robertson.

"Two of our brethren, Sir John Hare and Sir Herbert Beerbahm Tree, have joined England's greatest actor Sir Henry Irving in being recognized for knighthood by our king in recognition of their notable contributions to our profession." Hare and Tree, seated next to one another in the front row, turned to the cheering audience and gestured their thanks. Before seating themselves, they both spread their arms towards Benson, who acknowledged the clapping recognition of his own previous royal honor of knighthood.

Benson, referring to his notes, told the assemblage, "Before we recluse ourselves in the separate rooms set aside for our deliberations, I'd like to call upon several individuals who have been giving our topics considerable thought over the past several months, people who have assisted me in planning this important gathering, individuals who will be leading the discussion sessions with you. First, I'd like you to recognize Sir Squire Bancroft who some years ago met with leading actor-managers to discuss many of the topics we'll be considering today. As you know, Sir Bancroft was knighted in 1897, honoring his significant contributions to theatre in the United Kingdom. Sir Bancroft."

To uplifting applause, Bancroft strode slowly and deliberately to the speaker's stand. "Thank you, thank you all," he said in his booming baritone. "I can't tell you how honored and thrilled I am to be with you this morning. As you know, we're not the first nation to consider supporting a national theatre. France and Russia already have thriving national companies. Others are under the leadership of reigning monarchs. In fact, the first play that was claimed to be a production of the British National Theatre was performed seventy years ago, in 1848, in Effingham. That run didn't last more than several weeks. Forty years later, Nathan Wilson, the radical bookseller of the Royal Exchange, issued hundreds of pamphlets suggesting that a house for Shakespeare under public ownership be built. It never was. Our own late and great actor-manager colleague, Sir Henry Irving, tried to turn his own Lyceum Theatre into what was widely known as the 'defacto national theatre.' Successful for a short time, he staged both modern plays and large cast classics before going bankrupt in 1899. In 1907, William Archer and Harley Granville Barker, both of whom we are fortunate to have with us today, wrote the very relevant book entitled *The National Theatre: A Scheme and Estimates.* I'm sure most of you have read the book since it serves as the blueprint for this gathering. Our conference host, Frank Benson, has for years been producing Shakespeare's mighty works here in Stratford in hopes that here would be established a national theatre in the bard's memory. Let's have a hand of recognition for Papa's past efforts."

Applauding collectively as one, audience members verbally insisted that Benson rise from his first-row seat, which he did.

Bancroft continued his speech in a serious tone, "There are four essential theatrical ingredients all of you must consider in your deliberations today without which theatre would not exist: the audience, the stage, the actor, and the play itself. For a national theatre to be considered, these are its most important elements. First, you must recognize that the audience's role in the creative act of theatre is an indispensable factor that makes drama possible. Second, the physical medium of performance, the acting area, its shape and space, the stage structure, the playhouse and its size, how it affects the acting and the response to it is a vital feature. Third, as to acting, the style of the actor's performance absolutely determines the success or failure of the work as a whole and whether its purpose has been fulfilled and its presence and purpose perceived. Fourth, the written play itself is necessary to the other three elements, subject to the pressure of past ways and means, the tyrannical expectations of the audience, and the strengths and weaknesses of the human factor in the artistic undertaking. In short, ladies and gentlemen, all drama today is a body of aesthetic laws for performance and communication. That's why it's so important that we consider its future not only on a national basis but also as to how our recommendation may influence the rest of the world. Now, let us allow Harley Granville Barker to address you."

As he crossed in front of the crowd, Barker shook Bancroft's hand strongly and was heard to say, "Jolly good, old mate."

Barker, a veteran of all theatrical roles - writer, actor, director, producer, theatre manager, and now educator – had prepared a large chart for the visual benefit of the audience. In large letters the following information was exhibited:

Spectrum of conventional possibilities:

Rules pertaining to authors and their plays:

The play's form and styles; and its musical content

The play's genre: comedy, tragedy, etc. masque, mime, etc.

The degree of reality implies: natural, symbolic, poetic, or ritualistic

The play's plot and structure

The forms of language, devices of speech and dialogue

Barker began. "All of you realize the first necessity in the culture of theatre has to be the literature itself. Shakespeare wrote of kings, queens, generals, and nobles rather than the everyday life experiences of common people. His medieval colleagues followed suit, but, instead of following the Greeks and Romans with their gods, they chose monarchs and the upper class representatives as their major characters. The relevance of Norway's Henrik Ibsen and his 'reality plays' had great influence on the more modern direction of our country's theatre."

Pointing with a finger as if counting, he continued, "From all of you playwrights in our midst - and I note John Galsworthy, Laurence Houseman, Somerset Maugham, Allen Monkhouse, William Archer, and Bernard Shaw - we need your expertise to address the significant topics of the play's genre – the characters, where the play takes place, whether it is to garner laughter, sensitivity to tragic events, or is devoted to spiritualism or intellectualism or just plain entertainment. The believability factor is another element. Should our national theatre reflect only realism? Should it symbolize love, or loyalty, heroism, or failure? What is the play's story and how does it unravel? And the language itself? Is it dialectic like the works of the Abbey Theatre? Is it lofty and thought-provoking like the work of Shakespeare and the person now walking in his footsteps - J. B. Shaw? Good, I see several of you taking notes. We can't wait for your thoughtful reactions to this kind of dialogue." Barker took his seat.

Next, Benson introduced Lewis Casson, husband of prominent actress Sybil Thorndike and a member of Annie Horniman's original Manchester Repertory Company.

Amid some murmuring throughout the large room, Casson, with his deep resonating theatrical voice, in his fatherly manner, commanded attention."Let me add to what

Harley has suggested. In considering a national theatre, I'm naturally partial to the actor. I, like many of you, have been one all my life. What would we, as actors, want to transmit to our audience,? The lyrical and thoughtful words of Shakespeare or Marlow, the significant messages of George Shaw, or the sometime shocking dialogue of Sir Arthur Wing Pinero and his theatre of ideas? Would you want to concentrate on one aspect of theatre or both historical and contemporary works? How are the actor's signals translated in performance? Let me try to answer that question because, in short, the actor is the translator of what a playwright wants to share with his audience. He is the one who has to present the written words and the stage surroundings to the minds and emotions of those viewing a performance. Should the actor's mode of performance be naturalistic or representative or surrealistic? What dictates his movement, his changing of position, gestures, facial expressions, and his choice of characterization? What does his costume, mask, or make-up imply? How does his use of props and the décor setting and lighting affect the performance? What is the actor's physical acting area or playhouse, his spatial workplace? Is his performing platform an arena or thrust stage or is it framed by a proscenium arch? Actors and actresses, when we come together in a few minutes, these are the experiences I urge you to remember and which to think about as you ponder your own desires of our nation's future theatre movement. Thank you."

The highly regarded George Bernard Shaw was the next featured speaker. Enthusiastic applause followed his path to the head of the assemblage. "I'm a playwright. I imagine most of you already know that." Laughter. "But, first, and many of you hate me for it, I was a critic. I was an evaluative member of the audience. My task was somewhat, like Lewis expressed, that of an actor. I was also an interpreter – an interpreter of what I had witnessed in a full scale production, sharing my own impressions with readers of newspapers - potential audience members. Accordingly, that makes me a professional audience interpreter now because that's who I still write for. Most of you also know that the Lord Chamberlain and I didn't agree on some of the material I included in my scripts. You're also aware that several plays of which I was most proud were performed in America before they became accepted in my own country."

"I didn't realize that they were produced first in America," Ashley proclaimed quietly. "That's criminal."

Shaw continued, "When I write, I think not only of my subjects and the messages I want to transmit. I consider the audience's expectations. What are their individual and collective desires from the work they witness? These expectations are dependent on the place and time of the audience members, and their cultural experiences and assumptions, their religious and economical persuasions, their educational experiences, and their grasp and degree of imaginative perception. Theatre thrives in a simple metaphor. As in theatre, things stand for things rather than being those things. Or, as this room represents a world, you now represent an entire society. Remember, it was the French playwright Eugene Scribe, who taught us about the well-made play. 'The first rule is clarity,' he said. 'There has to be a reason for servants to clear a room. Each piece of dialogue should advance the plot or reveal character. We must arouse and maintain suspense.' As I've said so often," Shaw said, in his native Irish accent, "Make 'em laugh. Make 'em weep. Make 'em want. Provide them with a sense of waiting for something to happen. Use surprise. I look forward to gathering with my fellow playwrights to ponder our auspicious cause."

Several voices in the crowd reacted to Shaw's introductory words with "Hear! Hear!"

Next, Basil Dean, also a member of Annie Horniman's first Manchester Company, stood in front of his theatrical peers. "Isn't this exciting?" he asked. "This is the first time in the history of our nation that the future of British theatre is actually going to be considered seriously and charted by people of the theatre. I heartily welcome you, looking forward to the recommendations that will be forthcoming from this unique and talented body of theatre professionals. Before I introduce you to the 'mother of repertory theatre,' I want to briefly address the amateur and educational theatre movement taking place at this very moment in our country. Will all of the university professors and managers and performers in amateur theatre groups please rise?"

Perhaps, twenty men and a few women stood in front of their seats and welcomed the applause given them.

After they re-seated themselves, Dean continued. "We're all, those of us in professional theatre, delighted to have all of you with us. If we address the significant issue of a national theatre, we must have a foundation of well-informed, well-trained, well-read, and well-prepared advocates to perform theatre in every village and community, to prepare themselves for professional venues, to carry the message of the 'culture of drama' into our classrooms, into our churches, and into the hearts and minds of our people. We'll not be telling you the productions you should perform or the subjects you should teach or study. We're hoping that you'll be telling us what we need to do to nationalize our profession. Thank you all for being with us today. Now, it is my honor to introduce our next speaker. Though as yet still unmarried, she's still the 'mother of repertory theatre in the United Kingdom,' Annie Horniman. She'll be making her entrance shortly. She wanted to make it suspenseful."

"Phillip and I met her on a train to Liverpool several

years ago," Ashley whispered to Richard. "We told her we were secret agents. I'm not sure she really believed us."

Dean continued describing Miss Horniman's ventures with Ireland's Abbey Theatre, her becoming close friends with playwrights W. B. Yeats and G. B. Shaw, her hiring now prominent director Ben Iden Payne when he was just a bit player. He spoke lovingly of his own first encounters with her in Manchester when she formed England's first repertory company in the Gaiety Theatre she had revamped. "Will any members of that first company who are in the auditorium this morning please rise?" he asked.

Scattered throughout the hall, several now famous personages rose from their seats to a continuous clapping of hands: Sybil Thorndike and Lewis Casson, side by side; Ben Iden Payne, who had just returned for the conference from America; Herbert Lomas, Miss Darrah, Charles Bibby, and several other recognizable faces.

Dean glanced at his notes and went on, "The first play she opened was on Saturday, 11 April 1908, and I remember it well. It was written by the chap who grew up here in Stratford, William Shakespeare. It was his popular *Measure for Measure*, without lavish settings and costumes, presented on a bare two-level stage with Mr. William Poel as producer." Dean waved a hand at Poel sitting in the front row. "Mr. Poel, as several of you have experienced, has his own special technique of delivering Shakespeare. This method, mind you, he and other imitators have performed at previous festivals here in Stratford." A number of audience members nodded knowingly, recalling their own rehearsals with Poel who forced them to carefully articulate Shakespeare's lines to deliver them in sing-song fashion to emphasize the rhythm of his words.

Dean went on, "Miss Horniman was a business woman in a male-dominated artistic world and delighted in the challenge of making her theatre both an artistic and commercial success. She spoke to the Manchester public about her repertory dream. To her, repertory meant 'storehouse.' Just as library shelves held used books waiting to be taken from its shelves and be reused, to her, plays that had already been produced and justified were also ready to be used again. By changing the play two or three times a week, actors would not grow stale, and their supporters could come to the theatre more than one time a week to see them act. I know, for I was one of her early cast members, at that time quite young."

Many in the audience knew that Dean had originated the term, "scene stealer," with his crafty portrayal of protagonist Jack in Galsworthy's *The Silver Box*.

"Additionally, new plays, just like new books, could be added to the shelves. In this way, a community spirit would grow between the actors, the playwrights, and their audiences. She was the first to encourage new authors to write for the theatre and to mold her company to perform new and untried scripts. To her, the movement was meant to be a democratic art, embracing the widest possible audiences. To me, Annie has already provided us with a model for England's national theatre. Ladies and gentlemen, Miss Annie Horniman."

As she entered the room through large rear doors, the audience rose as one, all applauding. She was dressed in academic garb, with a dark velvet flowing robe and squared scholar's academic cap in celebration of the honorary Master's degree she had received ten years ago from the University of Manchester. This was in recognition of her contribution to her adopted city and to the cause of drama. She also wore her famous brooch, a silver dragon-shaped pendant, five inches long and emblazoned with over three hundred opals.

As she made her way down the center aisle, Ashley again

whispered to Richard, "And I thought she was just a crazy old buzzard." Richard pouted.

Miss Horniman began with her soft matronly voice, "Thank you. Thank you. I appreciate Mr. Dean's kind words and, hopefully, will speak as briefly as he has. As you can see, as usual, I'm without notes. My memories have held me in stead thus far, and, as I approach my sixtieth year, I hope they don't take leave of me during this address. I had considerable help in getting this rep scheme going. My first company of actors was drawn from Harley Granville Barker's and Frank Benson's companies, and William Poel's Elizabethan Stage Society. Fortunately, I was able to hire Ben Iden Payne as my first stage director. We attracted the very best of actors. I'm overwhelmed in seeing so many of you here today. We have, indeed, made theatre history together, have we not? Of our twelve productions in Manchester during our first season, which was an unequivocal success, artistically and financially, three were new plays, three were plays that had their first tours. One was foreign, a Sudermann play, and two were revivals. I am proud to have started the first permanent repertory theatre in England. We performed drama about real life, tried and true plays, Shakespeare and the classics for our audiences," she related.

Several members of the audience rose, cheering and applauding.

"Besides being a resident repertory company, we also became a touring company, taking our best plays to local villages. That first season, we gave the inaugural performance of Edward Garnett's *The Feud* and John Masefield's *Nan.* Even though I couldn't vote or hold public office and I had problems getting a drinking license for the theatre, I enjoyed being a woman in a man's world. And I still do."

There was a ripple of laughter and applause, especially among the ladies present.

Miss Horniman said that her company, in their acting, followed the group idea of a continuously changing programme and group responsibility for acting. An actor might play a minor character in one play, a star part in another. In their fourth year of existence, 1911, the company went to America to spread the good word about repertory theatre. They were enthusiastically received and asked to return. In 1912, they took a company of eighteen actors and their business manager to Canada, with eleven plays and fifty tons of scenery and properties.

"That's what I want to do, Richard, tour America," Ashley announced quietly in a serious tone.

Miss Horniman regaled. "The Gaiety ship was riding on the crest of a powerful wave, the white horse," the female captain boasted. "Besides Manchester, we played a six-week season in London at the Coronet Theatre, the first provincial repertory company to perform there. We also spent another three months in Canada and America to sell-out audiences. We grew to such a size we could accommodate two theatrical companies, one resident in Manchester, and one staging choices from our repertoire at the Royal Court Theatre in London for nine weeks. The newspapers reported our actors and stage direction as being of the highest standard. Unfortunately, the Great World War was about to unleash its fury and misery. Like others during this horrendous period, we moved to producing 'cheery plays.' We disbanded two years ago. I've spent these past months enjoying life, travelling, and giving advice, as I'm doing now," she said proudly. "Why did our theatre fail during the war? Who should bare the blame? I'll answer that question. We all should. It's our fault that theatre has entered this purgatory. As to starting a national theatre movement, let's stop talking and get doing."

Again, the audience rose together, all applauding enthusiastically.

Frank Benson again appeared before the theatrical crowd. Pointing his finger at the audience, he said, "Now, it's your turn. Please go to your assigned rooms. Remember, although theatre may still be active in London, it's isolated and remote in the rest of the country. Let's all do something about that!"

Everyone went to a room matching the number that had been pinned on their prepared name cards when they entered the lobby on their arrival.

Playwrights, including Sir Arthur Pinero, John Galsworthy, Laurence Houseman, Somerset Maugham, Allen Monkhouse, James Fagen, and John Drinkwater, whose play *Abraham Lincoln* had been an acknowledged success in London, followed Shaw to the Hamlet Room.

The few critics on hand went to the Macbeth Room with William Archer. Geoffrey Whitworth, who had just founded the British Drama League, and James Agate, the outspoken critic of the *London Sunday Times*, joined them.

The directors met with Barry Jackson and were assigned the Tempest Room. They included Robert Atkins, Peter Godfrey, Nugent Monck, Ben Iden Payne, William Poel, and Alan Wade.

The theatre managers, the largest group, under the leadership of Sir John Hare, who had been knighted in 1907, entered the Othello Room. Among them were William Armstrong, Lillian Baylis of the Old Vic, Annie Horniman, Gerald Lawrence, Miles Malleson, Albert Matthews, Fred Percy, Arthur Rose, Fred Terry, and Harcourt Williams.

The former actor-managers, probably the oldest gathering, appropriately, went to the Lear Room with Benson as their spokesperson.

Actors and actresses, among whom were Gracie Fields, Hermione Gingold, Helen Hayes, Gertrude Lawrence, Beatrice Lilly, Mrs. Partrick Campbell, Marion Terry, Ellen

Terry, Sybil Thorndike, and Dame May Whitty, along with such actors as Robert Atkins and J. Robin Hare, filled the Verona Room.

The amateur theatre representatives met in the Shrew Room; the academics in the Romeo and Juliet Room.

Frank Benson had held a briefing with the recorders early in the morning. Requesting that they try to take down as much information as they could, he indicated that their primary objective was to identify as many subjects as their groups considered and, especially, attempt, word for word, to capture any recommendations that were agreed upon regarding a national theatre. "The group leaders," he commented, "will each provide a summary to the reconvened audience. Your materials, I assure you, will be the basis for the report that Harley Granville Barker and I submit to the appropriate British government cultural officials."

Ashley joined Benson and the actor-manager group, while Richard went to the actors' Verona Room. For the next three hours all of the groups enthusiastically continued their discussions. At one in the afternoon, food was brought into each of the rooms and devoured quickly as the meetings went on. Promptly at three o' clock, a bell chimed and all the conferees reassembled in the main hall.

This time, it was Oscar Asche who greeted the returnees. Asche was perhaps the most prominent theatre manager of this period. Having begun his eventful career first touring with Frank Benson, his own oriental fantasy, *Chu Chin Chow* was still playing at His Majesty's Theatre, having opened to rave reviews in 1915. As the audience settled down, Asche requested that each of the discussion leaders join him at the front of the room where chairs awaited them

The presenters faithfully held to the fifteen minutes each had been allotted. By the third speaker, it was obvious that the collective opinions appeared to favor the continued development of theatre in Stratford to perpetuate Shakespeare and his contemporaries work, using the resident theatre model of Annie Horniman's Manchester Theatre Company. The British government should be encouraged to create a national theatre in London, which would have both resident and touring companies taking their best productions throughout the British Isles. The amateur theatres and university theatres would serve as the testing grounds for new plays and the training of playwrights, directors, performers, setting designers, and lighting technicians.

Many "bravos" were uttered as the group representatives shared what had occurred in their gathering places. By the time Benson rose for his anticipated summary, one could feel the enthusiasm and vigor of the audience.

When Benson began, he exclaimed, "I never in my life believed that so many with such diverse backgrounds and representing all the different aspects of theatrics could come to such a common threshold. I'm thrilled with your conclusions. I'm excited about the future of theatre in this country as long as it's in your hands. I declare our mission accomplished!"

Cheers rang throughout the hall as everyone appeared to be congratulating everyone else. Barker leaped to his feet and ran to Benson, hugging him warmly. "Now we've got the information and the support we need. Now, we can prepare our national theatre document."

They joined the departing throng, most heading for a nearby pub.

Richard said to Ashley, "I guess we'd better start writing. We promised to give our reports to Sir Benson tomorrow." They left for their hotel lodging.

The next day, they departed on separate trains, Ashley returning to Bristol, Richard to London. Before leaving, having spent the previous evening writing and talking, with little sleep accomplished, they had given their written reports to one of Benson's associates. He promised that he would be in touch with them soon.

Chapter 24
Among the Unemployed

London, 1920

Back in London, a non-paying guest in a flat shared with Rex Gerard, his Liverpool mate, Ashley took up the employment-search gauntlet. He regarded the task as a business venture. He was the product to be sold. First, he compiled a lengthy list of actors' agents from the most recent theatre magazines. Next, he identified all of the new plays announced for production in London during the next three months, the names and addresses of producers, where copies of the plays could be obtained, and the dates and places for auditions. Visiting the local printing shop, he laid out a new vitae summarizing his theatrical experiences with A.L.S. and the Liverpool and Birmingham rep companies. He included three photographs of himself in different costumes and poses. He mused, *I look rather handsome in this foot soldier's uniform. As an old beggar with beard, cane and ragged clothes, no one could recognize me. Am I not dashing as a well-dressed fop in my fifteenth-century outfit?*

Needing guidance as he attempted to begin his real-life profession in theatre, he spent two entire days preparing letters requesting referral suggestions from Richard Bates, Phillip Maggs, and Rosie St. John. He wrote lengthy letters to Sir Frank Benson, John Drinkwater, Arthur Asche, and Basil Dean. He even found time to send notes to the Townsends and to magician Marvelous Martin. He had one hundred curriculum vitae produced, and, upon taking them home, immediately began his letter-writing campaign.

Initially, he penned twenty-five personal letters to agents, several with whom he had been in previous contact, but mostly to those he had picked at random. Agents, he felt, were keys to an actor's life since many of them had previously provided talent to producers or were on friendly terms with them. They could influence casting decisions. As a relative unknown and a young one at that, Ashley felt he was at the bottom of the mix when it came to being selected as an actor.

It took a week before he could post all his solicitation letters. Next, he made up a master calendar of audition possibilities. Within a fortnight, from the letters he wrote to agents, he received only one telephone call and two mailed responses, none of which was encouraging. He had waited faithfully next to a friend's phone, which he had listed in his writings, hoping for a better agent response.

"Perhaps my wording was poor in the letters," he remarked to Rex one evening.

"No, Ashley, I think it's just your lack of acting experience. I'm only in this long run at the Majestic Theatre because of my stage manager's background. I'm not paid as a walk-on actor. Maybe you should be looking more for design or technical work," Rex suggested.

"I enjoy being onstage rather than backstage, Rex. Frankly, I feast on the adulation that goes with acting, that reaction of a live audience appreciating your performance. It gives me a sort of rush throughout my body when I'm before an audience. I just love pretending I'm in another person's body. I'm sure acting's in my blood."

"Well, somehow you need a transfusion, Ash. You've got to keep trying. Looking for work is part of an actor's life. When the play closes, you've got to strike out again."

Ashley took out his list of agents. "You're right. I just have to knock on the right doors."

For the next ten days, he walked London's streets, stopping at actors' agents' doors to drop off his resume with a note requesting an appointment. From theatrical notices and magazines, he also averaged an audition call at a theatre every other day. Usually, he spent a full day waiting for the chance to read a piece he carried or lines from a play to be produced, but he was never selected for a part. On the eleventh day, happily, he was invited into Cleve Smith's office to discuss representation. Smith had been suggested as a possible agent by Richard Bates. However, after several minutes, Smith indicated that Ashley lacked the necessary professional theatrical background and should seek other employment.

Responses to his letters to his friends Richard, Phillip, and Rosie brought only encouragement. There were no return letters from Benson, Drinkwater, Dean, or Asche. The only other response he received was from Eleanor Elder who wrote him a letter every week, inviting him to return to her company. He replied to her, indicating that now pursuing a professional career, he considered the A.L.S. as amateur theatre, gratefully insisting he would continue his quest in London. He also traded letters with his father who never failed to insist that he give up "this foolhardy chase of theatrical life and return home to follow a grocer's profession."

Two more weeks passed. Ashley had only one audition that was somewhat encouraging. Only a few actors had been called for a play about school children during the Great War, *Rising to the Occasion*. The producer, Thad Wooley, had written the play himself. It was a hero's story about a school-aged boy, lying about his age, who had entered the British Army and had been sent to the front in France. He had distinguished himself on the battlefield and returned home with a set of medals. His homecoming had been disastrous, with his former friends rejecting him because of his superior attitude, and the fact that he had not completed his schooling in preparation for the university. There was a part in the play that suited Ashley as one of the hero's former friends who had turned on him. Ashley had been encouraged by the scenes he had read with the young actor who had been selected to play the hero lead, Lawrence Olivier. They interacted well together, and Ashley had been impressed with the maturity Olivier exhibited. Olivier, himself, had encouraged Ashley, commenting on his convincing reading of his lines. Unfortunately, Wooley, admitting that Ashley performed well, felt he looked too much like Olivier facially and in stature and, thus, was unsuitable for the part. He dismissed Ashley with thanks.

Ashley was invited to another audition invitation at Her Majesty's Theatre. It was for the Shakespearean play, *Julius Caesar*, which was to open one month hence starring Robert Atkin. Ashley arrived at the backstage door at exactly nine-thirty a.m. He was ushered into the gas-lighted auditorium where at least two hundred people were already seated, all apparently prepared for an audition. As he looked around those seated, there was no one he recognized. He sat quietly reading the *London Globe*. At ten a.m., four men, all apparently in their forties, dressed in business attire, entered from the rear, marching behind one another down the aisle to the front row. Three of them sat down. The other, a tall, graceful, very distinguished gentleman, remained standing and introduced himself, "Good morning. Thank you all for coming. You'll all be auditioning for me, Thelman Richardson, the producer, and Mr. Rice Anderson, our stage manager."

Anderson rose and waved to the crowd.

"For Mr. Ned Wagner, our director."

Wagner stood and bowed before re-seating himself.

"And for the prominent actor who will be playing Julius Caesar, Robert Atkin."

Applause rang throughout the auditorium as the well-known actor stood, bowed, turned to his enthusiastic audience and opened his arms with gratitude, before sitting.

"We've asked all of you to bring a three-minute dramatic piece to read aloud," Richardson continued. "When your name is called, please stand by the stairs on stage right. When your name is called again, please go to the apron and deliver your presentation immediately from center stage directed to the four of us in the first row. We'll call upon you alphabetically, so, for many of you, you'll have a long wait. You may leave the theatre, but if you miss answering your call, we'll have to cancel your audition. Is that clear to everyone?"

"Yesses" rang through the auditorium.

"Amy Adams," called out Rice Anderson loudly. Elizabeth Abbott, Margaret Alcott. Please come to the staircase. You can begin as soon as you're onstage, Miss Adams." The three women hurried to the staircase footing, and Amy Adams began hurriedly reading her lines.

"Thank you, Miss Adams. We'll be in touch with you if necessary," Richardson said. "Next."

And so the auditions continued throughout the morning.

With eighty attendees at three minutes each, Ashley figured the tryouts would last into the evening, but many of those taking the stage were sent away before their time was up. At noon, Ashley was becoming quite restless and left the theatre for fish and chips at the closest eatery. When he returned to the theatre, the calls had reached the "p's," so he felt he would be called upon by late afternoon. He had picked up the *London Times* and had read every single article by the time he heard the "t's" being requested. At five p.m., he heard his name at last and rushed to the staircase. When his name was called a second time, he sped up the stairs, strolled to center stage and, nervously, and with some hesitation, began Hamlet's famous soliloquy:

"To be, or not to be, that is the question," Ashley began reading. He looked away from the four intense faces in the front row up at the balcony.

"Whether 'tis nobler in the mind to suffer the slings and arrows of outrageous fortune, or to take arms against a sea of bubbles. I mean troubles," He glanced at the producer who appeared to be scowling. There were murmurs from the audience.

Ashley continued, "And by opposing end them? To die, to weep. I mean sleep, no more; and by a sleep to say we end." *I'm not doing well,* he said to himself. "The heart-ache and the thousand natural shocks that flesh is heir to, 'tis a consummation devoutly to be wish'd..."

"Stop! Stop! Mr. Thronson. That's sufficient. Yes, sufficient. You should change your audition piece. That's quite beyond your range," said Thelman Richardson. "You may go."

Embarrassed, Ashley left the stage and the auditorium in haste and rushed to the haven of his flat. That night, he drowned his self disappointment in ill-afforded ale.

Two days later, having received a telephone call from a

theatrical agent, Paul Nugent, who had an office on Fleet Street, Ashley made an appointment for nine a.m. Dressed in his finest, he arrived on time at Nugent's office and introduced himself to the attendant. There were at least ten others in the waiting area. The woman said graciously, "I'm sorry, Mr. Thronson, but there will be a slight wait."

By three in the afternoon, others had also arrived, and all of the earlier visitors had been seen, as well as several of the late arrivals. Apparently, they had left by another entrance. Ashley, hungry, quite irritated by being ignored, approached the attendant and asked. "Why have I been kept waiting so long?"

"Oh, I'm sorry, Mr. Thronson, isn't it? Mr. Nugent is casting a play for a producer friend and holding auditions in his office. Would you like to make another appointment?"

"No, how much longer do you think it will take to see him?"

"He has no more appointments after four," was the response.

"I'll wait, then," Ashley responded. And he did.

At precisely five o'clock, Ashley was admitted to Nugent's office.

"What can I do for you, young man?" Nugent asked.

"I'm looking for representation from an actor's agent," Ashley responded. "You appear to have a good reputation."

"Thank you, my man," Nugent answered, fumbling through the papers on his desk. "I must have your resume somewhere in this pile."

"Here's another, sir," said Ashley as he passed one to the agent.

Skimming the resume, Nugent remarked, "I see you've done resident stock as an apprentice and you were a lorry driver for a touring theatre company. Where's your experience as an actor?"

Well, sir, I attended acting school in Bristol and I was a prompter for the Bensonians on a seaboard trip to American, and I did some acting and singing for the ALS. tour," Ashley said anxiously.

"That's not being on the real stage acting," Nugent responded. "I'm sorry. You're too inexperienced for me to consider representing you. My income depends on many actors having theatrical work. You just lack the qualifications."

"But, sir, I'm a talented actor. Miss Eleanor Elder used me in many different roles during the A.L.S. tour. I played leads, old men, and I even danced." *What's a little fib*, he mused. to himself.

"I'm sorry, son. I have to leave now. I'll see you to the door," Nugent said as he escorted Ashley out of his office. Once again, a disappointed young man returned to his flat.

Rex Girard greeted him at the door. "How did the interview go, Ash?" he asked.

"Not well at all," was the response. "And I'm running out of money. I doubt that my father will send me another shilling until I promise to return to Bristol and the grocery store."

"I've other news for you, Ash. It's not so good either. Have you read today's *Manchester Guardian*?"

"No, what's the news?" Ashley asked.

"There's a rather long story about Harley Granville Barker's meeting with the British National Arts Council."

"Oh, yes, about our meeting at Stratford to form a national theatre company," Ashley said.

"Right-o, but I'm so sorry to tell you the Council didn't agree with the report Barker presented. They felt the national concentration should be on promoting theatre and the arts in the schools, and on an amateur rather than a professional basis. They concluded that theatre was a business, not a responsibility of the government."

Ashley was silent, his disappointment apparent in his facial expression.

Girard sat next to him. "Ashley, I know you were hoping that a new national theatre company and one at Stratford dedicated to Shakespearean productions might bring cultural enlightenment to this country. That's not about to happen," he added.

Chapter 25
The Travelling Theatre Again

On the Road, 1920-21

Ashley had kept in close touch with Miss Eleanor Elder who had continued moving her Arts League Services touring group throughout England. Returning to his small flat in London's Soho district, he found a letter from her under his front door. It read:

> Dear Ashley:
>
> I hope all is well with you. Are you available? I need someone for a month, from late January to late February for a short ALS tour through the southeastern area. Rex Gerard has indicated you're available. I'd like you to drive the lorry, play several small roles in our one-acts, and, perhaps, sing a few ditties and dance. Of course, we'd also like you to help load and unload the settings and equipment.

> Are you still in contact with Rosie St. John? Might she, too, be able to join our touring company? I can offer you both ample salaries. If you are interested, please telephone me immediately. I need to move as rapidly as possible.
> Sincerely, Eleanor Elder

Ashley was excited. He had had absolutely no prospects from the last two months he had spent going from one theatrical agent's office to another on a daily basis and attending play auditions. Rosie had appeared in a Christmas pageant during the month of December, and he thought she might also be open to joining the A.L.S touring program. He ran to her nearby flat, which she shared with two other young aspiring actresses.

As Rosie opened her door, Ashley burst into the room. He ignored her roommates, both of whom were holding play scripts while seated on the two comfortable lounges that filled the small living room area. Eagerly, he explained to Rosie that Eleanor Elder had an offer neither of them should refuse, trying to convince her that they should see Miss Elder as soon as possible.

"But, Ashley, I may have a part in Todd Huntley's play that's opening next month at the Majestic," Rosie said.

"Rosie, that play won't open until March. I understand the producers haven't raised any front money yet. I also heard their lease for the Majestic won't begin until March. This tour would fit in perfectly. Besides, we have a chance to try out some of the new songs and dances we've practicing in the past."

"Yes, but those were designed for us to get jobs with variety shows, not the A.L.S. tour."

"What's the difference? Culture is culture, isn't it?" Ashley responded. "Come on. Get your coat. Eleanor Elder's flat's within walking distance."

Rosie complied.

The pair dashed the several blocks to Elder's residence. She opened her door after the first knock. "Ashley. Rosie. How good to see you. I'd hoped you might call me, Ashley. We can really use both of you."

For the next two hours, the three of them enthusiastically discussed the tour. There would be eight cast members. Rex Girard was to be stage manager, and Eleanor was to serve as the producer. Each performance would include a mixture of three dance numbers, four ballads or folk songs, a poetry reading, interspersed with three one-act plays. A gramophone would provide musical accompaniment. The ballet numbers would be exclusively performed by Hermoine Baddely, and a variety of ballroom dance routines peformed by Ashley and Rosie. Six different one-act plays would be presented, three of which would alternate for every performance, and there would be three singers, including Ashley and Rosie, to allow setting and property changes in between the one-acters.

"Remember, darlings," Elder reminded them. "We're bringing culture to these folks. We have to have considerable variety in our performance offerings to try and satisfy all our audiences, regardless of age, gender, education, or knowledge of theatrics."

"When do rehearsals start?" Rosie asked. "And where are you holding them?"

"Right here, Rosie, as we've done in the past. We're starting in seven days. I still have to round up three other cast members. As you know, we have to give credence to one-act plays. The sophisticated town doesn't want precisely the same thing as the remote village, and the League must cater to both. It must, indeed, contrive to introduce the touches of nature, which make them keen. When our travelling theater first toured, the list of available one-act plays was comparatively small, though it claimed some masterpieces of language and construction. Now, among the hundreds published every year, in addition to the thousands written, a producer has to hunt diligently for those worthy of production. There're so many imitations of what has been said or done before. Both the British Drama League and the A.L.S. helped incur rapid growth of the amateur dramatic movement, which is the sole summary of the one-act play."

"As you may recall, Miss Elder, I'm not a polished actor," Ashley admitted.

"I well remember your Boaer War performance," Miss Elder said with a slight giggle. "However, I'm counting on you to have gained some polish, Ashley," Elder answered. "You've got a fine voice, a manly physique, and you're handsome. Don't you agree, Rosie?"

"I do," said Rosie with a nod and a smile.

"Also, many fine writers have emerged through our League efforts. They're writing real stories about real people in real situations. They're much more believable; the acting is more natural. Amateur groups are flourishing. At the beginning of the A.L.S., there were comparatively few amateur play-producing groups. There were more operatic societies found in almost every town of size, all dedicated to producing Gilbert and Sullivan operas. Amateurs found proof through the simple staging of A.L.S. that plays could be successful with the barest minimum of stage equipment. People who had become accustomed to using their eyes only for silent films learned that it was a good thing to also be able to listen to voices as well."

"Have you already selected the six one-acts?" Ashley inquired.

"Yes, we have," Miss Elder responded. "We'll rotate among several. Barry Jackson, whom you know, Ashley, is a member of our A.L.S. Council. He sent me a translation of a fabulous French play by Henri Gheon, *The Farce of the Devil's Bridge.* It's a story about a holy hermit who has converted his neighborhood. The devil is jealous and sends a fiend to outwit the hermit, in the guise of a peddler. The hermit foils the peddler's plot to destroy people through their crossing an unsafe bridge and sends him back to the devil with nary a convert to evil. Other one-acts will include *The King of Barvander* and *O Death, Where Is Thy Sting?* both by Allan Monkhouse; *Pot Luck* by Gertrude Robins; *The Sun and Hall-Marked,* by John Galsworthy, which deals with the homecoming of a young soldier; and Gilbert Cannan's delightful imaginative comedy, *Everybody's Husband.* This is about a young bride on the eve of her wedding. She's visited by women of three preceding generations, all of whom agree that all men are alike – boring, unfaithful, and sex-crazed. Rosie, you can play one of the roles."

"You've selected quite a variety, haven't you?" Ashley remarked.

"Yes, and they all have small casts and only a few pieces of furniture and properties. The costumes and make-up will be simple. We're also going to use masks in some of the plays and productions. They're half-masks, which are comfortable to wear and very effective. The faces have been enlarged to abnormal proportions and the hair's made of silk or wool or dyed frayed-out materials. The value of the masks is that they provide good disguises for our actors and singers. They don't cause discomfort to them or muffle their voices. Even though an actor can't be as expressive as when his living eyes can be seen, every gesture of the hands and movement of the head or body becomes more emphasized. Additionally, the unchanging features can be greatly affected by theatrical lighting with changes of brightness and shadow. We've tried masks over the past year in our tours. We find audiences become more focused on exaggerated arm and body movement. We've used them in a variety of ways. A satirical monologue, 'The Eleventh Hour,' by Anthony Armstrong, takes place on Armistice Day, with one actor, changing masks, having a dialogue between a British inventor who manufactures armaments and a young German. The younger man, who was a member of a peace organization, wants to buy the plans of a new model of a machine gun in the interests of saving humanity. Turns out the inventor's only son has been killed by the German, with a hand grenade that he, the manufacturer, had invented. The final two minutes were played in silence with an enormously 'shocked' audience. The symbolism of the masks was uncanny."

During the next two weeks, the cast was assembled, rehearsals took place, and the fit-up, equipment and properties were prepared and loaded into the lorry, which the cast had already dubbed as T, standing for the Travelling Tour. Ashley and Rex were to drive the lorry, loaded to the gills, from London to the Company's first stop at King's Lynn. The rest of the troupe took the train. Ashley had been also assigned to keep the tour's log for the A.L.S. Board of Directors, to briefly record the Company's activities in each of its performance destinations around the southeast part of England.

Ashley and Rosie had worked hard together and had mastered three different ballroom dance routines and practiced four solos and two duets, from which they would be choosing their nightly acts. They continued changing records on the gramophone, constantly helping one another with the delivery and gesturing of their vocal numbers. With the dancing, all went quite well, since Ashley proved to be a rather smooth on his feet and Rosie was so light and coordinated. They made a striking pair as they swung their bodies to the invigorating music. Their singing improved with each rehearsal.

Ashley kept a meticulous log of the tour.

> 24 Jan, Tuesday, King's Lynn, Norfolk County. The cast arrived at the train station after their long trip from London. They climbed aboard T and were taken to the four homes where they were to be guests. The hospitality for them was several miles away from the hall, and the cast carried their own suitcases through the snow. We unpacked all the stage paraphernalia and costumes at the hall. It was an excellent opening night. However, one of our cast members had hidden away her dog in her dressing room, unbeknownst to Miss Elder, who wouldn't allow actors to bring their dogs on a tour. There was a scene in *The Farce* with one of our actors in a small replica of a fishing boat. He was supposed to be in the middle of a river, and the dog, having escaped the dressing room, approached him and hopped into the boat, apparently in search of his actress mistress. Michael Hogan looked at the dog and said, "You really swam a long way." Everyone in the hall collapsed with laughter. Miss Elder chastised the actress and sent her dog home.
>
> 25 Jan, Wednesday, Skettishham. The cast arrived by train at eleven in the morning and was taken to a hotel for lodging. They had rehearsed a new one-act on the journey. The lorry carried all the stuff by road and arrived before the cast. We played Circus Hall, a dreary, shapeless place. The show seemed organized, but we didn't have a big audience. When we performed *Pot Luck*, the silent portions kept being interrupted by noise of a prayer meeting taking place next door.

<u>26 Jan, Thursday, Burnham Market (Brancaster Bay)</u>. We had to make two trips with the lorry, which was so full the actors had to carry their own suitcases on the second trip. Rosie's was too heavy, and she had to send some of her clothing home. We couldn't get into the People's Hall until after one because of a lecture taking place. The hall was immense, which made setting up our much smaller fit-up difficult, a small stage and curtains in the middle of a huge structure. Felix Irwin played the part of an old lady, which was way out of his range. In the guise of an 80-year-old woman in an awful-looking dress, he resembled a young girl inserted in a bag of flower. Several of our actors corpsed during the one-acts. The prompter was kept very busy. Miss Elder recast the old lady's part with a younger one wearing a blond wig. She added another rehearsal in the hall after the performance to better prepare the corpsers.

<u>27 Jan, Friday, Blakeney</u>. We left Burnham Market with snow and ice and arrived in the same in Blakeney. This time, we sent the settings and equipment by train and drove the entire cast to our next stop. One of our hosts owned the mills where the performance was to be given. The hall had a low ceiling and hot pipes, which, when the stage was set in position, was just a tiny bit higher than our heads. Because of the snow, we couldn't get back to digs for rest or food, but we had a gigantic tea given by the host organization, a church group. There were no dressing rooms. We had to dress and make up in the wings. Audience wasn't large but seemed to enjoy themselves. One of our actors laughed for

no reason while on stage. Rex pulled him aside and lit into him. He told the man, who had also forgotten his lines the previous evening, that, if he didn't straighten out, he'd get the boot. He called him "a miserable disgrace to the acting profession." Rex informed him he was to remain as cool as ice on stage and not be distracted by anything but his role. He also told the actor if he continued to play with his coat during others' speeches, he'd cut his arms off. Rex kindly offered to work with him on his various one-act roles. He's a cut above for a stage manager.

Rosie and Ashley went to a local bookseller to obtain reading material for the little breaks that came between rehearsing and performing. Ashley bought a guidebook to the United States. Rosie found several novels she hadn't been able to obtain in London. "They," she reported to Ashley, "were romance books. You wouldn't understand them."

28 Jan, Saturday, Waybourne. Again, the setting and equipment went by train and the cast and their luggage by T. We were all assigned to guesthouses by our host organization, the local YMCA. They fed us in the cafeteria, and we gave our performance in a community center. Here, the audience was very disturbing. They all seemed to be uneasy. They spoke in loud voices, even during the performance. One woman kept moving in and out of her seated row, walking up the aisle and returning rather noisily. During Michael Hogan's Shakespearean soliloquy, when he recited the line, "All the world is a stage," a voice popped up with, "Here we go again, Mabel." It was a crazy night.

29 Jan, Sunday, Overstand. We had an active day here. We all arrived at the hall at 9:30 am, erected the fit-up, and unpacked. We stayed in an old dormitory where the beds were fine for young ladies but far too small for the males in our cast. One new female cast member came late during the morning. She had motored the previous day from Liverpool, where she had been playing with the rep company. The playing hall was in a school for small girls, all of whom came and looked through windows as we prepared the stage. We rehearsed three one-acts. Had a successful matinee, with encores for everything. Evening show was even better. Both one-acts gained roars of laughter, and, during the serious one later that night, the audience was deathly quiet. The performances were sheer fun.

30 Jan, Monday, Stalham. The performance here was a disaster. People fluffed their lines, scenery doors wouldn't open, a telephone rang, and it wasn't onstage. In the middle of the performance, a number of people rose from their seats and started to depart. One man turned and shouted, "This was the worst amateur theatre I've ever seen!" Another said loudly, "Your tour looks like it's over!" Walking to and leaning on the forestage apron, a disgruntled man in his 60s said sternly to the three actors on stage, "This was humiliating theatre. Don't you rehearse before you perform?" Rex took the stage and apologized to the remaining audience. He announced a brief intermission, and, in Miss Elder's absence, held a hasty meeting with cast and crew to "get serious and perform." The rest of the evening went more smoothly.

31 Jan & 1 Feb., Tuesday & Wednesday, Norwich. Of the two days here, the first was full of misery. T broke an axle about five miles outside of town and the brakes wouldn't hold. I stayed with lorry until help arrived. Nine others started to walk along the roadside with their luggage. It was very cold and rainy. A car stopped. There was only room for one, so Felix Irwin was elected to go ahead to get help. The others stayed where they were. Felix was first driven to Gisburn Arms, and then got another lift onto Norwich. He sent food via a passing motorist to the others who were marooned on the road. A huge lorry appeared at 5 p.m., and it was still raining and dark by the time we reached our stranded comrades who had been sitting put since twelve-thirty. The whole load was transferred from T to the lorry. Towing T, the lorry picked up the others in torrential downpours and mud into which we sank. A hired labourer even fell off the top of the lorry and hurt himself badly. He had to be assisted to a nearby cottage. It was a miserable day. At six, we reached the hall in Norwich. We unloaded, dropped our luggage at a very nice hotel, and were onstage by eight. After the performance that night, we danced and played the piano and rehearsed almost until dawn. The next day, I had the worst time of anyone. It was a tiring and dangerous day. T's rope tow to the lorry broke several times, and the brakes were totally out of action. It was T's swan song. The following day, Miss Elder had purchased train passes for all of us. We did a matinee and an evening performance, and, thankfully, all went well.

2, 4, 5 Feb., Thursday, Friday & Saturday, Great Yarmouth. These were easier days. We left Norwich with everything and everybody by train. We put in a hurried rehearsal of two one-acts on the train to the nonpaying audience of business travellers. Arrived at Great Yarmouth at one. Several cast members went shopping. We all gathered at the station hotel where everyone stayed. We picked up our letters at the post office and rehearsed the plays we were to perform again. We did three evening performances and a matinee. We rehearsed two new one-acts to add to our repertoire and performed them on the last night. We should have rehearsed them longer. One involved a duel with pistols. One of the guns didn't go off after the actor referee called the number "three." The actor who was to be shot, hit himself on the chest and said, "I'm having a heart attack." The other actor remarked, "That's because you smoked too much." The audience howled. Then one of the pistols was accidentally thrown into the audience and the actor had to ask to have it back. In the other one-act, Rex, playing the part of a servant, carried on sandwiches and two cups of tea. One cup contained the poison that was supposed to kill the antagonist. He tripped over a rumpled carpet and the tea and sandwiches went flying all over the stage. One of the sandwiches, loaded with salad dressing, landed on the head of a man in the first row. The audience was all in total laughter. So was the cast. Miss Elder brought down the curtain, screaming, "You're all sacked." Rex bawled everyone out, had each one help pick up the mess then stepped in front of the curtain and told the audience the scene would be started again. When the curtain rang

> up, everyone was still laughing. Rex pantomimed bringing in the tea and sandwiches, which couldn't be replaced on the spot. The one-act was a disaster. Michael Hogan overplayed his role as the poisoned victim pretending he drank a nonexistent potion.

As an actor, Ashley had improved his performances steadily, playing mostly small roles in one-acts. Rosie would rehearse with him, reading the parts of the other actors, and he helped her practice her lines as well. However, Miss Elder was giving him more opportunities to play roles that would challenge him. He'd been a waiter, a salesman, a policeman, a detective, a soldier, and now had worked himself up to a leading role in a romantic one-acter about a young boy-meets-girl, courts-girl, loses-girl, regains-girl.

"Ashley, you're really becoming an actor. Your gestures, your voice control, your movement around the stage, your attention to make-up detail – they've all added up. You may have some talent, after all," Miss Elder told him after one rehearsal. "The rest of the cast has noticed it too, Ashley. Keep it up," she said.

"Frankly, I've had lots of help from Rex Gerard. He's tutored me on all my parts. Rosie has helped considerably as well. She's probably tired of playing all those roles in the one-acts we've been rehearsing."

"As I've always said, Ashley, you reach the art through the craft. You've been practicing the craft."

"Thank you, Miss Elder. I appreciate your good words. I believe I have to improve as an actor if I'm going to be able to go to America."

"Why is that, Ashley?" she responded.

"I'll have to go with a touring rep company," he answered. "The more different roles I can play, the more valuable I'd be to a theatre group. Particularly if some are difficult roles to play, older gentlemen, dashing soldiers, wealthy businessmen. You know what I'm talking about."

"But, Ashley, you've also learned a great deal about scenery building, make-up, stage lighting and sound. You're valuable in many ways. Certainly, being a lorry driver is also another skill you have. In fact, I'm going to add to your current duties and your salary. You're going to be our new ASM, our assistant stage manager."

"That's positively keen, Miss Elder. Thanks very much. Does Rex know he's about to have a new assistant?"

"Of course, Ashley. It was Rex's idea in the first place. He wants to train you to take over his job on the next A.L.S. tour."

"Aren't I a bit young to take on that responsibility?" Ashley asked.

"Yes, but you've matured a great deal on this trip, don't you think?"

> <u>6 Feb. Sunday Gorleston (nearby)</u>. We spent most of the morning setting up the stage because we were in a very small hall. It couldn't hold all of our scenery. Also a basket full of costumes had fallen into a muddy ditch. Fortunately, all were miraculously okay. We rehearsed another one-act, this one without sandwiches and tea. It's still not yet ready. Got a great ovation from the audience. Expected a poor house and critical audience but they appeared to enjoy themselves immensely.

> <u>7 Feb, Monday,</u> Lowestoft. Better house and larger audience here. Except that the females had to dress in a woodworker's shop next door to the hall. There were tools lying all around and a huge forge. The males were staying in a cottage down the street and

had to go out in the open and then up some stairs to get into hall. We rehearsed still another one-act called *The Severed Onion* in the afternoon. We included it in the three one-acts that night for the first time. They all went smoothly and were definite successes. Both Hermoine and Rosie received standing ovations for their respective dance and singing numbers. They had to add extra pieces, to the audience's delight.

<u>8 & 9 Feb, Tuesday & Wednesday, Southwold</u>. For both evening performances, the audiences weren't large but they seemed to enjoy themselves. On Tuesday night, however, Rosie, wearing a long, sweeping satin, tripped onstage and the skirt wrapped around the back of a rocking chair. She tried to loosen it, but the chair awkwardly followed her upstage. The audience began to titter and Elsie Bourn, playing the part of a maid, tried to help her get loose. The sight of Rosie's bare legs caused another wave of laughter, and what had been a serious one-act turned into a comedy. Both actresses took advantage of the moment and delivered their lines as if they were in a farce rather than a melodramatic situation. The audience accepted the change in mood from the serious to the farcical, which led to standing applause at the end of their skit.

<u>10 & 11 Feb, Thursday & Friday, Ipswich, Suffolk County</u>. The first night went well. The next night, Rex was wearing a clown's colourful suit, and, right in the middle of a scene, he dropped his large cane in the front row. He looked down and a woman said loudly, "I could use this." "No," said Rex, "I'll fall

if I can't retrieve it," and he thudded down on the stage. "Oh, my," said the woman, throwing the cane at the crumpled body. Fortunately, we'd also had an unexpected theatre critic from the *Manchester Guardian* attend one of our performances in Ipswich. His story follows:

Ashley had glued the following story in his journal:

Manchester Guardian 3rd Feb, 1921. "This remarkable but small group of players had a major goal to bring theatre to every hamlet in Britain. This is a large and encompassing plan and it includes lectures about theatre and experimental work in music, dance, drama, poetry reading, and monologues. It's hard to name what all they do except that it's variety. One can doubt that art can be brought in entirely by advocating it, but it seems to be working. If this delightful group journeying round the counties of England cannot make converts, it would be like a church without a congregation, and that it is not."

The log continued:

12 Feb, Thursday, Harwich. This was a convenient hall near the train station and it was also attractive. The sponsoring group brought us tea while we set up and we finished shortly after five. The hall was packed to the rear doors with an audience that truly enjoyed the show.

13, 14, & 15 Feb, Friday, Saturday & Sunday, Colchester, Essex County. We played in a large drill hall, performing nine different one-acts for two different evening performances and a matinee. The large hall was only half full, but they were good audiences. A death in her family took Hermoine home. We replaced her in Colchester with a 15-year-old ballet dancer whose mother was an amateur actress. Mum joined us in two one-acts, and we found she had a lovely singing voice as well. Both Sarah and her mother, Diane, are now members of our company for the rest of the tour.

16 Feb, Monday, Clacton. Everything went smoothly here. Our host group, a Church of England club, gave us a huge banquet before the performance, and we were so full it was hard to walk around the stage. They even served us snacks in our hotel after the show. We sang and danced until two in the morning.

17 Feb, Tuesday, Clemsford. We played in a charming hall with a primitive dressing situation. Everyone had to share one big room, but the fit-up looked perfect. We surrounded it with a portable proscenium of plain wood. The show was a colossal success. It seemed to be an intelligent, involved audience. Some people who love dance had to travel a long distance for our performance. Many had walked several miles across hills in bitter weather to get to the hall. With Sarah, we did a new ballet for their benefit. In the large estate where we all stayed, our host and hostess had alarmed us about Clemsford. Miners who dislike strangers, especially actors, mostly inhabited it. We had no trouble at all.

18 Feb, Wednesday, Maldon. The hall here was a dingy place with dark chimneystacks. Our host and hostess made us feel comfortable, and, in a short time, we became very attached to them. They fed us well, provided comfortable rooms, and really enjoyed our performances. They gave praise to each and every one of us. We gave our show in a secondary school. Many of the townspeople were artists and craftsmen. Their collective works were displayed in the school and in the windows of all the shops in town. It was a surprisingly quiet and interested audience, much to the contrary of that expected.

19 & 20 Feb, Thursday & Friday, Southend on Sea. The first was a day of surprising experiences. We rented a large lorry and with cast, sets, and equipment, drove to this lovely seacoast location. We stopped in a small village for a refreshing lunch, however, shortly thereafter, we ran into rainfall. The scenery was lovely but the lorry I was driving seemed ill, making noises like a stomach growling. We tinkered with the engine and it sounded better after an hour or so. Got lost in another village. We were inside an ancient wall that went on and on, encircling the town. We also had trouble getting the large vehicle through one of the few gates. Next, we came to an incredibly steep hill. We all got out of the lorry and walked up. Got to digs at five, had hot soup and whiskey, and were ready for our performance at eight.

21 Feb, Saturday, Romford. Training here, we breakfasted at eleven. We were all still exhausted

from the previous day. We set up, ate our lunch in the hall, and we all went to our digs at Miss Perkins stately home. We gave our show in the gymnasium of the local college. All the one-acts went well. We all found ourselves writing letters after the show.

22 Feb. We all returned to London.

End of journal.

In April, the group was on the road again. Ashley had given over the tour journal to Rosie. A.L.S. officials had informed him that his writing was "too homey." Hermoine had rejoined the company and Sarah and her mother remained with the travelling troupe. They toured counties from Essex to Suffolk to Kent, to Sussex and Hampshire. Flowers and trees were blossoming. The weather was consistently good. The League had purchased a new lorry, dubbed TT, which Ashley drove. It was the largest one they had ever used and held everything and everybody. TT was a Lancia coach with high sides you couldn't see over when you stood. It had an enormous canvas sheet covering the baggage, which could also be used for shelter. The cast sat at one end with the luggage and stage furniture. The fit-up and equipment were at the other end. The biggest problem was that punctures occurred throughout each of their theatrical journeys. They had six punctures on one particular day. In May, they returned once again to Dorset and Somerset, before travelling to the "shires" - Wilshire, Berkshire, Warwickshire, Worcestershire, and Gloucestershire.

In July, Ashley was unemployed, with no immediate jobs in sight. Another A.L.S. tour in September was his only future possibility.

Chapter 26
The Brighton Repertory Company

Brighton, 1921

Phillip had invited Ashley to meet with him at noon on a Monday in August, at a local Brighton pub popular with the theatrical crowd. Leaving London on the Volks Railroad, one of the first railroad lines built in Southern England's Sussex County, circa 1883, Ashley arrived at ten-ish. He decided he'd first visit the Brighton Repertory Theatre Company's facility where Phillip was employed by the now very prominent producer, Oscar Asche. Ashley strolled casually down Kings Road on his way to Palace Pier.

Approximately seventy kilometers from London, the trip had taken one hour during which time he had perused a Brighton tourist guidebook. He learned that the Royal Pavilion, a handsome structure transformed for King George IV by architect John Nash, was used as a "summer castle" for royalty. The sumptuous leisure palace, completed in 1823, was nestled near the sea. It featured an Indian-themed exterior and an interior decorated with a Chinese motif. Originally a small fishing village known as Brighthelmston, Brighton's charming seventeenth-century cottages had now become well-attended greengrocer, butcher, flower and gift shops, and pubs. The weather-boarded former dwellings were colorfully clad with painted wooden planks as protection against the elements. Popular at first as a health resort on the English Channel, the now thriving city was considered "London-by-the-Sea" because of its attractive marina, its sophisticated downtown area, museums and art galleries, and the Royal Brighton Theatre, which had opened with a notable performance of *Hamlet* in 1807. Touring companies, primarily from London, performed regularly. In May of each year, the Brighton Festival, a special event of music, dance, and theatre, had also become a quite successful attraction.

The fashionable resort was home to Brighton University. The pebbled marina beach was across from a wide street filled with numerous hotels and restaurants, and several well-attended cinemas that had begun their showings in 1909. The major attraction, however, was the Palace Pier, with one of only a few aquariums in England; a broad boardwalk overlooking the ocean on all sides; a 1500-seat pavilion, which featured musical concerts, theatrical performances, vaudeville, magic shows; a Ferris wheel, a ten pin alley, a petting farm; and water rides in various crafts on the ocean below.

It was on the Palace Pier that Oscar Asche had leased a rectangular structure formerly used as a warehouse for storing fish. Within three months, he had converted the building into a 500-seat theatre he renamed the Brighton Playhouse. During that time, still involved with his smash London hit, *Chu Chin Chow*, Asche had hired a director,

Robert Atkin, a set designer, an experienced stage manager, an electrician, and a carpenter, and employed an acting company of fifteen, nine men and six women. He had also invited Phillip Maggs to join him as his special assistant.

Ashley had no trouble locating the Brighton Playhouse. The stage doorkeeper welcomed him enthusiastically when Ashley mentioned Phillip's invitation to meet him in Brighton. He learned that the new theatre had been operational for six months, and, after a modest beginning, was slowly becoming a relatively profitable venture. In theatre parlance, that meant all the bills were being paid on time. The company alternated a mixture of eight plays from Monday through Saturday, each one performed at three night shows and a matinee. Every two weeks, another play would be added. There would be a total of fifteen productions for the entire nine-month season from September through May.

Thus far, three of Shakespeare's works had been offered: the romantic *Romeo and Juliet*, the wistful *Midsummer Night's Dream,* and *Twelfth Night,* shockingly performed in modern dress. Oscar Wilde's comedic *The Ideal Husband,* Pinero's *Trelawny of the "Wells,"* and *An Englishman's Home*, a revived war tragedy that had enjoyed large and enthusiastic audiences for a short period during the Great War, were well received. Ibsen's translated *Ghosts* and *Hedda Gabler,* both naturalistic plays about common people, had been enormously popular. The final dramatic act is the symbolic shooting of a British war hero by a German raiding party, a grim reminder of difficult years nationwide. *The Liars,* by Henry Arthur Jones, was in rehearsal. The additional productions to be included in the repertory were Brandon Thomas' comedy, *Charley's Aunt; Bill of Divorcement* by Clemence Dane, a plea for easier divorce laws on the grounds of insanity; *Hobson's Choice* by Harold Brighouse; Ibsen's *A*

Doll's House; Shakespeare's dark tragedy, *Othello;* and a new play by an untried playwright, Thomas Wicks.

Ashley was impressed with the lavish beauty of the theatre interior, the efficient backstage area with large wings to the sides and a high ceiling to handle stage-high hanging curtains, and the modern lighting equipment. The dressing rooms were all large and comfortable, and a handsome green room, with tea always at the ready, was a convenient gathering place for the actors and crew.

Phillip had telegrammed Ashley to meet him at the Crippled Crow, a campy pub located in the Lanes, where the narrow streets and cobblestone alleyways were always crowded. Phillip paced with his noticeable limp in front of the pub, frequently scanning the milling throngs, searching for his longtime mate.

Ashley saw him first, and rushed to him, exclaiming, "Bully! Phillip, you're walking!"

Thrusting out his hand for a shake, Phillip said proudly, "Aye, Ash, this artificial leg works better than a real one. I'm even close to conquering my limp. Come on. Come inside. I've got a table waiting for us."

Once seated and after ordering "'alf a Bass" each, Ashley told Phillip he'd arrived on an early train and had already toured his place of employment. He asked, "Well, you've been here quite a spell. You must like repertory better than touring?"

The subject couldn't have been more appealing to Phillip. He'd dwelled on this question for some time and was prepared to respond at length. For the next several hours, with the waitress frequently refilling their glasses, they discussed the differences between repertory and touring theatre.

Phillip started it. "There's a glow about rep that can set you afire. You see the same faces in the audience every week.

You work with the same actors, but different producers. As an actor, you can even develop your own 'fan club.' It's more about creativity rather than just seeking applause and laughter with a touring production. Rep's the difference between a long-term romance and a chance encounter. You can use your own imagination and emotions as you portray different roles. You're allowed to play the person, not just the part. You grow with it. Rep shows you whether or not you're getting through to an audience. One actor friend told me, 'I act through instinct. I do what I feel is right. I try not to act but be absolutely real.' The intimacy and immediacy of drama becomes much more realistic than formalized. It's less stylized and more naturalized. Do you know what I mean?"

Ashley, shaking his head, said, "I don't agree. Rep is more like being a big fish in a little pond. It's an ego builder. Most actors play their roles much the same in every play. They perform themselves rather than their characters. They use the same mannerisms, the same quirks, the same tricks to get a laugh, the same business with a cigarette. They change the characters into themselves, not the reverse. They may wear different frocks and spiel out different lines, but they're still playing themselves. Much of the time, in rep, people are grossly miscast."

"Oh, bosh!" Phillip exclaimed. "That's just not true. They may be adored by old ladies with tea cups on Sunday afternoons, but rep demands more than the older conventional styles of acting. I've seen mostly solid performances in rep, and so have you. I've seen actors age forty years in a two-hour period and be very convincing. Don't you remember in Liverpool when Chauncey Porter played an 80-year-old when he was only 20? He was magnificent. The actor playing his son was 60. Chauncey had the audience in the palm of his hand. Besides, three jackets and a huge overcoat made him look ten stones fatter. His wig and beard and fabulous make-up fooled everyone from the front row back. Rep actors have a capacity you can't find with touring actors."

"I don't agree with you, Phillip. A good producer of a touring drama group - and I'm not talking about the variety the A.L.S. does - casts people in roles who are 'types.' They look like the characters they play. Their walks, mannerisms, clothes, hair, speech, and accents parrot the part. In rep, much of the time, people are given roles for which they're totally unsuited. They're miscast. Even wonderful actors can fail in parts that don't suit them. Look at some of our famous actor-managers in their sixties playing roles more adapted to younger actors. I mean, Hamlet isn't believable if his mother and uncle are younger than he is..."

"I know a fine actor who'd be marvelous in rep - Henry Johnston," interrupted Phillip. "But, because his wife's a leading lady in a touring company and he's not a leading-man type, all his parts are the butler, the policemen, or the village magistrate. Now, that's type casting of the wrong type."

"I remember Johnston," Ashley recalled. "He was truly great in that role he played as a lifeboat captain in one of the war plays in London."

"True, at least we agree on that person," Phillip responded. "To me, it's essential that actors be given the opportunity to be constantly challenged in their characterizations. One of the great outcomes of rep is reaping the benefits of playing roles with a wide range of discovery. One can explore different sides of his own nature. A woman can learn how to feel beautiful if that's required. She can even become ugly if that's called for. A serious actor can test out his comedic skills or adjust his sense of timing actions, experimenting from performance to performance to see the audience react."

"Come on, Phillip. Remember that young actress who played an 80-year-old woman when we had our London tour several years ago? She was way out of her range. She looked like what she was, a young girl with white flower all over her body and grey powder on her head. I think actors playing older roles usually look like they've been hit by a sack of flower. Really, would a tall, thin actor be convincing as Falstaff or an old orator more believable as Romeo?"

"But, Ash, acting is acting. That's why it's so dangerous and exciting. You're always on the edge of yourself and the part you're playing, on the verge so you can tip either way. That's what acting should be. Rep allows you the time to learn, to gain skills that are personally valuable in the long run. When we alternate, performing a straight play, then a modern play, and next, a comedy, and a classical play every week, we're extended. We're stretched to our limits. That's one of the reasons I'm not sorry about my accident."

"What do you mean, Phillip?

"Last week, we were rehearsing a play where the ingénue was supposed to be a Welsh maid. It was important to the plot. She didn't have a clue how to do it. Oscar called me over and said, 'Work with her.' She protested. 'I can't do that accent.' He said, 'Yes, you will. This is how you learn your craft. Work with Phillip. You'll be the Welsh maid.'"

"Was she?" asked Ashley.

"Most credibly. I'm working with her on other common accents - Irish, Scottish, and American. Shaw's and O'Casey's plays, in particular, demand the language authenticity. In fact, I'm on an educational mission myself. I've been jotting down everything our company's actors say when they speak of mistakes they've made when first entering the profession. Maybe, someday, I'll write a book about it. They talk about overplaying things, underplaying things, not knowing when to hold back, being too obvious, pacing, and timing. They're constantly sharing with one another, too. What do I do with my hands during that long speech you have in the second act? I don't want to distract the audience. What if I stroll over to the front of the stage, turn around and face you? Actors are constantly worrying about what they look like, what they sound like. Am I getting all the laughs on time? That's why rep's such a good training ground for actors."

"So's touring theatre," Ashley mused.

"I'm not denying that, Ash. I just believe that repertory theatre has given me the most practical experience I could possibly have. Both of us went into rep rather than the university after grammar school. All the great actors and producers came from rep. The experience they gained on stage in front of a paying audience was invaluable. Doing weekly rep gave them a sense of the craft of acting. You go through dozens of parts.

Yes, all the great ones started there. They reached the art by practicing the craft. Rep provided them a sense of British theatre. It helped them learn how everything worked – costumes, props, stage management. You turned your hands in everything. You gained a tolerance for what was going on. Most importantly, you learned what not to do, what an audience might not accept. You learned what you were good at and what not to do. When you're young, like us, you think you can do anything. Rep has taught me what I'm really good at and what I am very bad at. It taught me that I'd have a go at producing if I could. I know it's a hard discipline with low financial rewards. I'd be better off in my father's furniture store. However, I want artistic rewards, not financial ones. I want to keep learning this craft, making mistakes, watching seasoned actors ply their wares, members of a unified company at work making a production successful together."

"That's ripping, Phillip. I've noticed that there's a

growing difference between producing and directing these days."

"What do you mean?"

"Well, when we were younger and even before, plays were organized and produced by actor-managers, who also played the leading roles," Ashley explained.

"And now?" Phillip asked.

"Producers, many who are not actors, put up the money, cast the roles, and do all of the management. They hire directors to be responsible for the acting, the interpretation of parts, the blocking, the on-stage interaction."

"That's a good observation. I think you're right. That's what Asche does. In fact, that's what I have in mind for myself," Phillip said.

"I rather think you'd be good at that, Phillip."

"I continue picking up those stray bits of wisdom from my elders. I can recall when I didn't know what I was doing. I just did it. As you know, in Liverpool when I tried acting, two or three old hands didn't resent me at all. They'd say, 'When you do that, you face the audience.' 'Speak up or they won't hear you.' They gave me the basic things, the rhythm of a line, the cadence of a Shakespearean rhyme. I learned so much from them. To me, they were the tradition of theatre, which they handed down. They would say, 'Even if you're playing a small part, think of it as a leading role. Don't rush it just to get on and off stage.'"

"It's good you're still learning. How are you getting along with Oscar Asche and his other directors?" Ashley inquired.

"Swimmingly," Phillip replied. "Oscar's taught me so much in such a short time, lots of things we never picked up in Liverpool or Birmingham. Rep here has so much more depth than what we learned in acting classes and even in our two stints with rep companies. Oscar's directed three of the productions. He constantly points out the positive traits excellent actors possess. He encourages and praises them a lot. But he also dwells on the faulty habits of the less talented. He's given me a greater respect for outstanding acting. You really can't learn how to act. You may have the coveted 'it,' or you don't. This company is completing my own training. I've even learned how to fence, and on my fake leg! I'm in a setting where I've seen actors using scores of little tricks like shouting the last line as they leave the stage, banging a door to get a round of applause, or delivering a laugh line facing the audience. The best ones have developed their own special systems for learning lines. They maintain a readiness onstage no matter what's occurring around them. They have a sense of spontaneity even when they're repeating familiar lines. Working with other people performing the same scenes over and over again allows them to imbibe the craft. This becomes like osmosis when you're working with other skilled people. You watch; you learn. Your self-consciousness gives way to a unified effort. It takes the edge off your nerves, giving you a sense of professionalism as a member of a talented cast. I've never seen any of our actors have a problem with corpsing, for example. They either adlib their way through a scene or the other actors pitch in and help them through. It becomes a creative challenge rather than a mental lapse."

"I'll admit that rep gives one the opportunity to play a vast variety of roles. I like the idea of mixing up Shakespeare with more modern plays here in Brighton," Ashley commented.

"Playing a wide variety of roles provides the same function for an actor as a sketchbook does for an artist. You try on numerous roles for size. For some, you may not be entirely suitable. It gives you a sense of which characters you can give a go at. It stretches your own understanding of your real capabilities. It gives you the wonderful opportunity to fail. Rep stretches every muscle of an actor's being. You learn so much about so many plays and so many writers. You find out what you can do, what you have to work on, how to be subtle about problem areas, how to hold yourself on stage when someone else is delivering his lines. It teaches you the difference between how your make-up looks off stage and how it looks onstage. It lets you practice pacing, coming in on time, and, so important, the chemical balance between you and an audience. There's nothing else like rep. Most of your concentration is on doing the plays for which you're cast. You're amongst a tight knit family. You get to know your audience, and they you. One of the most valuable things you learn is to sustain the necessary energy you need from curtain up to curtain down."

"You've given this rep business a great deal of thought. I'm impressed, Phillip. Does this mean you're looking at directing as a profession?"

"I hope so, Ash. I really hope so. No one wants a crippled actor, do you think? But directing, that's another matter. It's much more interesting than working in my father's furniture store."

"But, you're too young. No producer would employ you, would they?"

"That's the problem. I think that the best directors are former actors. They really know the problems actors face. They tend to be like umpires, knowing what to do and what not to do. They plan all the rehearsals. They select their players. They plot out every onstage move. Every time there's a move onstage, there's a new stage picture for the audience to view. Movement's so important. You can't just have a static scene. I plan to make models of every set with cardboard figures I can use to think through the blocking and movement. During the last six months, I've worked with Robert Atkins doing Shakespeare and with Peter Godfrey, who's not much older than I am. Oscar intends to direct three plays, and he's bringing in Alan Wade and Nigel Monck to do the others. I intend to shadow their every move. I'm going to make myself indispensable to them."

"How can you do that? Aren't you more or less a foot servant for Oscar Asche now? Aren't you his special assistant?

"That's true. I primarily deliver messages for him, make tea, and fetch items he needs from time to time. Mostly, I take notes as he comments on the actors during rehearsals, and about problems around the theatre, especially with people. But, I've also been helping the other directors set up rehearsals, bringing them requested items and the like."

"You're the 'stage slave' then," aren't you? Have you ever thought of being a prompter? You remember? That's how I got to know Sir Frank Benson. Following the script during rehearsals gives you an idea of what each and every actor has to do, stage crosses to make, expressions to use, and you certainly get a good feeling for characterizations."

"That's a good thought, Ash. Thank you. I'll talk to Oscar about that. We have one of the cast members doing the prompting now."

"Benson was a wonderful producer, Phillip. But, he was primarily a classical one. He rarely directed any play besides Shakespeare. He'd insist on his own design of stage movement by actors since they depended so much on what lines they were speaking, where they were on the set, and who had the major speeches and warranted the audience's attention. He was pretty dictatorial."

"Don't you think that's important with Shakespeare, that every actor performs a role the way it's been done before? That's Shakespearean tradition, isn't it? That's another difference in directing in rep. I've watched Oscar closely. He'll plan the basic moves an actor makes, but he'll ask him why he's making a particular move. What are the feelings the character is trying to portray, and how should the lines be delivered? Is he happy, angry, confident, hesitant, or remorseful? He wants to know the reasons. He wants to put the feelings and action together with the actor. It's like a partnership. He's always looking for the motivation in either words or movement. He was certainly trained as a classical actor, but, now, he really pushes for realism, especially with contemporary plays, like *An Englishman's Home* and *Bill of Divorcement*."

"What about plays that took place twenty years ago, or French plays, or Ibsen?" Ashley asked.

"He always tries to adapt the setting and costumes to the time and place of the playwright's intention. It's almost a modern version of the Greek 'time, place, and manner' concept. He always tries to have the actor look at the words he's to speak from the character's point of view. Like other directors, he'll first have a read-through of the script. That way, everyone gets an idea of what the play's all about. He usually walks them through the action while they make notes in their script sides. Then, as the actors learn their lines and walk through their scenes, he has me take notes. He shares them with the cast members, either when they're all together or separately. He develops kind of a physical chemistry with each actor that's different. With the longtime professionals, he's more like a chum giving helpful suggestions. With younger actors, he's more authoritative but with a soft manner about him. He doesn't want to intimidate anyone and, with our resident cast, he works with each person differently. He wants only the most favorable results. And from the critic's reviews and the spirited actors we have, he gets them. He's a bloody good director, I think."

"Well, with our Liverpool and Birmingham rep experience, we ought to know how different directors work. Remember George Bellamy in Liverpool? He seemed to work primarily with the scenery and costumes and to forget about the meaning of the play. He'd demand a waste basket on stage so an actor had an excuse to cross upstage left to drop a piece of paper. The actor would say, 'Why?' He'd say, 'Because I said so!' He bragged that he could block an entire play the first day of rehearsal."

"I remember him, Ashley. How could anyone forget him? He'd even fall asleep during rehearsals and still give the actors his notes. I don't think he really knew what was going on. He left it all up to the actors. I'm still happy I glued him to that chair."

Laughing, Phillip continued, "What about John Drinkwater at Birmingham? I really liked his directing style. He'd grown up from amateur theatre and created his own rep company. He always had a broad vision about a play and strove to replicate it. He sent many actors to the London stage. He organized his time meticulously. Neither he nor the actors stood around very much. He'd call you onstage only when necessary. He'd divide his rehearsals into the scenes that actors played together rather than following the play chronologically. "That gave them more time to learn their lines, didn't it?"

"It certainly did. Breaking the play into segments makes a lot of sense. Oscar does that, and he gives notes to everyone. Like Benson, he's always talking about cricket, too. He likes to challenge the locals to matches whenever there's time. I was pretty good at it before I lost my leg."

"With the busy production schedule, how do you handle rehearsals, Phillip?" asked Ashley.

"First of all, we have Sundays off. However, that's the time the actors take to learn the lines for new plays and practice those for the ones coming up for the next week. On Mondays, we do a dress rehearsal for the play opening that night. The next three days, we try on a new play for size. We do a reading, a walk-through, and, at three p.m., we usually do a walk-through of the play we're performing on Thursday, Friday, and Saturday. It depends on how well we remember our lines. Much of the time, actors are working together, practicing. The director goes from one pair or group to the other, listening, offering suggestions. All of our directors want their actors to be active all the time, not waiting around for their scenes, but doing their bits out of sequence. They work fast and well and together. Oscar's been striving for both the actors and directors to establish their own originality, their own creativity. He doesn't want them to copy the London performances. He demands original work."

"What about scenery and costumes?" Ashley asked.

"Our scenic artist, Dudley Weston, is a pearl. He and his crew are constantly working on the scenery for our two shows per week, painting, building flats, and hanging curtains. He also gets help from the actors. Dudley has a basic box set he uses for most interiors, and he paints the flats according to the play. Furniture includes a sofa and several chairs and a dining room setup. He changes covers on the couch for every show. For exteriors, he has flats of all sizes and shapes - trees, rows of bushes. His sets don't wobble; they're very solid. All the doors open and close and have trustworthy handles. He knows all of the plants and flowers by season. He gets remnants of material and wall paper and borrows pictures, ornaments, furnishings, carpets and other properties from hotel lobbies, homes, and shops. Sometimes, he has to return items during the run of a show but always replaces them from elsewhere by opening curtain. He's a marvel.

"As to costumes, every one of our actors has a standard wardrobe that's personal property. For men, it's two ordinary walking suits and one evening dress suit, a sports jacket, brown and black shoes, shirts and ties. Women are required to have two ordinary day dresses, one evening dress, a two-piece suit, and several outfits. Usually, they sew their own dresses. Oscar buys all the costumes for the classics and Shakespearean plays."

"With so many plays and so few costumes, doesn't the audience recognize the actors' clothing shortages?"

"Ashley, our actors are very clever. The women can convert bedspreads into dresses; they put flowers and scarves over their blouses; they even trade with one another. Women can wear different pieces of clothing easier than men. The other night, George Handley came on stage with a grey suit; he'd put lines on it with tailor's chalk. Ray Gallant patted him on the back with a new piece of business and a big cloud of dust got some audience laughter."

"I remember in Birmingham, when several of the actors had custom double-sided suits made. Two suits, four costumes. Now, that's good planning. Do you have a make-up artist, too?

"No, Dudley Weston had several make-up sessions with the cast when they first arrived in Brighton. He emphasized their transforming their appearances for every play. He showed them how to do such tricky things as using a coin to get non-solid line wrinkles, making molds for false noses, and gluing on wigs and moustaches. He insists on the actors wearing gloves when they're playing older characters."

"Why is that?" Ashley asked.

"Hands really tell when a person is well along in years. With gloves, there's no problem.

Looking at his pocket watch, he said, "Well, Ashley, it's that time. I've got to get back to the theatre, and you have to catch the next train to London. "You don't have a job. What are you going to do?"

"I'll look for work for a while. I may go back to A.L.S. in September. They have a short tour planned heading to Hull, then Scarborough, then York. I could still drive TT, the lorry, dance and sing, and play a small role once in a while. We'll see."

"Ash, I'm really sorry. All I talked about was me. I didn't give you much of a chance."

"Phillip, I'm so happy for you. That's all I wanted to hear about. I hope you get that prompter's position."

"That's a good idea; I'll follow up on it. Ash, do you still crave to go to America?"

"Yes, of course," Ashley responded. "I want it more than anything." He waved fondly as he opened the door leading out of the pub. Phillip took a last drink of Bass and slowly limped towards the exit.

As he headed for the railroad station, Ashley mused, *I think I'll start taking director's notes from Eleanor Elder if I go on the next A.L.S. tour. She'd like that.*

Chapter 27
All's Well That Ends Well

London, 1921

While he re-entered his job search activity, Ashley moved into Soho digs in London, rooming with George Novinger, a non-acting former Bristol Grammar School friend and accountant. He would have preferred finding housing to share with Rosie, to whom he had become quite attached. He had even proposed marriage, which she rejected, not for lack of affection, but because of his limited funds. Neither of them had the income to accomplish much more than care for their own everyday necessities. Renting a London flat, furnishing it, and sharing food and money wasn't possible.

Rosie was finally in rehearsal at the Mermaid Theatre, playing the part of a nasty stepsister in the play *Robin's Nest*. The plot dealt with divorce and how newly separated parties could attempt further pursuit of happiness, while the young adult children they had borne were left in complete despair and financial disruption, departing from their chosen career paths. When Ashley attended one of her rehearsals, he remarked to Rosie, "You know, the theatre is just like the divorce in this play. The show closes, and you're out in the cold."

Robin's Nest opened to solid reviews and appeared to face a positive three-month run. Rosie had several favorable reports on her impressive acting by prominent reviewers and had inquiries from three producers on her future availability. Ashley had begun another daily quest for acting and, now, assistant stage managing opportunities. He had call-backs for a small part in Basil Dean's *Lion's of Escape* but lost the role to a more mature and experienced actor. He met with the managers of the Regent, Covent Garden, and the Gate theatres to no avail. To bide his time constructively, for ten solid weeks he worked unsalaried with noncommercial, but worthwhile London-based organizations including the Three Hundred Club, the Repertory Players, the Play Actors, and the Fellowship of Players, attempting to package plays as commercial productions for full-scale funded runs or touring opportunities.

During this period of active unemployment, he met often with Richard Bates, who had returned from his American and Scottish tours and was also seeking acting jobs. He also corresponded regularly with Phillip Maggs, still apprenticing in Brighton. On one occasion, at the Pig's Foot pub, Ashley suggested to Richard that he was seriously considering leaving theatre. "I'm going to try-out after try-out, Richard. I'm playing every kind of role I can without pay. I'm following every lead for acting or backstage posts that comes my way. I've even written to every repertory company in the country indicating my interest and availability," he said sadly. "I'm receiving neither positive responses nor any encouragement."

"But, Ashley, that's what theatre's all about. When the show closes, you have to find new work. In rep, that's not the case, but, in real theatre, that's reality. I have more experience than you do, and I'm having the same problem," said Richard. "My difficulty is that I'm too young for some parts, too old for others."

"But you've become very polished as an actor. I believe you can play any role you want, Richard. I don't see why no leads have come your way."

"You have to have a name to get the big parts, Ashley. You have to be able to draw an audience."

"I saw you as Hamlet at the Gate last month; the crowd was wild about your performance," said Ashley. "You're peerless as an actor."

"The play wasn't even reviewed in the newspaper, Ashley. No critics were in attendance. No one knew I even played Hamlet."

The young men continued their conversation until the pub closed and left for their respective flats. Nothing positive was gained from their exchange. Ashley had considered auditioning with Rosie for dancing sketches in musicals, but now, because of her nightly theatre commitment, she was unavailable. Nevertheless, they continued to meet weekly to rehearse new dance routines.

One afternoon, Ashley and Rosie were practicing a difficult Scottish reel in his flat, and Ashley tripped and fell. "Oh, bosh," he said as he tried to rise, "I'm getting clumsier and clumsier with every step."

"Ashley, let's sit down and discuss our dancing partnership."

"No, we have to practice. I'm all right," Ashley said.

"I'm sorry. It's not all right," Rosie responded. "The dancing's not all right and neither is our relationship. I think you're just using me as a dance partner, and that's all."

"No, Rosie, it's not like that. I'm still in love with you."

"No, Ashley. You're in love with yourself. Every time we talk, it's always about you, your career, you're becoming a well-known theatre manager, and you're going to America. I don't believe I'm really painted in the same picture."

"But, Rosie, you have it all wrong. We're in this together, aren't we?"

"No, we're not. If you must know, I'm seeing someone else, and he's taking me on a long holiday to France when my show closes next week."

"We're not going to see one another?"

"No, this is the end. I'm sorry, but this is the end." Rosie picked up her wrap and departed without another word. Ashley stood, stunned.

Ashley continued auditioning for acting roles. He tried to arrange meetings with every theatre manager in London, succeeding in five interviews for assistant stage manager, property, or scene moving posts, all to no avail. He had telegraphed his father for a loan, but his request had been rejected. His funds were close to depleation. He telephoned several of his friends for financial help. However, since all of them were also living hand to mouth in the theatre, he had no success. That is until he had a call from Phillip Maggs who was still in Brighton.

"Ashley, it's smashing to hear your voice. How's it going in London?"

"Poorly, to say the least," said Ashley. "I'm making the rounds until I'm positively dizzy. I don't even have a nibble."

"You can always come down and stay with me, Ash. I have plenty of room in my flat and two beds in the bedroom."

"I can't look for work in Brighton. I've got to find it here, in London."

"I understand."

"But, I could use a loan of maybe one hundred quid, Phillip. I'd pay you back as soon as I could. My father won't even lend me money. He wants me back in Bristol. Back at the market."

"I'll tell you what, Ash. If you come to Brighton for a few days, you can stay with me. I've been asked by Arthur to produce his newest play. We can't afford to pay you, but you could help me with some of the technical aspects. You were always better at that than I was. We can talk about a small loan when you're here."

"I'm on my way, Phillip. I've got just enough money for train fare. I'll meet you tomorrow at noon at the station."

The next day, stepping off the railway car with a small bag, Ashley saw Phillip, hurried to him, and grasped him in a warm hug. "It's really good to see you, Phillip. You're looking well. How are you walking?"

Laughing, Phillip hopped back and forth on both legs and said, "My fake leg is almost as good as my good one. I can almost dance a jig."

When they reached Phillip's modest two rooms, Phillip served ham sandwiches and bottles of local beer. When seated, Phillip handed Ashley a blue script. "This is the play Arthur wants me to produce. It's called *The Skin Game.* John Galsworthy wrote it. I'm going down to the theatre for a rehearsal. I'd like you to read it, and we can discuss it when I get back."

"I'd be happy to. I've always liked Galsworthy's work."

Both Phillip and Ashley had read and reread many of Galsworthy's plays while in acting school in Bristol. The playwright had grown up in Surrey, part of a wealthy family. He was educated at Harrow and, later, Oxford. He tried law for a time, but preferred travelling abroad to handle his family's shipping business interests. He became close friends with Joseph Conrad, then a first mate of a sailing vessel, who encouraged him to begin a writing career. His first book was a collection of short stories, *From the Four Winds,* which with subsequent works were published under the pen name of John Sinjohn. His first play, *The Silver Box* became a success. He followed up with *The Man of Property* and *Strife,* both of which addressed the British class system and social issues, which caused considerable controversy between the so-called Victorian advocates and the rising middle class.

Since this was a new creation, Ashley was not familiar with *The Skin Game.* It took several hours for him to digest it fully. He was moved emotionally by the story and the strong characters Galsworthy had developed. As soon as Phillip had returned from the theatre, they began their discussion.

"What did you think of the play, Ash? How did you like the plot?"

"It is intriguing, really. The timing is good. The war is over. I take it as a conflict between the old and the new British ways. Squire Hillcrist represents the old school with servants and old money. But it's dwindling, like mine, and he's trying to prevent his rich neighbor, Hornblower, from building factories next to his manor. Hornblower is a so-called self-made man and very wealthy."

"Good," said Phillip, "that's the gist of the story, but isn't there a larger conflict?"

"Right-o. Hornblower's son's wife. She was the 'other party' in two divorce cases. The family wants that subject to stay a secret."

"And the son doesn't know it either."

"Hornblower agrees to sell the land he planned to build

on for less than the auction price if the Squire withholds the information."

"But the couple stays together and Hillcrist gets the land. So everyone lives happily ever after, right?"

"Not necessarily. Galsworthy is pretty tricky. He lets the audience figure out what happens in the end. Clever fellow, no?"

"That's why I like the play so much, Ash. It has everything that was wrong about the war in it, the idea of the bungling generals who caused so much loss of life, the jealousy of the upper class when nobodies begin to become somebodies, the forgiveness of someone who has sinned but been given hope. I love it."

"Is that why Oscar Asche is allowing someone so young to produce it? Is that part of his hope?"

"I think so, Ashley. He's attempting to give me a voice, a means to sweep away some of the old with the new, to get fresh ideas. He's taking a big chance, but I'm going to give it all I can. There are sixteen roles in the play. I've memorized each of them and know exactly who I'll cast from our company. We have a strong group of actors. We'll have two weeks of rehearsal and one week of performance. Oscar has relieved me of all responsibilities except to get this play produced. He's still playing the lead in *Chu Chin Chow* in London and won't take over rehearsals until two days before *The Skin Game* opens."

"I don't understand, Phillip. I thought you were the producer."

"Come on, Ashley, how could someone in his early twenties be credited as a producer of a major first-offered play by a famous author? Besides, I've never produced before. Only a name like Oscar Asche could receive credit; Oscar chose the playwright and his play and is putting up the money to produce it. I'm just working with the actors and directing their scenes. Arthur will add the finishing touches."

"Sounds to me like you're doing all the work. But, in any case, how can I help you?"

"I can't pay you, Ash, but I can provide you with food and a bed for the next several weeks. All I ask in return is that you help plan the settings, props, and lighting. I just won't have time to do that all myself. I do have crew members in each of those areas, but I need someone to run the overall scheme. Will you do it?"

"I'll think about it, Phillip. I still have several auditions scheduled for next week in London. I'd really like a paying job. I need the money."

"I understand, Ash, but I really need you. This is my big opportunity to prove I can become a producer. Perhaps I can even pay you a few pounds per week out of my own salary."

"That would help, Phillip. I've already got some debts to repay. Okay. Lend me my round trip rail fare, and I'll return after picking up some clothes and personal items in Soho."

Phillip handed Ashley several quid. Ashley thanked him and left for the train station.

The next day, Oscar Asche arrived early in the morning to address his Brighton Company. He had met earlier with Phillip and had agreed on Phillip's selection of a cast.

The casting had been posted and the theatre company members gathered together for a briefing from Asche, all seated in a circle of chairs around him.

Asche began, "Friends, as you know, I'm still trodding the boards at Her Majesty's theatre. *Chu Chin Chow* has treated us all well financially, both me and you, our Brighton Company." I'm producing our next play, *The Skin Game*. I'm also in the early planning stages with both the playwright,

John Galsworthy, who you will be meeting soon, and my assistant, Phillip Maggs. As you well know, Phillip has become indispensible to me, a right arm as it were. He knows you, and he knows the play thoroughly. He will be spending the next two weeks with you in read-throughs, line and action-learning, in rehearsals, in the sensitive development of each of your characters and their interaction. Despite his youth, he has a great sensitivity for good theatre and realistic acting, for what's really dramatic. I will be travelling back and forth to London because of my own commitments but will be in close and constant touch with Phillip. As far as you all are concerned, Phillip is the producer of *The Skin Game*. I will be with you when it's ready to perform, to add credence and support. All right, Phillip, it's all yours."

Phillip rose to an enthusiastic round of applause.

When he had everyone's attention, he spoke. "You've all seen your parts on the bulletin board. I'm passing out your sides so you have something to use to learn your lines. I have the master script, so we'll begin by doing a reading through the whole play. That will give us all an idea as to where we can take this message that John Galsworthy has allowed us to transmit. This is a great play and we have a wonderful cast. Let's get to work."

During the next two weeks, the company continued to perform *The Notice* and *Two Brides and One Groom*, alternating each night, while rehearsing *The Skin Game* during the day. All the actors had spent special time reviewing their roles with Phillip. He worked with them carefully in spelling out what he was looking for in each scene, asking how their characters felt about their movements and words.

"Phillip, why do you keep questioning us on how the character feels? We have to feel like actors playing a role," Charles Anthony queried when they were alone one day.

"Charles, I want you all to step into the shoes of the

people you're playing instead of seemingly standing outside and watching yourself in your mind's eyes. This is what's known as realistic acting, being the person yourself, thinking like the individual, letting his words be your words, not the reverse. In every scene, I want you to live the situation as if it were reality. Let the character take over your being."

"That's not acting, Phillip. Acting is an interpretation of how your character speaks and moves. It's an impersonation rather than a personal transformation into that being."

"Charles, whatever you call it, I don't care, but I want you to be your character, not merely to play him as a role."

"I'll try," was the retort.

Phillip had similar discussions with each of the sixteen actors, having them write biographies of the characters they were playing from birth to the present time of the play, including descriptions of their imagined grandparents, parents, and siblings, the geographical areas where they had lived, the architecture and furnishing of their home, their habits, the books they read, and who their closest friends were.

By the time Ashley had returned a week later, Phillip was convinced that all the cast members were so familiar with the persons they were playing that they were far more convincing in their collective roles. "It's fascinating," Phillip said. "Their reactions to one another, the realistic moods they assume, and the delivery of their lines show each has become the character being portrayed. They, themselves, have become their roles, or rather the characters have become them."

"That's amazing, Phillip. I've sat through several rehearsed scenes that have seemed to exude a sort of electricity."

"I'd call it believability, Ash. It's not just imagining something's happening; it's witnessing it as if it's real. It's raising their acting to a higher, much more believable level.

If they're thoroughly familiar with their characters, the words and actions come more easily to them. Instead of playing the roles, they're living theirs."

"I'm beginning to see what you mean. It's a totally different approach you're taking. Richard Bates should be in this cast. He's made great gains as an actor."

"Speaking of Richard, I heard he was in France working on a film," Phillip said.

"That's interesting," Phillip responded. "Rosie's there, too."

"Oh, Ash, haven't you heard? They're together. They're a couple now."

Ashley was stunned.

"Where are you going?" Phillip called as Ashley suddenly rushed out of the room.

Slower, because of his artificial leg, Phillip finally found his friend on a park bench around the corner from the theatre. They both sat quietly for a long moment until Ashley finally said, "I should have known it. When Richard returned from the Scottish tour, Rosie and I spent some time with him together. I should have seen that something was happening between them."

"They never told you?" Phillip asked.

"I didn't have a clue," Ashley said sadly. "Not a clue."

Over the next days, both boys were busily engaged in their respective endeavors. Phillip continued to rehearse scenes separately with selected actors and then staged the entire play in its planned sequences three times each day before the evening performances. Ashley painted scenery, built staircases, roamed furniture stores in search of props, focused lighting instruments, and even helped with the costuming. Two days before opening night, Oscar Asche sat in the middle of the theatre to watch a complete run-through of *The Skin Game*. Phillip and Ashley sat on either side of him taking notes as he spoke of line deliveries, different positioning of actors and properties, movements about the stage. Phillip kept scribbling "upstage," "downstage," "cross" as Oscar called them out next to the names of the characters when specific lines were to be spoken. "Upstage." "Downstage." "Cross." It was obvious Oscar was attempting to reposition the actors as they delivered their lines.

As the cast and the backstage crew prepared the scenery and properties of the play's final act, Oscar Ashe and the boys spoke quietly together in the front rows of the empty theatre. "What's the matter, Oscar? Why do you want to change the blocking?" Phillip asked.

"Don't you see it? Time after time, an actor has his back to the audience when he's delivering a line. Often, there's very little movement. Remember, boys, theatre is an art because it presents different pictures, almost like a film. If you're portraying only one picture, you lose the audience. You need action, movement, something always happening on stage."

"Oscar," Phillip pleaded, "You're only looking at technique and elocution. You're looking at portrayal, at performing. You want all the actors to speak loudly so the audience can hear them and have some reason for their hand and body movements. That's not what I've asked of them. We're all agreed on the behavior of their characters, not impersonation, but personation, to live like and be that person. They're all looking for realism, for believability rather than imitation. This is what we've worked so hard on all these days. Please, Oscar, please. I plead with you. Don't change my style of production. Please, don't do it. Look, just watch the final act. You'll see what I mean. Can we stop taking notes so you can really get involved with what's going on on stage?"

Ashley remained silent but nodded his head positively as Phillip spoke.

"All right, Phillip," Asche said. "I've trusted you this far. I'll speak with you before I talk to the cast after this final act is over." The three sat back in their seats. Phillip was energized with nervousness while Ashley still was quiet. Oscar Asche began relaxing and even lit up a cigar. The curtain opened and the rehearsal continued.

The first of the final three scenes ran smoothly. Phillip was proud that the cast had worked hard to play their roles as if they were real persons rather than imitators. *They're not puppets*, he thought, *they're performers.* He glanced several times at Oscar Asche, but saw only a continuous attentive expression. Ashley displayed a slight smile and seemed enraptured with the onstage movements. When the stage lights dimmed after the first scene, he broke into applause, but one glance from Oscar silenced his hands. Oscar started to say something, and then broke off at the beginning of his sentence, again his face was impassive. In Phillip's judgment, the second and third final-act scenes flowed beautifully. He prayed Oscar was satisfied.

The curtain dropped with Phillip and Ashley applauding loudly. Oscar Asche rose, and, without a word, headed for the forestage stairs, and rapidly entered the stage through the side of the main curtain. The boys followed him, arriving as the entire cast and crew mingled onstage.

"Attention! Attention everyone!" Oscar Asche shouted. "Please come forward and circle me. I have something important to share."

The company members mumbled among themselves as they followed Asche's directions, unsure of what was next to come. Phillip and Ashley looked at one another fearing the forthcoming words.

"Actors all. As I sat in the theatre's third row center,

I was calling out notes on stage movement, gesture, and delivery. I wanted emoting, oration, solid theatrics, acting as it's been practiced my entire life. What I was seeing was not that style of acting. Each of you was far more believable than I had anticipated. Each of you became the character you were portraying. The play sang a melody of realism. In a word, you were all – magnificent." He clapped his hands loudly. "Phillip, he continued, "You've done a splendid job. You've convinced me with your experiment in reality. In fact, I'm pleased to invite all of you to join me on a three-month tour to New York to the Majestic Theatre. We'll leave within a fortnight. I'm taking *Chu Chin Chow*, and *Two Brides and One Groom* to the United States. And, after this rehearsal, I've decided to add *The Skin Game* in the naturalistic manner in which you've performed it. It represents a major innovative style of theatre that will be entirely new to the Americans. I need all of you because we'll offer the plays alternatively in repertory form."

Cheers, laughter, and applause followed as cast members presented themselves to Oscar Asche with thanks and gratitude. Ashley congratulated everyone, then stood silently, but pleased, to the side as the happy ensemble returned to their dressing rooms.

Oscar Asche came over to Ashley and Phillip with his right hand outstretched. "Phillip, you've astounded me. You're a rare talent. Will you come to America as my assistant producer?"

"Will I? Oh, Oscar. Thank you. Thank you. I'm just speechless," said Phillip.

"And Rupie," turning to him, Oscar continued, "Will you come with us as our assistant stage manager?"

I was [illegible] notes on [illegible] movement, gesture, and delivery. I watched, emoting, gesturing, and [illegible] acting [illegible] my entire [illegible]. What I was seeing was not that [illegible] each of you was far more believable than I had anticipated. Each of you became the character you [illegible] playing a melody of [illegible]. In a word, you were all magnificent. [illegible] talent [illegible]. Phillip has spoken [illegible]. You've done a splendid job. You've convinced me [illegible] in reality in [illegible] three-month tour [illegible] with a [illegible] in the [illegible] United States. And [illegible] in [illegible] a [illegible] style [illegible] because [illegible] form.

Cheers [illegible] applause followed as cast members [illegible] with [illegible] to the [illegible] to [illegible].

Oscar [illegible] came over to [illegible] with his right hand [illegible]. "[illegible] you [illegible]. Will you come to America as my [illegible] producer?"

"Will I, Mr. [illegible]? [illegible] you. Thank you. I'm [illegible] speechless," said Phillip.

[illegible] turning to [illegible] Oscar continued, "Will you come with us and assist in stage management?"

POSTSCRIPT

This "true-to-life" novel is roughly based on the many reminiscings my father, Ernest Leslie Thomas, shared with me during his busy life in the United States. He immigrated from England in the late twenties as a working actor and assistant stage manager. During his long and up-and-down career, he primarily worked as a theatrical house and company manager in California, including stints with the Hollywood Bowl and Greek Theaters, as well as stage managing for the Los Angeles Civic Light Opera Company. He was also a company manager for the Sacramento Music Circus and the La Jolla Playhouse. His most successful career role, however, was escorting theatrical companies across the United States from New York to California after successful Broadway runs. Called "second companies," and termed "acers," "ducers," and "tres," meaning from one to three performances in each toured city, Les made all the road arrangements: booking theatres and lodging, hiring stage crews, supervising actors and crews, co-coordinating publicity and promotion, and assuming all production and financial responsibilities. Preparation for all these different tasks, of course, was gained from his early theatrical experiences in England, to which this book is addressed.

ACKNOWLEDGEMENTS

This book is dedicated to my lifetime sweetheart and wife, Diane, our four sons - Greg and wife, Mary; Mark and wife, Meghan; Scott and wife, Chayree; and Chris, the book cover designer. It is also dedicated to our eight grandchildren: Jenny, Ian, Erin, Zander, Summer, River, Abby and Christopher. Other dedicatees include my late stepmother, Sunny, and stepsister, Pat, both of whom were devoted to my father and made the word "step" one of love and support. Additionally, I could not have completed the manuscript without the able counsel and editing of my friend and colleague, Liz Siertz Newman, who co-authored our English textbook, *Read, Write, Work*. Thanks to you all.